20.00

D0392299

20.00

WHEN ANGER HITS HOME

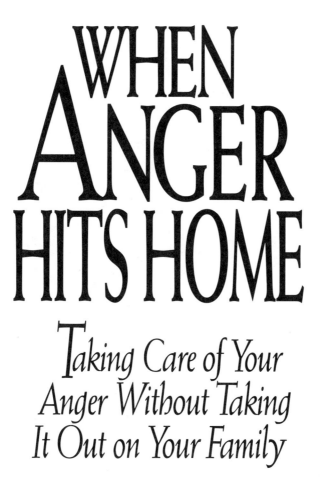

WHEN ANGER HITS HOME

Taking Care of Your Anger Without Taking It Out on Your Family

GARY JACKSON OLIVER
H. NORMAN WRIGHT

MOODY PRESS
CHICAGO

© 1992 by
GARY JACKSON OLIVER AND
H. NORMAN WRIGHT

All rights reserved. No part of this book may be reproduced in any form without permission in writing from the publisher, except in the case of brief quotations embodied in critical articles or reviews.

All Scripture quotations, unless noted otherwise, are from the *Holy Bible: New International Version.* Copyright © 1973, 1978, 1984, International Bible Society.

The use of selected references from various versions of the Bible in this publication does not necessarily imply publisher endorsement of the versions in their entirety.

ISBN 0-8024-9237-1

1 3 5 7 9 10 8 6 4 2

Printed in the United States of America

Dedicated to

My mother and father,
George and Leona Oliver,
and my sister, Marsha Oliver.

My mother and father,
Harry and Amelia Wright,
and my brother, Paul Fugleberg.

For their constant love,
faithfulness, and encouragement.
For teaching us what it means
to be a family.

For giving us the opportunity to learn
that all our emotions, including anger,
are a gift from God.

CONTENTS

1

THE MANY FACES OF ANGER

D ale tried to keep it all in, and so far he had succeeded. Sally's request to drive Joey to school because of the rain had made him ten minutes late to work. Dale wanted to tell her off, but he had no time that morning. He arrived to learn he had meetings until lunch. Lunch itself was interrupted when his boss gave him a must-do-five-minutes-ago task. On the way home the car sputtered and stopped on the road. Fortunately he was only a block from the service station. Unfortunately, impatient rush-hour drivers honked mercilessly as he and another driver tried to push his Ford to the side and up the garage driveway.

"Honey, the car's being repaired," he told his wife in a phone call a half hour later. Dale sounded surprisingly calm. But inside he was seething. With measured tones he said, "I hope to be home in another thirty minutes, once they put a new fuel pump in. Gotta go now . . . " Sally could not see Dale slamming down the receiver in disgust.

Wow, $210 for a fuel pump! We can't afford that! Dale's thoughts sped on. *And now she wants me to pick up some milk for supper. She thinks I've got a little free time. Ha! Well, I'll get me a candy bar then.*

But Dale forgot to shop. When he arrived home, Sally greeted him innocently enough. "Honey, I'm glad you're here. Did you get the milk?"

Dale exploded. He came like a heat-seeking missile. There was no warning. No alarms sounded. Everything had been calm. And then the missile exploded. Sally and little Joey, on the blast's receiving end, were devastated not only by the suddenness but by the intensity of the blast. The damage included wounded feelings and faltering esteem. The recovery from this onslaught took days.

The missile? Intense, unexpected, and uncalled-for anger.

On other occasions, anger is a snake, gliding silently and unseen through the underbrush. It may raise its head, promising a commitment but then disappears once more, its promise forgotten. Or the anger may slink by as a costly delay by someone who is full of weak excuses. Sometimes a withdrawing partner says, "I do love you" and then retreats into silence each time you bring up an important issue. The bite of this anger is not as blatant or devastating as the missile, but the results can be similar.

Anger. That controversial, misunderstood word. That controversial misunderstood emotion. It affects all of us, yet it continues to baffle us.

Even the so-called experts disagree. Some say, "Experience and express it." Others say, "Disown and repel it." But it is with us now and forever. We were created with the capacity to become angry.

One dictionary calls anger "a feeling of strong displeasure." Is that your definition, or do you couch it in other terms? How would you describe it? The above definition suggests that anger is manageable. It is like so many other feelings—neither right nor wrong in itself. The problem lies in its mishandling.

Too often we link any expression of anger with an explosion. Have you noticed some of the major synonyms used for anger? Wrath, rage, fury, hostility. These words paint the picture of anger out of control and running wild. They reflect an anger that is destructive. Some of us equate anger with our memories of the comic and television hero "The Incredible Hulk," an out-of-control, raging beast. This was anger uncontrolled. On the other hand, others would like to maintain a staid emotional composure like Mr. Spock, the emotionless Vulcan on the Star Trek TV series. He never allowed himself to be angry.

Often anger begins slowly. It starts as a slight arousal, a feeling of discomfort. We begin to notice changes in our body, especially a feeling of tension. Our pulse rate increases, and there is a surge of adrenaline. You've felt it, and so have I. It's been that way throughout history.

But anger wears many faces. Moses was livid with anger at the Hebrew people when they set up idol worship. And with the energy provided by his anger he was able to regain control of the people. David was consumed with anger when Nathan told him about the rich man stealing from the poor man. He used this anger to face his own pride and admit his own sin. Anger can be used in a creative way to resolve major social problems. Gandhi and Martin Luther King, Jr., put their anger to constructive reforms. A mother who first cried then became upset about her son's death caused by a drunk driver organized MADD (Mothers Against Drunk Drivers). Her anger, put to positive use, has created an organization that now promotes legislation and awareness programs to remove drunk drivers from the nation's roads.

POSITIVE ANGER

Anger can be used positively and creatively in many ways. For example, anger is a part of the grieving process following a loss. Here are several ways in which anger has been used positively.

A relative of an accident victim *convinced* the hospital chaplain staff to establish new and improved procedures for helping the survivors of sudden accidental deaths.

A parent *proposed* that warning signs be posted at a pond where his son drowned to help reduce similar accidental incidents.

A grandmother *requested* that parents of cancer victims be provided printed information about cancer as well as the location of support groups.

An adult son who lost his elderly father *organized* programs for a local convalescent home.

A young mother who lost her preschool age daughter *solicited* toy contributions from anyone she could to give to a local pediatric ward.

Notice the action words alone, which reflect how these people not only redirected their anger but also brought relief and a sense of control to their lives: convinced, proposed, requested, organized, and solicited.[1]

DESTRUCTIVE ANGER

But anger also wears an ugly face. Consider some of the destructive results of this emotion. People seem to go to extremes in their demonstration of anger, either outwardly or inwardly. Turn it outward too much, and it destroys others. Turn it inward too much, and it destroys us.

Not only did Cain misuse this emotion but so did Esau, Saul, the Pharisees, Attila the Hun, Adolf Hitler, and rulers in most of the countries of the world. Our history is a tragic drama of hostility and domination.

Anger motivates a person to hate, wound, damage, annihilate, despise, scorn, loathe, vilify, curse, ruin, and demolish. Under anger's curse, a man will ridicule, get even with, laugh at, humiliate, shame, criticize, bawl out, fight, crush, offend, or bully another person. All of these are definitely negative!

The first time we see the effects of anger in Scripture, they are very destructive. "But on Cain and his offering he did not look with favor. So Cain was very angry, and his face was downcast. Then the Lord said to Cain, 'Why are you angry?'" (Genesis 4:5-6a).

Cain was angry at his brother because Abel's sacrifice was acceptable and his own was not. Inwardly Cain experienced anger, and the result was murder (Genesis 4:8). Cain was alienated from his brother, from other people, and from God. His anger led to murder and to extreme loneliness.

Most everything in life has a price tag. Go into any store and rarely will you find anything that is free. Purchasing a new car may give us a feeling of elation, comfort, and prestige, but it costs. Expressing our anger can be a relief. It can influence or even control a situation. But it too has a price tag. Some of the costs may be obvious, such as a strained relationship—resistance or withdrawal of others when we come near them. Or a tension-filled marital relationship with spouses who are now combatants rather than lovers. Even though there are personal physiological costs to anger, the greatest price to be paid is in our interpersonal relationships.

Anger has its place and can be effective, but usually it is not. Our anger, carelessly expressed, will override the love, care, and appreciation that creates close relationships. The person who has a reputation for anger is soon given a wide berth. Indeed, the book of Proverbs recommends: "Make no friendships with a man given to anger, and with a wrathful man do not associate, Lest you learn his ways and get yourself into a snare" (22:24-25, Amp.*).

McKay vividly describes the anger's brutal barrier to relationships in *When Anger Hits*:

> Anger stuns. It frightens. It makes people feel bad about themselves. And of course it warns them to stop doing whatever is offending you. But people gradually become injured and resistant. As soon as they see you, they put on their emotional armor in preparation for the next upset. The more anger you express, the less effective your anger becomes, the less you are listened to, and the more cut off you may begin to feel from genuine closeness.[2]

Anger erects barriers. Anger leads to aggression; it doesn't reduce it. Each expression of anger adds to the stockpile of fuel.

Anger can be a very upsetting emotion. You may be afraid of your own anger because you saw people totally out of control. They didn't just experience anger, they raged! Perhaps you believe that healthy people don't have anger. You may regard anger as a dysfunction, and only dysfunctional families experience anger. Or perhaps you feel that you don't have the right to be angry at others.

Fear of Anger

We're afraid of the reaction of others when they witness our anger. We learn to ask ourselves, "What right do I have to be angry?" "What good will my anger do in this situation?" "Is it worth all the emotional energy that it's going to cost me?" And when we ask ourselves these questions and debate the answers, we end up using them as a gag to completely stifle the anger. It doesn't go away; it's just shut down and stored away waiting for an outlet.

We fear other people's anger because we equate the emotion with personal rejection. But we also learn to fear our own anger. We're afraid we will either lose control or do damage to others that can never be undone. I've talked to people who were afraid that if they let their anger out they would never be able to find the off button. The problem is that repressing your anger can bring about the very things you are afraid will happen if you were to express

The Amplified Bible.

your anger—depression, abrasiveness, and sullenness. You become a ticking time bomb, and no one knows when and where you will explode.

We're afraid that our anger will make us look inferior and inadequate. So we learn to *bury* our anger, *swallow* it, *stuff* it, or *bottle* it up. We fear anger because we have not been given the truth about anger, nor assistance in its expression, nor enough practice expressing it properly to trust ourselves. This book will show how to release your anger in a healthy manner, to your benefit and the benefit of those around you.

How We Feel Our Anger

There are various ways in which people feel their anger, as well as express it. Let's meet three kinds of angry people.[3]

Sam Slow Burner rarely feels anger at the time of an infraction. But over time, as he reflects upon what took place, the feelings begin to intensify. Some of the Slow Burners expend their energy in restraining any expression of their anger. Others see anger as a childish feeling and immediately experience guilt. They tend to turn their anger back against themselves. Other Slow Burners need time and privacy before they begin to feel their anger. When it does arrive, they are usually off by themselves and can reflect upon it.

Who do you know that is a Slow Burner? Perhaps you're not sure. You probably know some Slow Burners but are not aware of it. After all, they are hard to recognize because they don't let their anger out.

At times, Sam Slow Burner will accumulate a series of upsetting events and then overreact to some minor event with intense anger. At that point, his anger sails fast and furious, and his response is completely out of proportion to the current situation. Sam reacts more to the past than to the present situation.

In contrast, Tom Tinderbox feels his anger "quick as a flash," like a quickly igniting match. Slow Burners feel the anger slowly; Tinderboxes feel it immediately, though they refuse to express the anger, keeping it to themselves. Some feel it immediately, know why they are angry but deny themselves the right to feel it. Tom's motto is "Adults should always control themselves and be able to handle whatever difficulty arises." Once again guilt overrides the anger and kills any expression of it.

Other Tinderboxes know why they are angry and who is to blame, and they feel justified in being angry. These Tinderboxes rarely hold back the feeling. Their main decision is whether to focus their anger on the source or on something else!

Some Tinderboxes that are deeply troubled about how they feel their anger cannot figure out the reason for their feelings. This uncertainty makes their anger a burden, even though at times they may be able to identify several causes of their anger. Sometimes their anger is released. Other times it remains bottled up. Who do you know that might be a Tom (or Teresa) Tinderbox? What kind is he? How does his style affect you?

Another group of individuals, when questioned, claim they never experience anger. In fact, some of them say they can't recall a time when they felt angry. They are the Cool Heads. The first time I meant a Carl Cool Head, he was difficult to fathom. But Carl Cool Head does not seem to experience intense feelings of any kind. Some Cool Heads will say they experience some feelings such as embarrassment or annoyance, but definitely not anger.

How We Express Our Anger

There are various ways in which we feel our anger. But perhaps the area of greatest concern is how we express it. Meet four more people; they embody the various styles that are employed to release or express anger.

Stella Straight Shooter expresses her anger directly at the source of her irritation. Unfortunately, some members of the Straight Shooter clan fail to keep their anger directed at the irritating situation or behavior but go after the actual person. And some of them seem to have no fear of the results either. Fortunately, some Straight Shooters simply describe what has happened, why it was a problem, why they are angry, and what they would like done about the issue. Some are loud, while others remain calm and quiet. But they are definitely angry. These are the people who tend to get over their anger quickly. Those who use indirect approaches retain their anger, and it continues to live. Some of the indirect methods include withdrawal, avoidance, and even lack of consideration. Who is the Straight Shooter in your family?

Dan Deflector expresses his anger in such a way that those involved in causing the feeling don't even know about the anger. The anger is displaced against someone or something else, often less threatening than the actual source. Who is the Deflector in your family?

Karen Keeper holds in her anger until she is with people with whom she feels safe. Then she expresses her pent-up feelings. Some Keepers are quite selfish with their feelings, for they never share them with others. Others express their anger quite well, but through tears. Their hurt and frustration finds its release through crying, which may elicit sympathy and concern rather than rejection. Karen Keeper may choke up or sob; she may cry briefly. Her display may be public or private. For some people tears are their only outlet for their anger. Who is the Keeper in your family?

And finally, Randy Revenger likes to vent his anger by "evening the score." You probably have seen his seemingly funny bumper sticker on America's highways: "I don't get mad, I get even." The driver is serious. Randy and Rita Revenger simply wait for an opportunity to gain their revenge, and they enjoy it. They file away who did what to them, and in time they make the person pay.

The thinking underlying this style is interesting. Revengers believe the offender is responsible for, and thus deserving of, what the Revenger is now doing to get even. After all, "He brought it on himself. I'm only getting even, like I should." Randy Revenger tries to tell the target person what is being done to him. Men who use this approach tend to feel comfortable with it as an "instrument of justice."[4] Who is the "I'll get even" person in your family?

The actual tactics of these four responders take many specific forms. The ways we respond will greatly affect our co-workers and families. Unfortunately, most of these responses are destructive: at work they can wreak discord; at home, they leave insecurity, fear, bitterness, and other symptoms of an unhealthy, dysfunctional family. You may meet several family members (perhaps yourself) in this lineup.

THE AVENGING ANGEL

The avenging angel is a terror to behold. He does not merely express anger but attempts to dominate and crush others. You've seen these people even in public. So have I. I'll never forget the father I saw verbally crushing his son in front of dozens of others because of a simple mistake. You find them in restaurants, supermarkets, at amusement parks, and even at church. Their anger has to demean others. If they respond this way outside the home, imagine their actions behind closed doors.

Avengers are like a 2,000-horsepower engine spinning out of control. They have the power in their engine, but they don't know where the brakes are, and even if they did they might not know how to use them. All it takes is a slight infraction to ignite this engine and soon it is racing full speed ahead with rage or vindictiveness. The chaos is felt by everyone in the vicinity.

Avengers have a multitude of weapons available to them. Their toxic words are one of the main tools. Their words are frequently cruel, caustic, bitter, degrading, and judgmental. Their verbal missiles are targeted to contaminate and wound. The apostle James describes the impact of such missiles well: "The human tongue can be tamed by no man. It is (an undisciplined, irreconcilable) restless evil, full of death-bringing poison" (James 3:8, Amp.). Other weapons include exploitation, degrading, and even physical abuse.

Avengers have an addiction—they enjoy and continually seek discord through anger. Their method is to demolish the object of their anger. Retaliation is their forte.

THE CRITIC

Another tactic is to become a critic. Critics are much more common than avengers. But critics come in many different varieties. Have you met one of them? Perhaps you live with one.

There are *the blamers.* They avoid accepting responsibility for their actions by criticizing other people or blaming past experiences that cannot be changed or undone. Their anger is definitely directed outward. They are always looking to nail somebody else for "causing" their problems, misfortune, or misbehavior. They say, "This wouldn't have happened if it hadn't been for you. You're the cause of my troubles." They vent their anger by criticizing you for what you did wrong and for what you could have done better. The word "should" is a mainstay in their vocabulary: "You should have known better." "You should have done it my way." "You shouldn't have said that."

Another negative critic is *the angry joker.* Humor is a positive method of relating to others. I like to laugh and joke. If something is funny, even in a serious context, I have difficulty containing my laughter. But angry jokers make others the butt of their humor. They specialize in laughing at people instead of laughing with them. Their facial expressions and tone of voice carry the barb so well.

I see this often in husbands who subtly criticize their partners' characteristics, skills, or weaknesses by joking about them in public. A husband says at a dinner party with friends, "My wife serves hamburger for dinner so often that I'm thinking about erecting golden arches in the front yard." That may be anger masquerading as humor. Or a wife says in the couples' Sunday school class, "Jim sings so badly in church that I'm tempted to volunteer for full-time nursery duty at 11:00 A.M. so I don't have to listen to him." Is that humor or anger?

When you confront the joker about his or her stinging humor, the reply often is, "Take it easy. I was just kidding. Can't you take a joke?" This response reminds me of Proverbs 26:18-19: "Like a madman shooting firebrands or deadly arrows, is a man who deceives his neighbor and says, 'I was only joking!'" You know his humor was just camouflage for anger.

A third kind of critic is *the fault-finder,* or *the flaw-finder.* This person seems to have an insatiable need to point out others' defects. Many are perfectionists. But flaw-finders are only interested in revealing the faults of others.

The fault-finder scrutinizes people, watching for the more obscure, trivial details of what people say, what they remember, what they do, and what they did in the past. She has a great filing system. When she spies even the most minor error or deviation from the norm, she is quick to expose and correct it. Her displeasure is obvious. She shows off the defects she finds in people as if they were trophies. And do you know what is so maddening about this person? She usually does what she does with a smile, saying, "I'm just trying to be helpful."

If it seems you can never please this person, you're right—you can't. Her critical eye always will find flaws. Often this display of anger is coming from the need to always be in control. If you confront her about her anger, you will often receive two responses, shock and denial.

If you think you've got it all together, the fault-finder comes along to expose your weaknesses and tear you apart.[4]

Another kind of angry critic at large in the world is *the cannibal.* These people don't criticize in a joking manner or settle for mere nitpicking. They go for the jugular. They devour family members and co-workers for breakfast, lunch, dinner, and between-meal snacks! They attack through the most severe forms of personal criticism and put downs with complete disregard for the feelings of others. Often their facial expressions reflect their anger.[5]

You've heard their biting remarks:

"You've got to be kidding. No one believes that kind of stuff anymore."

"A mature person wouldn't get upset over that. Shape up."

"What an idiot you are! You made seven mistakes on your spelling test. How could anyone be so stupid?"

"Another disaster for dinner. I wish your mother would have taught you how to cook before I married you."

"You're late for work again. At least you're consistent."

The cannibals are the personification of Proverbs 12:18: "There is one who speaks rashly like the thrusts of the sword" (NASB*).

These four types of critics all have the same basic characteristic: destruction. Destructive critics may say they are only interested in remodeling you into a better person by sharing a little constructive criticism. In reality, they are not experts in construction, but in demolition. They are intent on putting you down, tearing you down, punishing you, and manipulating you. Their brand of response does not nourish; it poisons.[6]

Destructive, angry criticism usually includes four elements:

1. *Accusation.* The critics use all-encompassing, accusatory terms such as *always, should, ought,* and *never.* They say: "You *ought* to have done better," "You are *always* so sloppy," "You *never* listen to me." These are words and phrases of anger—listen for them.

New American Standard Bible.

2. *Guilt.* A typical critical attack is designed to make the target feel guilty. For example: "I am so disappointed in you. I counted on you, and you let me down." "You must not care for me very much or you wouldn't have forgotten my birthday." Parents often use this destructive tool on their children and on each other. It's a safe, subtle form of camouflaged anger. Watch out for this one.

3. *Intimidation.* Some critics use such intimidating tactics as expressions of impatience and outbursts of anger to convey their disapproval. For example, a man paces the floor fussing and fuming noisily as his wife takes too much time getting ready for their evening out. Or an employer stomps through the office shouting angrily, "The next person who takes a two-hour lunch break will be fired!" They have periodic outbursts like the avenger.

4. *Resentment.* This form of destructive anger is often expressed by the person who uses his memory as an ammunition dump. Resentful individuals dig into the past to use your offenses, hasty words, and mistakes as weapons against you. They say things like: "You've been doing this for months." "I remember that nasty remark you made seven years ago." "You're just like your father. He used to treat me the same way." When you don't have a memory as sharp as this person's, you're at a disadvantage.

THE PASSIVE-AGGRESSIVE

They're hard to handle. They're clever. They deny. They're often quite skilled and successful in their expression of anger. We call them the passive-aggressives, or PA's, because coming out straight with their anger is difficult for a couple of reasons: They would have to admit they're angry, which is one of the reasons they've selected their pattern in the first place. And second, they would have to give up something that works for them.

Like the critic, the passive-aggressive expresses anger using criticism and resentment, coupled with a desire for revenge. This person tries to get even, and he does so in subtle but distinct ways.

A passive aggressive lets out his anger by procrastinating. Putting off responsibilities or delaying doing something for someone else is an excellent way to vent one's displeasure. But it's not obvious, and it's difficult for others to label the action as angry.

The PA can more easily handle being labeled "irresponsible" or "lazy" than being labeled "angry." Subtle stubbornness is another expression, as is forgetting or avoidance. This behavior is usually anger that the individuals wouldn't dare express in an open manner.

Forgetting is such a handy way to express anger since the responsibility can be turned back against the other person. "Are you *sure* you asked me?" or, "Are you *sure* that was the time we agreed upon?" "I'm so sorry you had to wait in the rain. But I was *sure you* said to pick you up at 10:30, and not at 10:00. Well, anyway, you can get some dry clothes at home." With responses such as these you begin to wonder and doubt yourself. The truth is, you were set up! You end up feeling responsible.

How else do passive-aggressives behave? They use their spouse's car and leave it a mess along with an empty gas tank. They say they will take care of paying a bill but conveniently forget, and you get the call from the gas company. They take money out of their partner's wallet and fail to let them know about it. During the viewing of a favorite TV program the passive-aggressive walks over and turns the channel to something he wants to watch.

Sarcasm is a "nice" way to be angry. They give two messages at one time, a compliment and a put-down. "You look so young I didn't recognize you." "Your new suit is radical, but I like it."

Other forms include the obstructionist who is always against everything or tends to make simple things complex. The angry person on a church board is the one who, when votes don't go his way, often makes the meeting drag on and on. I've seen passive-aggressives act as though they don't understand the simplest instructions. You may even notice a slight smile or smirk on their face, but confronting about this usually doesn't work. They play innocent, and if you ever suggest that they are angry you get a "Who me? I'm not angry at all." You end up wondering if you're not the one with the major problem!

Well, there they are. Not too pleasant, are they? But passive-aggressives are all around us. This kind of response can develop into a lifestyle. (See chapter 13 to learn about the three styles of responding to anger, the passive, the aggressive, and the assertive.)

WARNING SIGNS

Do you listen to signals? I hope so. Signals are there for a purpose. We have them on street corners to let us know when to go or when to stop. Those signals are there to keep us alive and well. Ignoring them leads to destruction.

Sometimes people signal us to warn or alert us to something we are not fully aware of at that moment. Those signals are for our own benefit. We learn to listen to them. But one of the signals of life that we don't always listen to is anger. It is a message system telling us that something is not right. We may be hurt, needs may be unmet, our rights have been violated, or we have recognized an injustice. Anger tells us that there is something in our life that needs to be addressed.

Anger is an emotion you feel. There is a reason and purpose for your anger. Too often we associate feeling angry with venting anger. The two do not necessarily go together.

When you are angry, ask yourself, "What am I really feeling? Is it anger? What is causing it?" Unrealistic, you say. No. Nor is it difficult to learn, though it may take time. Most of us have learned patterns of anger response, but we can relearn. We can change.

I've heard counselees make statements that indicate a desire to change. If you can make the following statements, or want to know the answers to the following questions, this book is for you:

"I'm tired of not knowing what it is that angers me all the time. I want to find the cause." Do you know what angers you?

"I want to discover who is responsible for my anger. Is it them or is it me?" Do you know who is responsible for your anger?

"I want to express my anger in a way that I feel good about, without always feeling guilt afterwards." Have you learned to do this yet? Is guilt a follow-up to your anger?

"I want to learn to express my anger without hurting others and without becoming defensive and attacking." Have you achieved this yet?

"I want to know what my anger will cost me if I express it. I know there are some risks involved. I need to identify them." What does your anger cost you? Have you measured the results?

Perhaps a major question is this one, which we all need to answer. "Is the way you are handling your anger working for you? Is it healthy and balanced?" If not, you don't have anything to lose by trying a new pattern.

Take Action

1. Each time you experience anger, ask yourself, "Is my anger helping me or hurting me?" Write down what it accomplished.

2. Think of the last two times you got angry. What was the cause?

   _____

   _____

3. Starting today begin to "observe" how you handle your anger. Begin an Anger Log to record your data. Completing the log will assist you in pinpointing problem areas that you need to work on. More instruction for your log will appear in chapter 11. For now, just begin a simple log of observations for a nine-day period, beginning today. Complete the Anger Log on the next page.

My Anger Log

Day	1	2	3	4	5	6	7	8	9
mes do ____ each day inwardly or outwardly? Place a number for each day.									
Intensity On the average, from 1-10 what is the intensity of your anger today; 10 is most intense, 1 is barely breathing.									
Duration How many minutes do you usually remain angry? Use an average.									
Negative Expression How many times does your anger lead to negative expression?									
Positive Expression How many times does your anger lead to positive expression?									
Disturbs relationships On the average, did your anger today help or hinder relationships? (9 is most helpful; 1 is a disaster.)									

4. Fill out the Anger Expressions chart. Consider the last two times you got angry at each person and how you expressed it. Now observe how you express your anger the next time you get angry at each person. These three columns cover all the styles and types described in this chapter.

ANGER EXPRESSIONS

(1) Mark with a check (✔) how you expressed anger to each person most recently.

Person	Hold it back	Indirect	Direct
Spouse	_____	_____	_____
Children	_____	_____	_____
Parents	_____	_____	_____
Employer	_____	_____	_____
Co-worker	_____	_____	_____
Friends	_____	_____	_____

Which type of expression do you tend to use most?

What can you do to make your anger expression healthier and more productive?

(2) Think about the following people toward whom you might express anger. How do they respond when you express anger? Write down how you will respond the next time.

Person	Response	How I will respond differently the next time
Spouse	_____	_____
Children	_____	_____
Mother	_____	_____
Father	_____	_____
Boss	_____	_____
Friends (who)	_____	_____

(3) Think of a constant provoking behavior or situation and then think of a change that you can make when all else fails.

NOTES

1. Carol Staudacher. *Beyond Grief* (Oakland, Calif.: New Harbinger Publications, 1987). p. 19, adapted.

2. Matthew McKay, Peter D. Rogers, Judith McCoy. *When Anger Hurts* (Oakland, Calif.: New Harbinger Publications, 1989), p. 33.

3. The seven kinds of angry people described in "How We Feel Anger" and "How We Express Anger" are based on categories developed by Jeanne M. Plas and Kathleen V. Hoover-Dempsey, *Working Up a Storm* (New York: Ballantine, 1988).

4. Plas and Hoover-Dempsey, *Working Up a Storm*, pps. 37-72, adapted.

5. Jerry Greenwood, *Be the Person You Were Meant to Be* (New York, NY: Dell, 1979), pp. 224-26, adapted.

6. Ibid.

2

ANGER IN YOUR FAMILY TREE

When my wife and I stay at various bed and breakfast inns, we enjoy looking at the various antique furnishings. Intricate patterns adorn the many different quilts. We marvel at the various colors and shapes of cloth that are stitched together into a pleasing design.

Patterns—our lives are filled with them. Have you ever noticed the intricacies of spider webs? There are various types, and definite patterns hold the webs together and make them functional.

You and I came out of family backgrounds with many patterns, one of which was probably anger. We all had role models who had their own way of displaying anger as well as responding to our display of anger. Think about it. How was anger expressed in your family? How did family members respond to your anger?

Consider the family stories of these five different adults:

"In my family my brother slammed doors and threw glasses. Is that why I overreact when I hear loud noises?"

"In my family my mom cried herself to sleep. It was her way of expressing her anger."

"In my family my uncle would lock himself in the garage for hours. That's the only way he knew how to handle his angry feelings."

"In my family my father went to doctors for years with aches and pains. He never showed his anger. It went to his stomach."

"In my family my sister was always smiling but always late and accident-prone. She said she was never angry. I knew better."

CHILDHOOD MEMORIES

As we move through our childhood years we begin to file information about anger in our memory bank. Some people learn that anger in the family is a sin at the top of the list of major offenses. Raising voices is never acceptable if you want love and approval. In a repressed atmosphere you may have learned not only to hide your anger from others but also from yourself. Anger still existed, but its presence wasn't acknowledged.

One day Fred told me how anger had affected him. "For years I experienced difficulty swallowing, and it wasn't just when I ate either. It happened constantly. Sometimes it was embarrassing, and I became very self-conscious about it. I was afraid that everyone around me could see it. I just thought I was constructed differently from others. But that wasn't it at all. I discovered that all my life I had been swallowing all right, swallowing my anger! I just stuffed it down, and in time my body began to rebel against this emotional gorging."

Jim expressed his family's handling of anger in another way: "I jokingly called my family the war zone. Except it was no joke. Everyone had his array of weapons. Verbal hand grenades were the worst. When they went off innocent bystanders got hit by the angry shrapnel. Screaming, fighting and put-downs were the order of the day. Perhaps that's why I handle work so well. It's like it's a reflection of my past family. I'm accustomed to it."

CHILDHOOD MODELS

Think about your family.
How did your father express anger?
How did your mother express anger?
How did a sibling express anger?
How did a favorite adult express anger?
How did a church leader express anger?
How did one of your friends express anger?
How did each of these people respond to you when you expressed anger?

Do you see any correlation between the way in which you feel and express anger now and your background?

Most of us did not learn appropriate patterns for handling anger, and this lack may generate fear. Our parents modeled actions that were not always right. For instance, consider how you might respond today, as an adult, if you saw one parent do a slow silent burn for days on end. How might you respond today if you saw both parents using the silent treatment with one another and going through you to convey information to their partner?

Was there anyone as you were growing up who taught you how to properly express your anger? Or did they try to turn off your anger? Most adults have so many questions about anger and feel so uncertain about it they are usually uncomfortable with the anger they see in their own child or adolescent. This pattern is then passed on from parent to child and on to the next generation.

Who carried the anger in your family of origin? Often one parent or family member ends up carrying the anger for other family members. He becomes the family's "designated angry member." Often other members behave in such a way that they trigger the angry person's anger as a means of getting him to express their own anger for them. It's safer that way. Their own expression of anger actually comes out through the designated angry family member.

Have you ever wondered why you react the way you do? If you came from a healthy family you probably received accurate and adequate information about feeling angry. If you came from an unhealthy family you probably received inaccurate and inadequate information about feeling angry.

Some adults had a parent who was a silent sulker. Others had a parent who played the martyr. Yet others had parents who were screamers or raging hulks. To the child, that was anger in action. No matter what the style, how you saw your parents handling their anger influenced how you handle your anger now. Your past shapes your present handling of your emotions.[1]

THE ANGER LEGACY

Jim was a typical example of past displays of anger dictating the present. He lived in fear of anger, anyone's anger, but especially that of Betty, his wife. Whenever she became angry at him, Jim withdrew from her in fear and anger. This in turn threatened and further angered her. Thus, not only was Jim afraid of Betty's feelings, but his own behavior would set them off.

His behavior and response to Betty was a mirror image of him and his mother. Jim's mother was a combination of intense loving and intense anger. The problem was he never knew which it would be! And his father responded to his mother exactly as Jim did with Betty. He had learned the interactive pattern well. It's not uncommon in your adult life to put your mother or father's face upon your spouse.

Every family provides their children with a legacy of anger— some healthy and some unhealthy. Some of us can recall our parents' anger toward us; others cannot. And every parent's response to the same behavior can vary.

In my counseling I ask people several questions. The answers are often the same.

"When you were a child and you disappointed your parents, how did they respond?"

"They were angry with me," many people say.

"When you were a child and you argued with your parents, how did they respond?"

"With anger."

"When you were a child and you went against their advice, how did they respond?"

"With anger."

"When you were a child and you didn't live up to your parents' expectations, how did they respond?

"They got very angry."

"Where was the healthy correction, empathy, love, encouragement and support?"

"I never saw it," many say.

I have also asked people questions about their own response to their parents' reactions.

"When your parents criticized you, how did you feel?"

Some say guilty, others afraid, a few sad, and many angry.

"When your parents tried to control you, how did you feel?"

"They made me feel guilty," some say. "I was afraid but also angry," others say. A few felt sad.

Among other questions I ask are:

"When your parents told you what you should think or feel, how did you feel?"

"When your parents made demands on you, how did you feel?"

"When your parents tried to live their lives through you, how did you feel?"

"When your parents told you what they expected from you, how did you feel?"

The answers are the same: guilty, afraid, sad, angry.

"When your parents hurt you in any way, how did you feel?"

"I felt very angry," most reply.

Where did we learn our angry responses? It should be obvious by now.

LIKE FATHER, LIKE SON

Jerry sat in my office and described the rage storming inside him the previous day. The young man had been surprised by the intensity of what he felt. He knew it was out of proportion to what transpired between his wife and him. After talking about it for a while, Jerry said with some chagrin, "I guess I was cut out of the same stone as my dad."

With some questioning he slowly revealed that rarely did his father appear irritated, upset, or angry at home. But once every three to four months all of the father's accumulated hurts and frustrations exploded onto the unlikely person who was closest. Jerry learned the same pattern so well.

One man expressed himself in this way: "I actually enjoy my anger. Sometimes it's cruel, but hey, that's life. You gotta get hurt sometime. I like seeing people squirm when I come uncorked. I guess you could say I'm unregenerately angry. I like to make trouble. I have a lot of energy, and this is one way to get rid of it. How did I become like this? I don't know. Somewhere I guess I saw it. And then I discovered it worked. So why should I change?"

MAINTAINING CONTROL

Jill, a thirty-four-year-old mother, could handle irritations some days, and other days she became a tinderbox, igniting at the slightest provocation.

Without any thought, she would rage at anyone in sight, regardless of their innocence or guilt. Later Jill told me why she was reacting in this way.

"For twenty-four years of my life I was not allowed by my parents to show any anger or irritation. Any display was met with immediate disapproval and resistance. I felt overcontrolled and repressed, but now I'm not going to hold anything back. If I feel it, I'm going to let it fly. Except, I still don't show much around them. Everyone else gets it. My only concern is what if this gets worse over the years. Then what? I don't want it to. But I don't want to stuff it, either."

Her response was a classic example of being overcontrolled in a dysfunctional family and responding by swinging from repressing rage to expressing it. Jill disliked the repression of the first twenty-four years, but now she was actually afraid of the intensity of her anger. A balance had not been attained. "I guess I'm trying to make up for those twenty-four years."

"How many years have you been expressing your anger?" I asked.

"Ten," Jill said, and she appeared deep in thought when I asked the next question, "Does that mean you will continue to express your anger in this way for the next fourteen years to make it balance out?"

Her look was more than thoughtful. It was shock. No one had ever put into words what she was doing. Her loss of control showed that she was still being controlled by her parents. Fortunately, she had the desire to bring about a change in her life.

But many people who think they are free from the pattern of their past are still held captive, as their present response is a reaction rather than a clear choice.

DENYING THE FEELINGS

Perhaps one of the worst displays of anger in a family is no display—anger is purposely not expressed. In many homes the family appears to be calm and unified. The parents appear consistently stable and on an even keel. Anger is not expressed except for tight lips and piercing eyes or extended silence. It is definitely not seen in children, for it is not allowed. They are taught two harmful guidelines for their life, "You do not feel anger and you do not show anger."

These children are being taught a life-debilitating pattern of denial. You may have learned this pattern as a child. Or, as an adult, you may be teaching your own child this behavior. The denial of any emotion leads to an accumulation of it and soon there is an overabundance with no proper avenue of drainage. Denying an emotion means you have turned its energy back against yourself and you are slowly destroying yourself and your potential.

David Viscott, a psychologist and author, describes the consequences of pent-up anger.

> When we hold in feelings, we distort the world around us. We really do not believe what we profess to be true and so we doubt our judgment. We make villains out of the people we love and begin to lose belief in ourselves as well. We become more interested in being right than in making peace. Although we hold feelings back to stay in control, doing so makes us feel fragile and at risk of going out of control. Our anger builds. We struggle to keep from exploding. We take it out on innocent people. We are easily triggered by minor frustrations.[2]

Consider the behavior of sharks. In several instances a captured shark being lifted out of the water has begun thrashing about violently trying to strike back at whatever has taken him out of his normal habitat. Unable to find a victim, he takes his fury out on himself. He opens his jaws, twists himself, and begins to rip chunks of flesh out of his own body. In his frenzy to attack, he misdirects and becomes self-destructive. So do we. Denial leads to repression, and the only outlets left are depression, elevated blood pressure, headaches, anxiety attacks, and ulcers. We become our own worst enemy.

Our other choice is to face the fact that what we were taught and learned was wrong. It was contrary to the way in which God created us and wants us to live. It's time to change.

Tim was honest about his anger. He told me, "I finally learned to label what I was feeling and let others know when I'm upset. I just feel better when all the cards are out on the table. And I know the reason I do it. I'm reacting against the pattern I saw between Mom and Dad. It was classic.

"Mom was one of those caretaker women. You know, the kind that does everything for you. She used to get so angry at Dad because he was slow to do things. She'd complain about all the things he didn't do and then before he could do anything, she would do it! But she would run around and complain and gripe in an angry voice. The angrier she got, the more energy she had, and she drove all of us nuts. Dad would give up and withdraw, and you can imagine how that set her off even more. It was a great vicious circle. There's no way I want that as a part of my life."

GUILT AND ANGER

Guilt is a frequent companion of anger. Guilt generates anger and perpetuates anger. And anger leads to more guilt. If anger has no place to go, it must turn into something, so why not guilt? We can feel guilty over the unexpressed anger toward others. And guilt is often being angry with yourself. You don't feel good about your feelings and who you are.

Guilt is the legacy of an angry family. It's an undesired inheritance. If you grew up with angry people, have you identified the residue of guilt? Guilt has its own style of expression.

Have you made the connection between the two feelings yet? Those who feel guilty ignore the positives in life. Joy is not part of their experience. They reinforce negatives. Many people cannot admit to their own anger, but its energy comes out in negativism, which can interfere with other people's joy.

Guilty adults have a difficult time directing their feeling toward their bottled-up anger. So they react inappropriately, and, because their response doesn't even make sense to them, they end up feeling guilty over their reaction, and the cycle continues.

Anger held in is often rehearsed in the mind. Past hurts and embarrassments are relived in the imagination with a sense of vengeance and retaliation. And if these angry fantasies continue to reside and are held in, the guilt is fed and grows. The anger and the guilt continue to feed on themselves, and it's difficult to break the cycle.

Ironically, a controlling family member usually feels more out of control than other members. Because he feels out of control of his own feelings, he tries to control how others feel. If you have a controller in your family tree, he/she really wants your love, but the individual probably has tried to get it in a way that has pushed you away or generated anger. And when others don't submit to the person's control, the weapons come out. Some are subtle. Others are blatant. Threats, intimidation, reminding others of how much they do and how others need them are frequent expressions of control. Their anger has many forms of expression. And controllers experience anger easily since they are wounded easily.

Jim, age thirty-eight, was an engineer. When he came home after a tough day, the tension level began to rise and the family would try not to upset Jim more. Even the family dog seemed to withdraw and seek out a safer sanctuary. Jim often berated his children about their homework. He began by checking whether they had begun it, and later would check to be sure they had done the schoolwork as well as their household chores. He would return several times to check up on their progress. "Are you doing your homework like I asked, Jan? What's wrong, Bob, can't you stick to it? You might as well learn good habits now. You won't be a success later if you don't start now."

Each time Jim returned, he repeated his previous tirade. And when they finished their tasks, he had to review what they had done one final time. He did this not only to make sure they understood but to demonstrate that he was in charge and they had to comply with his wishes.

When you grow up with a controller in your family, you soon develop a sensitive antenna that alerts you to any hint of control on the part of others. You easily become angry whenever you encounter someone like this. Who likes to be controlled, anyway? Even a dependent person is angry at the controller even though the resentment is buried and only comes out indirectly.

ABUSE AND ANGER

If you came from a home that was abusive in any way, you know firsthand about anger. An abusive home has anger as the head of the family. You may have had bruises on the outside that were obvious. But bruises on the inside are not obvious. Abuse can be sexual, physical, or emotional. All are expressions of anger. Sally's words reflect what many of my clients say: "Given a choice between physical and emotional abuse, give me the physical. It's obvious. Others can see it, and you get sympathy. Physical abuse only messes you up outside. Emotional abuse messes you up on the inside, and you have to carry the brunt of their anger by yourself. You don't get as much support when you're emotionally abused."

Sally had a right to detest such abuse. The Scriptures clearly warn fathers about verbal abuse, a common form of emotional abuse. "Fathers, do not provoke or irritate or fret your children—do not be hard on them or harass them; lest they become discouraged and sullen and morose and feel inferior and frustrated; do not break their spirit" (Colossians 3:21, Amp.).

Parental anger will leave inner and outer bruises on the children. The results are long lasting in some cases and guide the direction of that person's life for years to come. Unfortunately, verbal abusers get away with their damaging tactics more than the physical abusers. Some hold nothing back. Their anger includes degrading comments about their children. Their attacks are vicious, and they are oblivious to the damage that they do to their child's self-esteem.

PSYCHOLOGICAL ABUSE

Many expressions of anger are labeled psychological maltreatment. This is anger expressed as an attack on *who* the child is and *how* he responds to life. Consider the five ways in light of your own upbringing. Did you ever experience these?

Rejection. Your worth wasn't acknowledged nor were your needs.

Isolation. You were cut off from normal social experiences and were made to believe that you were all alone in the world.

Terror. You were verbally assaulted and learned to live in fear.

Being ignored. You were deprived of all of the life experiences and stimulation that you needed. Consequently you grew up having been stifled emotionally and intellectually.

Being corrupted. You were forced to engage in activities that were deviant and thus have difficulty fitting in emotionally.[3]

These five acts are all expressions of abuse and anger and they do have lasting results.

Some verbal abuse (anger) falls under the falsehood of guidance or help. Parents or other family members justify their put-downs and harsh statements. "Hey, I'm trying to help you. Don't you want my help? I know what's good for you." This is still an angry parent.

Too often abusive parents are unable to see their behavior as abusive, and that is why they continue in this pattern without ever seeking help. They deny what they do to themselves, other family members, and the outside world as well. Why does this happen? There are several reasons. It's a way to avoid feeling guilty or to avoid the effort and pain of trying to make changes in their life. The denial also lets the parent avoid facing the fact that he/she also was unloved as a child. Therefore parents often tend to do what was done to them even though they hated it.[4]

ABUSE AND PERFECTION

Perfectionistic parents are abusers. Shocking? Perhaps, but they do abuse in yet another way. If they are true perfectionists they abuse themselves as well as others. The unrealistic standards and expectations they have for themselves and others make a child think he is becoming a failure. Children of a perfectionist often wither emotionally because of lack of encouragement and affirmation. Perfectionists have tunnel vision. They see only results and only recognize 100 percent. A grade of B+ or A- is not recognized; instead the child hears, "Why wasn't this an A?" The child completes 95 percent of an arduous task but is not recognized; the 5 percent undone becomes the negative focus.

Perfectionists are angry people. They are angry because they never can accomplish what they want to; nor can their family. They live in a constant state of frustration: no one has ever had lasting success as a perfectionist.

THE CONSEQUENCES OF ABUSE

A child who was punished excessively by any means often ends up with a pool of raging anger over the injustices. An abused child carries damage into adult life. As an adult it is likely that he now responds to those abuses in one of three different ways: (1) he behaves and responds to others in a way that tends to elicit other people's anger; (2) he is angry at what happened and wants to get back at others; or (3) he has tremendous guilt and feelings of unworthiness.

The second outcome, trying to get back at others, is due to the typical absence of their parents. Adults who are abuse victims focus their anger on other people and reap the results of this anger. Their anger alienates others because it's an anger driven by vengeance. Their energy in adulthood is misdirected and limits the development of their potential in life.

Because they were punished so much, they perpetuate the pattern of punishment in their own life through excessive work, being ruthless with others, over-moralizing, or being excessively self-righteous. One of the saddest and strangest responses is their inability to accept gracious love and acceptance from others who are capable of giving it to them. This inability is the result of their feelings of unworthiness. They reject love or act in a way to discourage its expression.

For instance, June would answer every compliment she received with a nonloving explanation. Once she said, "You don't have any idea why I did that, do you? Well, it's not what you think." When her children came to give her hugs, she would push them away with such statements as, "Not now, can't you see I'm busy?" and, "Stop it. I don't have time for this."

Concerning the third outcome, many abuse victims fear rejection. Overly sensitive people carry the fear of anticipated rejection with them throughout their lives. Some lay awake at night rehearsing what they think people say about them or might say to them. Many who were verbally abused see anger where it doesn't exist. They expect it, anticipate it and read it into other people's reactions. They have difficulty sorting through what is real and what isn't. They have difficulty accepting the positive and the potential for being accepted.

Part of the reason that anger toward family members generates guilt is because being angry at these people is guilt producing. After all, you are supposed to love them. You may be especially prone toward guilt if it was used as a weapon in your family. (Chapter 12 discusses in detail the causes of abuse and ways to stop abuse as a response to anger.)

GUILT AS CONTROL

Perhaps a family member used one of the more subtle forms of anger against you—pouting. If they were displeased with you, they may have withdrawn and pouted. Then how did you feel? Probably a bit guilty. Then perhaps you complied with what they wanted you to do.

Some parents or siblings use hidden agendas to control their family. It's a sure way to create the conditions for anger.

Hanna is shopping with her thirty-year-old son as he looks for a new sport coat. She never comes out straight with a directive but instead asks, "Son, do you really think that you need a new sport coat at this time in your life?" What does her son hear in that question? "You don't need it." How will he feel if he goes ahead and makes the purchase—guilty. How will he feel if he doesn't—angry. He's caught. Perhaps you've felt caught in a bind such as this.

Your family tree did bear fruit. But it may not be the fruit you want. Are you satisfied today with your style and expression of anger? Is it really yours? It should reflect something that you have developed; however, it could be only a bitter legacy that continues to control your life.

An End to Childhood Patterns

A difficulty that many people face is being stuck in the memories of anger in the home when they were children. Often the family pattern that you see today is the memory of your childhood. The parent you see today is the memory of your childhood. That pattern can remain with your childhood memories, imprisoning both the family pattern and yourself. This may prevent you from changing your anger approach and style of expression. Or you may learn to express anger in a new and healthy manner.

You may wish the expression of anger in your family had been different. It wasn't then. It may not be now. Your parents and siblings may be the same. But what about you? You can be stuck with their pattern. You can deny your feelings or the pain you once experienced. Or as an adult you can address those issues and change your anger response.

You cannot change your past experiences by pretending they didn't happen. But you can change their effect and continued expression in your own life. It's your choice. The next chapter will help you begin to understand how to properly respond to your anger, dismissing common myths about anger, and uncovering important truths about anger's purpose in your life.

TAKE CHARGE

1. Did your parents engage in verbal abuse when they were angry with you? The abuse can be a put-down, double message, moralizing to create guilt, sarcasm, or ridiculing humor. Consider the following comments and check any you heard (or similar words) while growing up at home.

   ☐ "When are you going to get smart? Sometimes you are really dumb" (a put-down).

   ☐ "I'm glad you're listening for a change. If you would do it more often, you might learn something" (double message).

   ☐ "You should always obey me. Remember, God says to honor your parents. When you don't, you make God angry. If you would obey me, God would be happy with you" (moralizing or acting pious to create guilt).

   ☐ "You are so smart, aren't you? We won't have to send you to college, 'cause you know so much now" (sarcasm).

   ☐ "Can't you take a joke? I was only kidding. Get a sense of humor, for pete's sake!" (clever, I-didn't-mean-it comment after teasing the child).

2. Review the above statements and ask yourself as an adult (and a parent) whether you have made any of these comments. You may be repeating a family pattern. Put an "A" for adult in front of any of the statements you have said in the past year.

3. You may have responded to your parent's criticism like most people, with guilt, fear, sadness, or anger. Today, how do you respond to criticism as an adult? (Check all that apply.)

   ☐ I feel guilty.   ☐ I feel afraid.
   ☐ I get sad.   ☐ I get angry.
   ☐ I seek revenge.   ☐ Other: _____.

4. Who do you feel attempted to control you when you were a child. How was this accomplished? _____
_____

NOTES

1. Dennis and Matthew Linn, *Healing Life's Hurts* (New York: Paulist Press, 1978), p. 102-3, adapted.
2. David Viscott, *I Love You, Let's Work It Out* (New York: Simon and Schuster, 1987), p. 67.
3. Victoria Secunda. *When You and Your Mother Can't Be Friends* (New York: Delacorte, 1990) p. 25.
4. Ibid., p. 37.

3

THE MYTHS OF ANGER

D avid Burke's last words were tainted by vengeance. "Hi, Ray, I think it's sort of ironic that we end up like this," he scribbled on an air sickness bag. "I asked for some leniency for my family, remember? Well I got none and you'll get none."

Before writing that fateful note to his boss, the former PSA flight attendant had left one final telephone message. It was tinged with love.

"Jackie, this is David. I'm on my way to San Francisco, Flight 1771. I love you. I really wish I could say more, but I do love you."

No one knows what Ray Thomson told David Burke when he fired him for allegedly pocketing $69 in in-flight cocktail receipts. Those who knew Ray Thomson described him as quiet but confident, the kind of guy who didn't take guff.

Whatever Thomson said, Burke didn't buy it. Unemployed, spurned by his girlfriend, he apparently began making quiet but methodical preparations for a bizarre murder-suicide mission that would kill a planeload of people.

On Monday all of the rejection, all of the suppressed and hidden anger exploded 22,000 feet over central California. Shots splintered the calm of a routine commuter flight, and if his calculated death plan of revenge succeeded, at least one shot probably tore into Thomson.

The pilot radioed, "I have an emergency . . . gunfire." Sounds of a tremendous scuffle would be heard later on a cockpit voice recorder tape. A groan. A gasp. Then PSA flight 1771 plunged nose first into a cattle ranch in San Luis Obispo County.

A few days later, David's father, Altamont Burke, tried to make sense of the tragedy. "My son was a gentle guy, but don't talk any trash to him," he said.

Burke, Thomson, and forty-one other persons died, their bodies ripped apart and flung across acres of green hillside. Lying in the rubble was a .44 caliber magnum with six cartridges spent.

Also found in the carnage was the air sickness bag that spelled out the apparent motive for mass murder.[1]

From many of the newspaper reports and interviews with family and friends it was clear that David Burke did not appear to be the typical angry person. You might be asking yourself just what do we mean by a "typical angry person"? That's an important question. But let's turn it around. How would *you* describe the "typical" angry person? When you think of anger or angry people what comes into your mind? What do angry people look like? What do angry people sound like? What does it feel like to be around someone who is frequently and visibly angry?

That last question contains one of the key words many people use to identify an angry person. That word is *visibly*. One of the many myths regarding anger is that if a person doesn't look or appear to be angry, then he doesn't have a problem with anger; he is clearly not an angry person.

After reading chapter 1 of this book, you probably realize that anger is a complex emotion. It can disguise itself in many ways. One of the major reasons that the emotion of anger has gained a primarily negative reputation is that there is so much misinformation about what anger is and can be. This misinformation has produced a lot of misunderstanding. It is truly unfortunate that the mostly incorrect and inaccurate information far outweighs the true and accurate facts regarding this powerful and potentially positive emotion.

Many of these misunderstandings have been sanctioned by our society and have become myths—fiction that has become accepted as fact. For the past several years I have collected some of the most common cultural myths regarding anger. I would like you to read through the following list of anger myths. If *at any time in your life* you have either outwardly agreed with a particular statement or have by your actions functioned as if it were true, place an

A for agree in the blank in front of the statement. For those statements that you have never believed to be true, place a D for disagree in the blank. Remember that your response does not necessarily indicate your current belief but rather those statements that you have at some time in your life accepted.

_____ 1. God is love, and anger is the opposite of love. Therefore God is against anger, and whenever we allow ourselves to get angry we are sinning.

_____ 2. If a person doesn't look or sound angry, he doesn't have a problem with anger.

_____ 3. Anger always leads to some form of violence, and therefore it is never good to be angry.

_____ 4. If you express anger to someone you love, it will destroy the relationship. Anger and love don't mix.

_____ 5. The best way to deal with anger is to ignore it. If you ignore anger it will go away.

_____ 6. The best way to deal with anger is to stuff it. Expressing anger breeds even more anger and leads to loss of control.

_____ 7. The best way to deal with anger is to dump it. Just get all of that anger out of your system. You and everyone else will feel better when you express it.

_____ 8. Nice people don't get angry.

If you marked the letter A next to even one of the above statements then don't think of skipping to the next chapter. This chapter has some important information that you can't afford to miss. Let's explore each one of these myths.

Myth #1: *God is love, and anger is the opposite of love. Therefore God is against anger, and whenever we get angry we are sinning.*

This particular myth, or variations of it, is one of the most common misconceptions about anger. I'm not sure how it got started, but I recently discovered for myself one of the ways in which it is perpetuated.

The senior pastor at our church had asked me to give a series of three messages on anger for the evening services. On the first Sunday of the series, I was driving my family home from the morning service. As my wife and I were discussing one of the points of the Sunday school lesson, Matt, my five-year-old, interrupted with "Dad, guess what I learned in Sunday school today?"

"I don't know, son, but I sure would like to know."

"Well," he said after a short pause, "did you know that whenever you get angry you are sinning?"

I couldn't believe my ears. My five-year-old son had been taught in Sunday school one of the major misconceptions of anger that I would be debunking in my evening message. Matt's teacher is not alone in accepting this myth. Many Christians don't understand the Bible's teaching about the emotion of anger. The topic first appears in Genesis 4:5; the last reference to anger is found in Revelation 19:15. In the Old Testament alone anger is mentioned 455 times, and 375 of those references deal with God's anger. If God displays anger, the emotion cannot be sinful.

The Old Testament reports numerous instances in which God expresses anger or is described as being angry. God is described as being angry with the people of Israel for their rebellion—His ego was bruised because man wouldn't be subject to Him. His anger, however, had its source in His love, not in hate. It resulted in discipline and acts of love designed to restore a broken relationship with Him. God's anger revealed how much God really cared. It revealed His patience. It revealed Himself. God's anger arises out of love.

One of the reasons many individuals fall prey to myth #1, one friend suggests, is that they confuse anger and hate. Anger is an emotion. Hate is an emotion. Anger is not hate. Hate is not anger. Hate is the opposite of love. Anger is the opposite of apathy. Is God's anger qualitatively different from man's anger?

With men and women, anger often arises out of bitterness and hatred. In fact, the association is so strong in some people's minds that anger and hatred are often seen as synonymous. Anger becomes a sign of hatred. This error can make it difficult to understand God's anger. Some Bible teachers have never clearly seen the distinction between anger and hate. They seem to teach that God is a primarily punitive God who acts out of His hate for certain people. This thinking implies a very small and insecure God—one who gets upset at every offense to His pride. God turns quickly, then, from love to hate, depending on His mood at the moment.

This confusion of anger with hate can only be corrected by a careful study of Scripture. Consider, for example, Psalm 106. The psalmist declares in verse 40 that "the Lord was angry with His people." It is clear that the rebellion of His people caused the anger. But further reading shows this not to be the emotion of hate. The response is not of punishment but of discipline and correction. Yes, he did hand them over to their enemies. But then: "Many times he delivered them . . . he took note of their distress . . . he remembered his covenant . . . out of his great love he relented" (43-45).

These are not acts of hate. Here we see God's anger arise out of love. It is a means whereby God communicates His character. It is intended to convey that discipline has its foundations in love. Anger brings reality to the seriousness of the relationship.

In the middle of writing this chapter I received a phone call from a friend who, for years, has been struggling with being a workaholic, with taking on too many projects. He has used his busyness as a way to run from and avoid dealing with both personal and relationship issues. When he told me about his schedule for the next several months I told him that I was angry with him. My anger was not caused by hatred for him—just the opposite. My anger arose because of my love for him and my deep concern for his health and well-being.

Unless we are able to make a clear distinction between anger and hate it will be difficult for our hearts to be truly free to love. Love will express itself at times as anger. Recently my son Nathan was in a hurry to get to his friend's house. He jumped on his bike and rode down our driveway and out into the street without first looking both ways for cars. I could see a car coming towards him and yelled at Nathan to get out of the middle of the street. After the car passed I went over to him to remind him of the importance of looking both ways before crossing the street. The first thing he said was "Thanks, Dad."

Then Nathan looked up at me and asked, "Dad, are you mad at me?"

"No, pal," I replied, "I was afraid you might get hurt." He knew that I didn't hate him but that my love for him and my fear for his safety led to the strong response.

Paul destroys the myth that all anger is sin when he says: "Be angry and yet do not sin; do not let the sun go down on your anger, and do not give the devil an opportunity." (Ephesians 4:26-27, NASB). The translators of the *New American Standard Version* of the Bible accurately translate the meaning of the original Greek text of verse 26 in which we are given two commands. Do be angry but don't sin. Paul makes clear that while it is normal to experience anger, we can choose to express that anger in ways that are not sinful.

This distinction between having anger and expressing anger is crucial. In fact, a basic error of many of the anger myths is the failure to make this distinction. The experience of anger is a normal and natural one. As part of being made in God's image, humans have emotions, and one of those emotions is anger. Like all of God's gifts, anger has tremendous potential for good. On the other hand, the expression of anger is optional. We can choose to express our anger in healthy or unhealthy ways—in ways that heal or in ways that hurt. We can allow our anger to dominate and control us, or we can, with God's help and with a little bit of work, learn how to make the emotion of anger work for us rather than against us. We can develop healthy and constructive expressions of anger.

The experience of anger is not optional, but the expression of anger is. I can be angry and sin, or I can be angry and not sin. The sin does not lie in the fact of my experience of the emotion of anger but rather in how I choose to express it.

For each one of these anger myths a few corrections can be made to turn an anger myth into an anger fact. Here is the first:

Anger Fact #1: *God is love and one expression of God's love for us is that He created us in His image.* Since God has emotions, we have emotions. Although the experience of the emotion of anger is not optional, we can choose our expression of anger. God is glorified and we are both healthier and happier when we choose to express the emotion of anger in healthy and constructive ways.

Myth #2: *If a person doesn't look or sound angry he doesn't have an anger problem.*

Over the past twenty years I have administered a particular psychological test to several thousand individuals. One of the scales on this test measures anger. Countless times, individuals have scored high on the anger scale. When I tell them this fact, many respond with surprise and even shock. "I never yell at my wife or my kids. In fact I rarely even raise my voice. This must be a mistake—anyone who knows me can tell you that I'm not an angry person."

Myth #2 assumes that whenever we experience an emotion we are probably aware of it and it can't help but show itself on our faces. It is true that some individuals have a difficult time disguising what they feel. Even a stranger can look at the person's face or listen to his voice and tell what is going on inside. But a lot of people wear a straight face and rein in their emotions.

Many people at times are angry but are not aware of it or, if they are, have learned to repress, suppress, deny, or ignore it. Consider the vengeful flight attendant David Burke. Many described Burke as gentle, someone who did not appear to be an angry man. But he did have an anger problem. His inability or unwillingness to deal with his anger in constructive ways led to the destruction of himself and forty-two innocent people.

Anger Fact #2: *Just because you don't look or feel angry does not mean you don't have a problem with anger.* Anyone who does not understand and appreciate the potential value of anger may have a problem with anger. Anyone who hasn't identified his typical pattern of dealing with anger and hasn't developed healthy ways to express his anger does have a problem with anger.

Myth #3: *Anger always leads to some form of violence, and therefore it is never good to be angry.*

Most people we have met *say* they don't believe this particular myth. The vast majority of people who have responded to our questionnaire on anger myths have indicated that they have never believed or accepted myth #3. However, in sitting down with couples and discussing their individual ways of dealing with anger, one spouse will make the observation that while his or her partner may not consciously agree with this myth, in the actual behavior the partner functions as if this were true.

Carol is a good example of this situation. Carol and her husband, Mike, have five children. For many years Carol stayed at home with the primary responsibility for raising the children. But in recent years she has been very successful in business. Carol and Mike first came in seeking help in resolving their conflicts. They had struggled for many years trying to solve both marital and parenting kinds of problems. Most of the time they settled on a short-term compromise but were never able to identify or deal with the core issues.

"I am not an angry person," Carol said with some pride. "In fact, I rarely feel anger as an emotion," she said as Mike and I listened. However, Carol admitted that she was frequently forgetful, tended to avoid problems, was often late, liked to change the subject, and had some good skills in the use of subtle sarcasm.

In taking a brief history of each person's family-of-origin, I learned Carol's father had been an alcoholic. "But I don't think I've been affected by his alcoholism," she added quickly. "Our family had healthy relationships." Carol was the oldest child in a dysfunctional family, but she did not recognize herself as being the product of a dysfunctional family.

Carol, the oldest child, began to talk about how she would wait up for her father on weekend nights. "I would keep my bedroom window open and listen for how he would drive the car into the driveway, how he would slam the car door, the sound of his walking up the steps. Then, of course, I would listen for the sound of his voice and watch for a certain look on his face. Certain nonverbal signs always told me whether or not he would be beating Mom that night. I always knew if I had to gather up my brothers and sisters and get them out of the way."

"Whenever Dad got angry he would either beat on Mom or one of the kids." she added.

At an early age, Carol had learned to equate anger with violence. To her, the experience of anger and its expression through violence had become synonymous. Because she had vowed to herself that she would never be like her father, she simply denied any feelings of anger, and she believed that if she was never violent she could not be angry. Over a period of several months, Carol and Mike were helped to distinguish between the experience of anger and the various ways in which anger can be expressed. Carol learned that while she had frequently felt the emotion of anger, she had simply found different ways to express it. Although her passive and indirect expressions of anger were not as violent as her father's active and direct expressions, both her father and Carol handled their anger in unhealthy ways.

Carol's denial of anger served to obscure and hide her true hurts and needs and concerns both from Mike and from herself. Therefore, both of them were frustrated, unfulfilled, and had, at best, a superficial relationship.

Anger expressed in violent ways is not the only possibility. In later chapters we will be presenting a number of healthy and constructive ways to express anger. As Carol and Mike learned how to better understand and deal with the emotion of anger, they became free to identify and deal with core issues in their marriage and thus experience the deep intimacy that each one was seeking.

It is obvious that Anger Myth #3 is just that, a myth. How could you reword and correct Anger Myth #3 and turn it into an Anger Fact? Write your response in the space below:

Anger Fact #3: _____

_____

Myth #4: *If you express anger to someone you love, it will destroy the relationship*. Anger and love just don't mix.

Jim and Barb's marriage had begun like most. They both had many hopes, dreams, and expectations. During their courtship they had talked for hours on end and almost never disagreed. Even on the rare occasions when they did disagree it was never difficult or painful. They took the time to honestly share their ideas and, as a result of the discussion, went away from the disagreement with a stronger sense of understanding and oneness.

Within the first six months of marriage it became clear that Jim was much more of an introvert than Barb. When he came home from work he wanted to be alone for a while to rest and relax, to get his mind off the day's work and recharge his batteries. Barb was much more of an extrovert. When she came home from work she wanted the exact opposite. She wanted to tell Jim about the events of the day, to talk about what she had done, who she had seen. Then she would plan some activity for the evening, preferably with their friends.

With each passing month their differences became more obvious. Jim became increasingly frustrated with what he interpreted as Barb's incessant desire to talk and to be around people and her insensitivity to his need for some space. Barb became increasingly frustrated with what she interpreted as Jim's intentional distance, his unwillingness to share, and his seeming antisocial tendencies.

As their frustration increased, so did their anger. Both Jim and Barb had been raised in good Christian homes. They both believed that it was wrong to get angry and that expressing anger could jeopardize their marriage. At this point, they didn't understand that while everybody experiences anger there are a variety of constructive ways to express that anger. To them, any expression of anger was negative.

So what did they do? Jim dealt with his anger by hiding. He continued to retreat more and more into his computer and into his love of watching sports on television. Consciously, he felt a lot of pressure from Barb to perform and be someone he wasn't. Unconsciously, he felt misunderstood and unloved.

Barb dealt with her anger in an opposite but equally ineffective kind of way. She began to involve herself in more activities. She took on extra jobs at work. She became more active at church by joining the choir and teaching a third-grade Sunday school class.

Consciously, Barb felt deserted by Jim. *The computer and television have become more important to him than I am*, she told herself (but not Jim). She felt misunderstood, unaccepted, and unloved.

What was happening to their relationship? By not expressing and dealing with their anger, Barb and Jim were destroying their relationship. They were becoming married singles.

It is important to understand that while anger and love are separate emotions, the deeper the caring the deeper the potential for frustration. That can lead to much anger. By not being in touch with and communicating their anger to each other, Barb and Jim were not allowing the other person to understand their hurts and frustrations. By not sharing their hurts and frustrations they could not understand each other better and thus more effectively love each other.

In the sometimes delightful process of two individuals becoming one in their marriage, differences will arise. Those differences are what brought the two together. Yet those crucial differences can become the source of their greatest frustration and pain. Those differences provide the strength and balance in the relationship. The process of negotiating those differences is what allows our hearts to be knit together as one, to experience the breadth and depth of what true love can be.

Anger Fact #4: *If I am aware of my anger and choose to express it to someone I love in healthy ways, the anger can be used of God to help strengthen and enrich our relationship.* Both love and anger are God-given emotions that can strengthen and enrich any relationship.

Myth #5: *The best way to deal with anger is to ignore it. If you ignore anger it will go away.*

Imagine that you are driving down the street and you notice that the red warning light has appeared in the upper corner of your dash. You are running a bit late and don't have the time to check the source of the problem. You decide to simply ignore it. After all, if it just came on it can't be serious. After driving a few more miles the red light begins to bother you. You reach across the seat into your briefcase and pull out a small yellow Post-It® note and place it over the red warning light. Now that you can't see the warning light you feel much better.

What would you do if you were that driver? Does ignoring the warning light make good sense? Would it help your car run better or get to its destination faster? *Of course not!* However, what many people would never think of doing with their automobile they do on a daily basis with their emotions and thus with their body. One of the many potentially positive aspects of anger is that it can serve as an effective warning system. (We will discuss this in a later chapter.) Healthy anger can alert us to and help us identify problems and needs. Such a warning often can provide us the energy to do something about them.

Anger myth #5 really has two parts and both are erroneous. The first part suggests that ignoring anger can be healthy. The second part suggests that anger and the issues that led to it will somehow disappear. To say that ignoring our anger is healthy makes about as much sense as saying that it is healthy to ignore chest pain. Ignoring anger can be hazardous to your health.

On a short-term basis ignoring our anger may seem like a wise choice. Like the driver, we simply cover up the red warning light. There are usually few, if any, immediate consequences. At the moment the light was covered, the car didn't stop. In fact, not only did the car keep on running but there was no longer any irritating red warning light to contend with. Unfortunately in most cases, the car cannot run very long. And when it does break down, the repair bill invariably will be much more expensive than if the driver had heeded the warning.

Over the years I've discovered that whenever we ignore or bury an emotion it is buried alive. At some time and in some way that ignored or buried emotion will express itself—physically, psychologically, or spiritually. This principle is especially true as it relates to the powerful emotion of anger. What are some of the long-term costs of ignoring our anger?

A rapidly growing body of research strongly suggests the detrimental effects on your health of ignoring anger. A twelve-year longitudinal study of 10,000 people revealed that those who suppressed anger were more than twice as likely to die of heart disease as those who expressed anger in healthy ways. A twenty-five-year study showed that people with high hostility scores had higher incidence of heart disease; they were also five times more likely to die by age fifty from all causes of disease than their low-scoring counterparts. Other research over a twenty-year period correlated higher hostility scores not only with increased rates of coronary heart disease but also with incidence of cancer, accidents, and suicide.[2]

Carl Simonton and his psychologist wife, Stefanie Matthews-Simonton, have done significant work with cancer victims. The results of their research suggest that there is a cancer-prone personality, that certain combinations of traits make some people especially vulnerable to cancer. Some of these characteristics include a tendency to hold resentment, an inability or unwillingness to forgive, a tendency towards self-pity, an impaired ability to develop and maintain meaningful long-term relationships, and a very poor self-image.[3]

Anger Fact #5: *Anger is one of the most powerful of all the emotions, and ignoring your experiences of anger is usually hazardous to your emotional, psychological, physical, and spiritual* *health.* Ignoring anger is an unhealthy choice. In the short-term it hinders us from dealing with the real issues, and in the long-term it significantly increases the probability of physical problems.

Myth #6: *The best way to deal with anger is to stuff it.* Expressing anger breeds even more anger and leads to loss of control.

Stuffing anger? Isn't that the same thing as ignoring anger? What's the difference? When I ignore my anger I don't acknowledge it. I may not even be aware of it; and if I am, I pretend the anger isn't important and doesn't really exist. When I stuff my anger I am very much aware of my anger but I choose to keep it in, to stuff it. For whatever reason—fear of offending someone, fear of losing control, or perhaps fear of looking bad—stuffing it appears to be the healthiest option.

In his book, *Free for the Taking,* missionary Joseph Cooke tells how he tried to suppress his anger:

> . . . Squelching our feelings never pays. In fact, it's rather like plugging up a steam vent in a boiler. When the steam is stopped in one place, it will come out somewhere else. Either that or the whole business will blow up in your face. And bottled-up feelings are just the same. If you bite down your anger, for example, it often comes out in another form that is more difficult to deal with. It changes into sullenness, self-pity, depression, or snide, cutting remarks . . .
>
> Not only may bottled-up emotions come out sideways in various unpleasant forms; they also may build up pressure until they simply have to burst and when they do, someone is almost always bound to get hurt. I remember that for years of my life, I worked to bring my emotions under control. Over and over again, as they cropped up, I would master them in my attempt to achieve what looked like a gracious . . . Christian spirit. Eventually I had nearly everybody fooled, even in a measure my own wife. But it was all a fake. . . . The time came when the whole works blew up in my face, in an emotional breakdown. All the things that had been buried so long came out in the open. Frankly, there was no healing, no recovery, no building a new life for me until all those feelings were sorted out, and until I learned to know them for what they were, accept them, and find some way of expressing them honestly and nondestructively.[4]

Anger Fact #6: *Choose a healthy way to express your anger.* Anger Fact #6 is similar to Anger Fact #5. Unhealthy expressions of anger breed even more anger. They can be destructive and lead to loss of control. Healthy expressions of anger allow you to deal with the root issues and lessen the likelihood of more anger. They are constructive and lead to greater control.

Myth #7: *The best way to deal with anger is to dump it.* Just let all of your anger come forth.

Direct the anger at someone, get it out of your system. You and everyone else will be better off for it. This popular myth sounds good and, on the surface, seems to make sense. Unfortunately, it is not true. A classic example of someone who seems to have believed and practiced this myth is the late football coach Woody Hayes. A *Time* magazine reporter wrote about the sad dismissal of the out-of-contol coach:

> Coach Wayne Woodrow Hayes, sixty-five, the autocrat of Ohio State football for twenty-eight years, was fired after assaulting an opposing player. . . . Violent outbursts were a hallmark of his coaching career. "Woody's idea of sublimating," an acquaintance once said, "is to hit someone." . . . The people closest to him never seemed to lose patience. . . . Yet he was always frighteningly—even pathologically—at the mercy of private demons. "When we lose a game, nobody's madder at me than me," he said five years ago. "When I look into the mirror in the morning, I want to take a swing at me." Literally. After losing to Iowa in 1963, Hayes slashed his face with a large ring on his left hand. Pacing the sidelines, he sometimes bit into the fleshy heel of his hand until it bled. Even a heart attack in 1974 did not make Hayes ease up.[5]

Today when many people think of Coach Woody Hayes they think of a man who was a success at coaching college football but who was a failure at understanding and dealing with his emotions. It is possible for some people to be successful at what they do, at least for a while, and to be a failure in who they are. For a while Hayes was able to get by with his unhealthy ways of expressing his anger, but eventually they caught up with him. He lost the job he so dearly loved. He was fired and disgraced. His legacy was tarnished.

Both practical experience and recent research suggests that just talking about our anger and/or dumping it does not reduce it. In fact, just the opposite takes place—it rehearses and enlarges it. Several recent studies indicate that in the vast majority of cases "ventilation," or dumping of anger, does not in any way act as a catharsis. On the contrary, the individuals in these studies became more hostile rather than less hostile as a result of dumping their anger.[6]

Anger Fact #7: *When you are angry and when you are in doubt about what you want to do, stop and think.* Don't ignore it, don't stuff it, and don't dump it. Take time to understand your feeling of anger, and you will be better able to choose a healthy and constructive way to express it.

Myth #8: *Nice people don't get angry.*

Nice people love. Nice people are compassionate. Nice people are concerned, the myth says. However, nice people also can be discouraged. They can experience hurt, frustration, and fear. Nice people experience anger.

One of the occupational hazards of being human is that we experience emotions—*all* the emotions, including the very basic human emotion of anger. From the nursery to the nursing home the emotion of anger is a universal experience.

Feeling the emotion of anger has nothing to do with being naughty or nice. But when we talk about how we express the emotion of anger, that is a different story. We can choose to express our anger in ways that help or that hinder, in ways that build or that destroy. We can be irresponsible and allow the emotion of anger to control us and express that anger in cruel and violent ways. We can also be wise and choose to express that anger in healthy and positive ways. That's what this book is all about.

Anger Fact #8: *Everyone experiences anger.* Anger is a fact of life. Smart people choose to understand their anger. Healthy people choose to express anger in constructive ways.

Take Action

1. An important first step in helping to develop healthier ways of responding to anger is to identify and become more aware of our existing unhealthy patterns.

Take a few minutes to review the list of anger myths found on page 45. From this list of eight anger myths pick the three that have been most influential in your life. Using three- by five-inch cards, write each unhealthy anger myth on one side and the healthy anger fact on the other side.

2. Carry these 3 x 5 cards with you and for the next thirty days look at them several times a day. You might be surprised at how powerful this simple exercise can be.

Notes

1. Susan Peck. "Mission of Madness," *Long Beach Telegram*, December 18, 1987, p. A1, 6-7.
2. For a discussion of these and other related studies see Matthew McKay, Peter D. Rogers, and Judith McKay, *When Anger Hurts* (Oakland, Calif.: New Harbinger Publication, 1989), pp. 23-32; and Redford Williams, *The Trusting Heart* (New York: Time, 1989), pp. 49-71.
3. Carl Simonton and Stefanie Matthews-Simonton, "Belief Systems and Management of the Emotional Aspects of Malignancy," *Journal of Transpersonal Psychology* 7 (1974):29-47.
4. Joseph Cooke, *Celebration of Grace*, (Grand Rapids, Mich.: Zondervan, 1991), n.p. Previously published as *Free for the Taking*, (Old Tappan, N.J.: Revell, 1975), pp. 109-10.
5. "Violent World of Woody Hayes," *Time*, January 15, 1979, p. 54.
6. Carol Tavris, *Anger: The Misunderstood Emotion* (New York: Simon and Schuster, 1982), pp. 120-50.

4

MADE IN GOD'S IMAGE— EMOTIONS INCLUDED

I 've come to see that I'm afraid of my feelings," Paul said softly. After a long pause he added, "I don't know who I am emotionally, and it scares me to death. I don't think I even know how or what to feel."

For seven years, Paul had been the successful pastor of a large evangelical church. He prided himself on how hard he worked and on how much of his time was spent "serving the Lord." He had viewed his addiction to work as spirituality, and he placed a lot of pressure on his staff to work as hard as he did.

If you had talked with Paul two years earlier he would have told you that he had the perfect marriage, the perfect family, and the perfect ministry. But when his children entered adolescence, they began to challenge him and sometimes rebel. Meanwhile, his wife had become more assertive about her frustration with their lack of meaningful communication and intimacy. The easy answers weren't working anymore.

Paul began to lose his enthusiasm and intensity for ministry. He found himself becoming frustrated at little things that never would have bothered him before. He became more and more negative and critical and found himself face-to-face with a dimension of his life he had worked hard to ignore. He was a wounded healer who had no idea how to understand, let alone deal with, his own pain.

Karen, a successful business manager at a large company, was respected for her commitment and her dependability. Around the office she was known as the one who could always be counted on to spend the extra time to get the job done. The office motto was "If you need something done, ask Karen." At church she was respected for her "unselfishness" and her "servant heart." Her friends at church also knew her to be the kind of person who wouldn't say no.

However, during the past six months Karen had become aware of feelings of bitterness and resentment. She found herself withdrawing from usual activities and avoiding people. In the past two months she had to fight off feelings of wanting to tell people off. She had been able to handle the bitterness and resentment, but the emotion of anger scared her.

Karen had grown up in a small midwestern community. She told me her parents were leaders in the local church. "In our home, emotions were rarely discussed. I never heard my parents say, 'I love you,' and I don't remember them showing any love to each other. The only display of emotions I can remember was hearing my parents yell at each other behind closed doors." This was usually followed by several days of her parents not talking to each other.

"In my family it wasn't OK to express feelings." Karen added. "At an early age we built emotional dams to keep from feeling the pain. I think it was a way to avoid falling into our fear and our sadness."

Both Paul and Karen had come for counseling seeking help in dealing with their anger. They knew that the way they were responding to their anger was a problem. What they did not know was that the root problem was that neither one of them understood the anger. Nor did they know how to deal with their emotions.

At some point they had decided that feelings couldn't be trusted; feelings weren't important. They stopped listening to their feelings, they ignored them, they tried to make them disappear. They both pursued excellence in becoming busy doing other things. Part of their motivation was healthy; they truly cared about people and wanted to help them. But an unhealthy part existed also; they were ignoring the tensions in their own lives as they served others. Busyness can be an effective, temporary anesthetic for emotions. But it is short-term—the pain will return.

The stories of Paul and Karen are similar to those of hundreds of people I have worked with. Their frustration and pain is all too common. Many Christians struggle with their emotions due in part to an inadequate understanding of what it means to be made in God's image and thus have an inaccurate view of emotions. I was fortunate to be raised in a conservative, Bible-believing church; yet as I recall my early training I can't remember one message on emotions and the Christian life.

EMOTIONS AND OUR SPIRITUALITY

Before we consider the role of anger in the family we need to have a basic understanding of emotions. We will have only limited success in dealing with specific emotions, such as anger, unless we understand what emotions are, where they come from, why God gave them to us, and how they function.

Jesus shed His blood on the cross to save men and women from the consequences of their sins and to give each of us eternal life. We call that *justification*. Christ sent the Holy Spirit to indwell us and help us "become conformed to the likeness of his Son" (Romans 8:29). We call that *sanctification*.

Christ died to make a difference in our life. Unfortunately, for some Christians the difference is primarily external or at best intellectual. They are still influenced by old thought patterns and controlled by their emotions. Their lives are still dominated by fear, hurt, frustration, anger, or depression. They have become stuck in relational and emotional ruts and rarely experience the joy of their salvation.

Some get discouraged and feel guilty because they still have those struggles. This creates a problem. Do I share my questions and struggles with others and risk appearing immature and unspiritual? Or do I deny my problems and pretend that everything is going great? Rather than risk the humiliation and possible rejection that might come from revealing their feelings, many Christians ignore their problems and stuff their emotions. But eventually this creates an even greater problem. We can only pretend for so long.

New Creatures But . . .

Part of the problem comes from a misunderstanding of 2 Corinthians 5:17. The King James translation reads: "Therefore if any man be in Christ, he is a new creature: old things are passed away; behold, all things are become new." I have heard some teachers state that if you still struggle with old habits and patterns then it is clear that *all* things haven't become new, and maybe you aren't really saved.

Although wonderful things take place when we ask Christ into our heart, not *all* things become new. Body and soul are not immediately and totally transformed.

When I was born-again God became my Father, my spirit was transformed, and I was transferred from the kingdom of darkness to the kingdom of light. However, I didn't receive a new body and I didn't get a new soul or personality. In the area of my mind I didn't become more intelligent nor did old painful memories disappear overnight. In the area of my emotions I found I still struggled with anger, lust, and depression. In the area of the will my deeply ingrained habit patterns didn't immediately vanish. The process of becoming "conformed to the likeness of his Son" (Romans 8:29*a*) and becoming "the righteousness of God in Him" (2 Corinthians 5:21, NASB) takes time. Maturity is indeed a process.

When we ask Christ into our hearts, a radical transformation takes place. However, the consequences that sin has had on our mind, will, and emotions do not immediately disappear. I believe that an important part of the process of sanctification involves the healing of our damaged emotions.

One of the most significant aspects of being a person is that we were created in God's image. We bear the image of and in specific ways resemble our Creator. Even though the image of God in men and women was damaged and distorted by sin, we are still image-bearers.

When God created us in His image He gave us mind, will, and emotions. As image-bearers we have the capacity to feel, to think, and to make choices. Francis Schaeffer said that "as God is a person, He feels, thinks, and acts: so I am a person, who feels, thinks and acts."

FACTS AND FEELINGS TOGETHER

It is unfortunate that over the years many Christians have emphasized the mind and the will to the exclusion of the emotions. Some are more comfortable with facts than feelings, others with ideas than with people. Many of us have been led to believe that spiritual maturity consists primarily of acquiring facts or head knowledge. The more propositional truth we can cram in our craniums the more spiritual we will become. Some have taught that if we fill our mind with the "right" information and make the "right" choices our emotions will take care of themselves and automatically follow right behind.

The obvious implication is that emotions aren't important. Certainly they are not worth paying much attention to. Yet maturity is more than the acquisition of facts and head knowledge. True maturity involves the transformation of the total person. It involves becoming conformed to Christ in our mind, our will, and our emotions.

Head knowledge is important, yet true spirituality is much more than what I know or don't know. True spiritual maturity includes growth and development in the understanding and expressing of our emotions. God's Word is clear that the fundamental mark of a Christian is not merely what or how much he or she knows but how he or she lives.

"By this all men will know that you are my disciples, if you love one another," Christ said (John 13:35). When Christ met Peter by the Sea of Galilee He didn't give him a lecture on the correct way to catch fish. He asked, "Do you love me?" (John 21:15)

Emotions are important. Emotions enhance our ability to be in relationship with God and with one another. But due to the Fall and the effects of sin in our lives, our emotions, like our mind and our will, have become damaged and distorted. For many the emotions that God gave to make life more meaningful instead make life more miserable.

EMOTIONS: PART OF WHO WE ARE

The Bible has a lot to say about emotions. From Genesis through Revelation we read about God's emotions and the emotions of men and women He created. In the New Testament we find that Christ experienced and expressed a wide range of emotions including love, compassion, joy, fear, sorrow, discouragement, frustration, hurt, loneliness, and anger.

Our emotions influence almost every aspect of our lives. God speaks to us through our emotions. They are like a sixth sense. Emotions help us to monitor our needs, make us aware of good and evil, provide motivation and energy for growth and change. Emotions give us the vigor, power, and impetus for living.

THREE WAYS TO RESPOND

Sin has led to our responding to emotions in one of two unhealthy ways. First, we can deny or ignore our emotions. From this perspective the intellectual is more important than the emotional. In its extreme form head knowledge is deified and emotions are suspect. Emotions at best are unimportant and at worst a mark of immaturity. Unfortunately when we ignore or minimize the emotional realities of our life it distorts our perspective, limits our perception, and leads us to distrust our experience. We often tend to deny or ignore the very things God wants to use to help us grow.

Second, we can allow ourselves to be controlled by our emotions. This is an equally dangerous position. From this perspective the intellect is suspect. "If I don't feel it then I can't trust it," say those who embrace emotions exclusively. Consider the consequences. When Saul allowed his jealousy over David's popularity and success to be in control, he was not able to learn from his mistakes (1 Samuel 18-20). With the Jews at Kadesh-Barnea, anger and fear limited their ability to recall what God had done for them. With Elijah under the juniper tree, fear and depression caused him to lose perspective and want to die.

Whether you deny or ignore your emotions (option #1) or you embrace them and ignore your intellect (option #2), your response is not healthy.

By God's grace there is a third option. The healthy response is to view our emotions from God's perspective and to bring them into harmony with our mind. Maturity involves the whole person. It is impossible to be spiritually mature and emotionally immature. True maturity involves a balance among our heart, head, and will; among our feeling, thinking, and doing. Each one is important.

Each one was designed by God for our good. Each one is a manifestation of the image of God in us.

An important part of the process of sanctification is the healing of our damaged emotions. God wants to help us recover from the effects of sin on this key dimension of our personality, to restore healthy God-designed balance among our ability to think, choose, and feel.

Defining Our Emotions

What exactly are emotions? I've asked that question to numerous groups and the most common response is "Emotions are what I feel." That's a true statement and many people use feelings and emotions interchangeably, yet it doesn't give us a definition. It's similar to trying to define air by saying "Air is what I breathe." Most people are surprised that something as common as emotions can be so difficult to define.

"I am fearfully and wonderfully made," King David declared (Psalm 139:14). In no place is the complexity of God's creation more evident than in our emotional makeup. Our emotions are complex. The experience of emotions involve sensory, skeletal, motor, autonomic, and cognitive systems.

There are several ways to define emotion. Let's start with a formal definition. Webster defines emotion as "a psychic and physical reaction subjectively experienced as strong feeling and physiologically involving changes that prepare the body for immediate vigorous action." *Vigorous action* are the key words. The word *emotion* is derived from the Latin word *emovare*, which means "to move." Thus emotion involves motion, movement, and energy. I heard one speaker say that emotion should be spelled E-motion since emotions are energy in motion.

Finkelhor calls emotions the driving forces of our lives:

> [Emotions are the] motivating forces of our lives, driving us to go ahead, pushing us backward, stopping us completely, determining what we do, how we feel, what we want, and whether we get what we want. Our hates, loves, fears, and what to do about them are determined by our emotional structure. There is nothing in our lives that does not have the emotional factor as its mainspring. It gives us power, or makes us weak, operates for our benefit or to our detriment, for our happiness or confusion.[1]

What are some of the most common emotions? During scores of seminars and workshops, I've asked participants to make a list of frequently experienced emotions. The groups have listed as few as eleven and as many as eighty-two different examples of what they considered emotions. Interestingly, the group that came up with only eleven was a group of men and the group that listed eighty-two was composed of women. Here are thirty emotions that are most frequently listed.

loved	happy
pleased	angry
surprised	accepted
confident	bored
concerned	elated
confused	embarrassed
fearful	excited
frustrated	hurt
frightened	humiliated
glad	grieving
generous	depressed
scared	terrified
lonely	proud
uncomfortable	worried
unsure	sad

COMMON CHARACTERISTICS

If we are to move toward emotional maturity, we must be able to recognize certain features of all emotions. One of the most helpful ways to understand emotions is to look at some characteristics that emotions have in common.

EMOTIONS AFFECT EVERYONE

Characteristic #1: Emotions affect every person.

Tom was a tall, athletic man in his mid-fifties. He had grown up in the Sand Hills of western Nebraska and had been a cattle rancher all his life. When he came into my office the first thing he said was, "I want you to know that I'm just not an emotional kind of guy." He went on to explain that some people, especially women, have a lot of emotions and some people don't. He was convinced that he was someone who didn't have or need many emotions. That philosophy had worked for most of his life. However, when land prices fell and he found out that his wife had cancer, his emotion-free world began to crumble.

Some people are more aware of their emotions than others, but the experience of emotions isn't optional. Regardless of your gender, age, race, or socioeconomic level, emotions are an integral part of your standard equipment. The only thing that's optional is how we choose to express them. I can't always choose what I'm going to feel. But I can choose how long I feel it. With God's help we can change our emotional pattern.

EMOTIONS ARE NEITHER GOOD NOR BAD

Characteristic #2: Emotions are neither constructive nor destructive; emotions are neutral. What we do with them, however, will have a positive or negative impact on our lives.

Several authors and some speakers have labeled emotions good and bad, right and wrong, or constructive and destructive. I even heard someone give one list of emotions we should cultivate and another list of emotions we should at all costs avoid.

There aren't any good or bad emotions. However, emotions can have a good or bad effect on our lives. Consider the emotion of love. Most people would view love as a positive emotion. Yet in Proverbs we are warned to guard our affections because they influence everything else in our lives. Indeed, when we allow love to get out of control or attach love to the wrong person or thing it can blind us to reality and have a devastating effect.

For example, narcissism involves an immature, self-centered and inordinate love of self that narrows our world and limits our ability to grow. It was a narcissist who wrote the poem:

> *I love myself, I think I'm grand*
> *I go to the movies and I hold my hand,*
> *I put my arms around my waist,*
> *And when I get fresh I slap my face.*

As we discussed in chapter 2, anger is usually viewed as a negative emotion. When anger is out of control it can have a devastating effect. Anger provides a source of power that can be used for good or for evil.

When we understand our anger and choose to express it in healthy kinds of ways it has enormous potential for good. One reason people talk about good and bad emotions is their failure to separate an emotion, with its arousal and corresponding physiological changes, from the behaviors a person makes in response to that emotion. Maturity involves learning how to distinguish between the emotion and how we choose to express that emotion.

What a person feels is one thing. What he chooses to do in response to that feeling is another. The very same emotion can be constructive or destructive. The degree to which our emotions help us or hinder us depends on the degree to which we acknowledge them, understand them, choose to channel them through our thought life, and view them from a balanced, healthy perspective.

EMOTIONS CAN DECEIVE US

Characteristic #3: We can have strong emotions and not be aware of them.

One of the psychological tests we use in our clinic has a scale that measures hostility. On one occasion a man scored 96 out of a possible 100 points. When I started to discuss this with him he interrupted and in a loud voice stated, "These test results are wrong. I am not an angry man!" The expression on his wife's face told me different. It was difficult for him to even admit the possibility that he was at times dominated by his anger.

Whether we engage in denial, suppresssion, or simply are unaware of them, our emotions influence our daily life. As characteristic #1 declares, emotions affect everyone.

EMOTIONS ARE OUR RESPONSE TO THOUGHTS OR EVENTS

Characteristic #4: Emotions have a stimulus/response effect.

We most frequently have emotions in response to a thought that takes place in our inner world or an event in our outer world. Thinking and feeling are related. When we have new experiences we attach different emotions to those experiences depending upon our interpretation of that experience. When we interpret ideas or events consistently we will usually have the same emotional response. That response can become a habit, and that habit becomes a part of our emotional pattern. For many of us this emotional pattern is unconscious and automatic.

For example, whenever I hear the hymn "When I Survey the Wondrous Cross," I am especially moved. Tears often form in my eyes, a lump rises in my throat, and sometimes I have a difficult time singing. I don't remember when I first heard this classic hymn. It was uneventful, and the song had no more meaning than most others. However, as I have gotten older the words to that song have taken on new meaning. Now I can even hear an instrumental version of the hymn on the radio and experience an emotional response.

WE LEARN EMOTIONAL RESPONSES

Characteristic #5: Most emotional responses are learned.

Different people can have a different emotional response to the same event. The kind of emotion we experience is to a great degree determined by the meaning or interpretation we make of that event. What excites and energizes one person can bring panic and emotional paralysis to another. Several factors influence our emotional responses, including childhood experiences, where we were raised, and our personality type.

One of the most important factors is our home environment. Some of us grew up in homes similar to the one Karen described at the beginning of this chapter. In such homes emotions were not modeled or discussed. The few emotions that were expressed were kept behind closed doors. There were no names given to them and no healthy opportunities for understanding them.

Others grew up in homes where emotional expression was punished and emotional repression was reinforced. Children raised in this environment either consciously or unconsciously told themselves that it wasn't safe to feel. For the sake of survival their minds were trained to ignore emotions, filter them out, or, when one accidently crept up to the surface, stuff it back down.

In this kind of environment they weren't free to learn how to experience or express their God-given emotions. The only thing that felt safe was not to feel. They became emotionally numb. Now, as adults, they are faced with the task of unlearning old dysfunctional patterns and replacing them with healthy new patterns. But that task is easier said than done.

Another significant factor is gender. Men generally remain more hesitant that women to express emotion. I grew up in a time when being a "man's man" meant being unemotional. Society didn't reward or honor sensitive men. There were few models. If a man expressed any emotion it was most likely to be anger, and the anger probably would have an unhealthy expression. Even today, with a men's movement asking men to understand themselves, many young men don't know how to spell intimacy.

EMOTIONS CAN CONTROL OUR ACTIONS

Characteristic #6: Our emotions will control us if we don't understand how to control them.

Several years ago I spoke to a group of mothers of preschoolers. They had asked me to talk about emotions. "It is important for us to understand and control our emotions," I said at one point. A young woman quickly raised her hand to disagree. She interpreted my use of the term *control* to mean that we should ignore our emotions and keep them under control.

"Thanks for giving me the opportunity to make an important clarification. Actually, when I said '*control*' I did not mean ignore," I began, and the startled woman listened intently.

For the person who wants to be healthy and mature, ignoring emotions is not an option. To ignore your emotions can take an enormous amount of energy. And even then you can't ignore them indefinitely. We can only anesthetize ourselves just so long. Emotional repression eventually leads to self-destructive behaviors and addictions, such as working too much, eating too little, eating too much, alcohol and drug dependence, compulsive spending, sexual addictions, not sleeping enough, sleeping too much, and controlling behaviors.

The word *control* means to guide or manage and can refer to the skill involved in using a tool. The professional craftsman has a variety of tools in his tool chest. It takes time and effort to learn how to effectively and safely use those tools. Some tools are more necessary and effective in some situations and totally ineffective or useless in others. The effectiveness of the tool depends on the skill of the craftsman.

Our emotions are like tools. It takes time and effort to learn about our emotions. Through trial and error we learn when we can trust our emotions and when we can't. Controlling our emotions requires developing greater skill in understanding our emotions and then managing how we choose to express them. Healthy people are more likely to understand themselves and more accurately perceive the feelings of others.

EXPRESSED EMOTIONS YIELD HEALTHY RELATIONSHIPS

Characteristic #7: Expressed emotions are the currency of healthy relationships.

Unfortunately, many of us don't know how to express our emotions. The deeper the emotion the more difficult it is to communicate. We may cry at the wrong time, laugh at the wrong time, or get angry at the wrong time. We've had years of training on how to communicate our ideas with clarity yet precious little training in clearly communicating our feelings. When we do try we come on too strong or not strong enough. We get embarrassed. People misunderstand us. We decide it's safer not to risk the humiliation of being rejected or laughed at so we don't share.

"Better is open rebuke than hidden love," writes Solomon (Proverbs 27:5). It is better to be rebuked and corrected for a fault or a mistake than to be the object of love that is kept hidden inside and not communicated. Have you ever had the experience of thinking someone was a friend and when you needed his encouragement and support the person was not there? These kinds of friends are like a river that runs dry when you are in need of a drink of water.

When you express your emotions you understand yourself— and others—better. You have the opportunity to confirm or disconfirm what you are feeling. When you conceal your emotions they become more complex and difficult for you to understand. Withholding your emotions can distort your view of the world and isolate you from others. When we don't express our emotions others don't know what is most important to us.

This principle is illustrated in Proverbs 27:19: "As water reflects a face, so a man's heart reflects the man." Just as water can reflect a person's face, through the heart or emotional responses of another we can find our heart reflected. As we are willing to risk opening up and revealing our heart's deepest longings, we truly know ourselves and become known by others. The people that I understand the best and feel closest to are those who have shared their emotions with me and with whom I have been able to share my emotions.

Emotions were made to be expressed. They are the lifeline to healthy relationships. They provide the passion and intensity needed to initiate and sustain meaningful relationships. "I can only know that much of myself which I have had the courage to confide to you,"[2] John Powell wrote. When we express our emotions it helps us better understand who we are and what is important to us.

TAKE ACTION

1. Thank God for making you in His image. Thank Him for your mind, your will, and your emotions.

2. Ask God to help you better understand the role of emotions in becoming a mature man or woman. Don't be afraid of your emotions. See them for what they are—a gift from God. Be open to learning about your emotions.

3. Consider your own emotional patterns.
   What emotions do you frequently experience? _____
   What are the emotions that you rarely experience? _____
   What emotions are easy for you to express? _____
   What emotions are difficult for you to express? _____
   What aspect of your emotional pattern would you like to change? _____
   _____

4. Pick one emotion you want to understand better and that you believe God would have you develop more effective skills in expressing.
   Define that emotion. _____
   _____

   Make a list of what you consider to be unhealthy and healthy expressions of that emotion.

Are there any models from Scripture of healthy expressions of that emotion?

What are three specific ways you can begin to change your response pattern?

NOTES

1. Dorothy C. Finkelhor, *How to Make Your Emotions Work for You* (New York: Berkley Medallion, 1973), pp. 23-24.
2. John Powell, *Why Am I Afraid to Tell You Who I Am?* (Chicago: Argus, 1969), pp. 25.

5

THE GIFT OF ANGER

What's the first thought that comes to mind when you hear the word *love*?

Perhaps it's a special person you love and you know loves you. It could be a particular time of your life when feelings of love filled your every waking moment. Some people's minds fill with warm, wonderful memories when they hear the word. Most people associate love with "good" feelings, such as happiness, comfort, security, delight, hope, and joy.

What's the first thought that comes to your mind when you hear the word *anger*? Is it your mom or dad yelling at you when you were a child? Is it your child spilling milk for the twenty-seventh time that day? Maybe it's the critical voice of your parent asking, "Where are you going? When will you be back?" Perhaps it's the whine of your adolescent asking, "Do I have to?" The word *anger,* unlike *love,* does not fill the mind with warm, wonderful memories. Maybe it's the feel of your heart pounding while hoping that no one notices how hard you are working to maintain control.

During the past twenty years we have led many retreats dealing with emotions. Whenever we ask for a word association to anger the suggestions are invariably 99 percent negative. Clearly the vast majority of people view anger from an almost exclusively negative perspective.

Both love and anger are emotions. Both love and anger were created by God. Both love and anger are talked about in the Bible,

God's Word. Yet love is viewed as a positive emotion, and anger is viewed as a negative emotion.

Anger, however, can be constructive. Believe it or not, anger is a gift from God. It can be used for good purposes, if it is expressed properly. Still, many people have a totally unfavorable view of anger, and you may find it difficult to believe anger is a healthy emotion. It is. And when the energy from this emotion is constructively redirected, you benefit.

Keys to Understanding Anger

How can anger mobilize us rather than neutralize us? In what ways can this unwelcome and potentially destructive emotion be considered a gift to be used rather than a time-bomb to be avoided at all costs? There are certain keys that help us to unwrap anger's positive potential. Understanding these keys is the first step in allowing God to help us use the emotion of anger in a constructive way in our marriage and family relationships. Here are five keys to unwrapping the gift of anger and understanding this emotion.

1. ANGER IS A GOD-GIVEN EMOTION

I recently came across an article that talked about "the deadly sin of anger." Does Scripture label anger as a sin? No, it does not. If anger is a sin then God is capable of sin, because there are numerous references in Scripture to God's anger. Indeed, anger is a God-given emotion. As anger fact #1 (p. 48) indicates, God gives us all our emotions, including anger. He is glorified when we express this emotion in constructive ways.

Although the emotion of anger is not a sin (see Anger Myth #1, p. 45), we can respond to the emotion of anger in ways that lead to sin. That is one reason why Scriptures in both the Old and New Testament teach us to be slow to anger (see Proverbs 16:32 and James 1:19).

The starting point then for the positive use of anger is to understand that it is a God-given emotion. God has anger and because we were made in His image we have anger. As such it has all of the characteristics of emotions discussed in the last chapter.

Anger is not an evil emotion. Anger is not in itself a destructive emotion. Anger isn't necessarily dangerous. Unfortunately, many people confuse the emotion of anger with the ways some people choose to express or act out that emotion. Many people confuse anger and aggression. Anger is not the same as aggression. Anger is an emotion, aggression is an action.

When we don't understand our anger and allow it to get out of control it can lead to aggressive behaviors that are sinful, dangerous, destructive, and even deadly. But the emotion of anger isn't the problem. The real problem is the mismanagement and misunderstanding of the emotion. It is the emotional immaturity of the individual who allows himself or herself to be controlled by the anger-energy.

We can't always control when or how we experience anger. However, with God's help we can learn to control how we choose to interpret and express that emotion. Because God has made us rational creatures, we are free to choose how we will respond to external events. In fact we have more control than we give ourselves credit for. Often, however, our past experiences, memories, and patterns of response tend to hinder us from exercising this control, but with understanding, time, and practice we can overcome these influences and develop constructive and healthy responses to our anger.

2. ANGER IS A SECONDARY EMOTION

Anger is a warning sign, a clue to underlying attitudes. Anger is designed to help us detect improper and potentially destructive attitudes. For example, consider the anger of Joseph's brothers (Genesis 37). As one of the younger children in a family of twelve brothers, Joseph was the favorite child. His father loved him more than all his brothers and paid him special attention. Jacob gave Joseph special gifts and honored Joseph more than the others.

This favoritism was blatant, and his brothers were hurt and became jealous. When you are a child growing up it's very painful to know that no matter what you do, you will never be quite good enough. Because a parent favored one child over the others, the brothers felt they were second best. Their hurt and frustration soon turned into bitterness and resentment.

When bitterness and resentment are allowed to smolder, it doesn't take long for them to flare up into aggression and violence. That's exactly what happened. At first "they plotted against him to put him to death" (37:18). But Reuben convinced his brothers not to kill Joseph. Instead they sold him to a caravan of Ishmaelites for twenty shekels of silver, the equivalent of about $19. Joseph was then taken to Egypt and sold to Potiphar, the captain of Pharaoh's bodyguard.

This story has been used to illustrate the dangers of anger. Actually it is an illustration of what can happen when we ignore the warnings of anger and allow it to deteriorate into bitterness, resentment, and hatred, and then escalate into aggression and violence. It's an example of what can happen when we don't utilize the gift of anger in the ways God designed it to be used.

Notice that anger was not the first emotion that Joseph's brothers experienced. They first felt hurt, rejection, and jealousy. The anger came later. Anger is rarely the first feeling that comes in a situation. It is frequently a symptom of something else. Thus it is a secondary emotion and a warning sign of a more fundamental issue.

Anger may be the first emotion we are aware of, but it's rarely the first emotion we experience. The emotions that most frequently precede anger are fear, hurt, or frustration. These initial feelings are often painful. Not only are they painful, but they also can drain us of energy and increase our sense of vulnerability.

At an early age many of us learned that anger can divert our attention from these more painful emotions. If I get angry I can avoid or at least minimize my pain. Perhaps I can even influence or change the source of my anger. It doesn't take long to learn that it's easier to feel anger than it is to feel pain. Anger provides an increase of energy. It can decrease our sense of vulnerability and thus increase our sense of security.

3. ANGER WEARS MANY DISGUISES

We do not always recognize anger, because it manifests itself in ways other than a strong physical or verbal response. What are some of the most common disguises anger can take? When we begrudge, scorn, insult, and disdain others or when we feel annoyed, offended, bitter, fed up, or repulsed, we are probably experiencing some form of anger. Some people are angry when they become sarcastic, tense, or cross; or they are feeling frustration, exasperation, or wrath. Anger can also manifest itself as criticism, silence, intimidation, hypochondria, numerous petty complaints, depression, gossip, and blame.

Even such passive-aggressive behaviors as stubbornness, half-hearted efforts, forgetfulness, and laziness can be evidence of an angry spirit. An important part of learning how to make our anger work for us is to be able to identify the many masks or disguises of anger.

4. ANGER IS A FREQUENTLY FELT EMOTION

"I never get angry," John said proudly. "I grew up in a home that was characterized by self-control and as a young boy I learned to control my anger." John had been referred to me by his physician. He had complained of stomach pains for several years. His internist had run all the tests known to medicine and had concluded the cause wasn't physical. The symptoms were physical, but they were being caused by something else. Like many people, John was frequently feeling anger, and the emotion, expressed inward, was wreaking havoc with his body.

People experience the emotion of anger with greater frequency than we would like to admit. From the number of times God's anger is mentioned in Scripture, it is obvious that He also frequently experiences that emotion. I've seen several studies that suggest that most people experience some form of anger at least eight times a day. It may not always be identified as anger, but it is a form of anger.

We not only don't recognize our anger at times, but often we are unwilling to admit it, as key #5 emphasizes.

5. ANGER IS ONE OF THE MOST DIFFICULT EMOTIONS TO ADMIT

When is the last time you admitted that you were angry? What did it feel like? Did you feel a little ashamed or embarrassed? One reason anger is so difficult for many people to deal with is that we are not comfortable admitting that we are angry.

This is especially true for many Christians who believe that all anger is a sign of spiritual immaturity and weakness. When they do acknowledge their anger they usually described themselves as being discouraged, frustrated, sad, worried, depressed, annoyed, or irritated. That is much easier than looking someone straight in the eyes and say, "I am angry."

What makes it even more difficult is that often the source of our anger has been something silly or insignificant.

Virtually everyone I have met, myself included, has experienced anger over little things. That should encourage you—you are not alone in your anger. At one time or another every one of us has overreacted to what in retrospect was clearly a minor event. If your friends knew some of the puny things you've gotten upset about they would probably laugh so hard their sides would ache. But then you would laugh too if you knew some of the things they had overreacted to.

IN HARM'S WAY

These five keys can open the gift of anger, permitting its healthy expression and making you aware of other, underlying needs in your life. Grasping those keys—learning to manage and express your anger properly—is not always an easy task. But it is well worthwhile. The alternative—accepting unhealthy anger—will keep the doors to emotional health locked. Consider the two major consequences of continuing with unhealthy anger: hurting others and hurting yourself.

HARMING OTHERS

The first time I heard the story on the local news program I couldn't believe it. The reporter said that a man had been shot in his car while driving on the freeway. Apparently he had pulled in front of another driver, and that driver thought he had been cut off. The second driver, irate at what he considered the rude and intentional behavior of the first, reached for a gun he kept in his car. In a fit of "You can't do that!" he pulled up next to the man who had cut him off and shot him. The first driver died moments later.

Since that time I have heard and read numerous similar stories. It may start with a clenched fist, an obscene gesture, or a few poorly chosen words from one irritated driver to another. Traffic congestion, a rush to get somewhere, and often the heat of summer combine to create tension for a driver; with the one final straw, someone cutting him off or honking at him, the incensed driver is ready to dump his anger. The outcome can range from someone being run off the road, to being pulled out of the car and given a severe beating, to shots being fired.

These violent incidents don't take place just between strangers. Some of the most devastating examples of violence occur between people who know and even love each other. Every year millions of children are shaken and battered by out-of-control parents. Every year millions of women are battered and bruised by raging husbands. The majority of all homicides are committed by people who knew the victim. Nearly a third of all policemen killed were attacked while breaking up domestic arguments.

In one study a psychiatrist interviewed more than one hundred inmates convicted of murder and concluded that most were not what we would call "angry people." In most cases they had never learned how to deal with little issues—and had allowed emotions to build and build. In these cases their emotions were finally expressed in an out-of-control and violent way.[1]

When people don't understand, listen to, and learn from their anger, the anger can become more intense and turn into rage. At this point the person faces a much more difficult problem. The energy of rage is much more powerful and much more difficult to direct than the energy of anger. If anger is 10,000 volts of energy, then rage is 100,000 volts. When rage isn't dealt with it can easily turn into aggression and then to violence.

HARMING YOURSELF

Although the potentially harmful effect of anger on others is obvious, the harmful effects of anger on ourselves are a bit more subtle, but nonetheless real.

An increasing amount of scientific evidence clearly suggests that the ways in which we handle our emotions or allow them to handle us is a major factor in our physical well-being. In his book, *None of These Diseases,* S.I. McMillen, a medical doctor, cites more than fifty diseases that can be triggered by the mismanagement of our emotions. Then he describes the danger of mismanaged emotions—hate, bitterness, and anger.

> The moment I start hating a man I become his slave. I can't enjoy my work anymore because he even controls my thoughts. My resentments release excessive stress hormones and I become fatigued after only a few hours of work. The work I formerly enjoyed is now drudgery. Even vacations lose their pleasure. It may be a luxurious car that I drive along a lake fringed with the multicolored au-

tumnal beauty of maple, oak and birch. But moping in my resentment, I might as well be driving a hearse in mud and rain.

The man I hate hounds me wherever I go. I can't escape his tyrannical grasp on my mind. When the waiter serves me steamed lobster and clams, with asparagus, crisp salad and strawberry shortcake smothered with ice cream, it might as well be stale bread and water. My teeth chew the food and I swallow it, but the man I hate will not allow me to enjoy it.

King Solomon must have had a similar experience, for he wrote: "Better a dish of vegetables, with love, than the best beef served with hatred."

The man I hate may be many miles from my bedroom, but, more cruel than any slave driver, he whips my thoughts into such a frenzy that my inner spring mattress becomes a rack of torture. The lowliest of the serfs can sleep, but not I. I really must acknowledge that I am, indeed, a slave to every man on whom I pour the vials of my wrath.[2]

It is obvious that understanding anger and healthy anger management is good preventative mental health. Numerous medical studies have shown that poor emotional health can be a key predictor of early physical deterioration. One of the most interesting long-term studies has been conducted by George Valliant of the psychiatry department at Cambridge Hospital in Cambridge, Massachusetts. In studies that have been in progress since the 1940s involving the same group of men, Valliant has found that the determining factors in health and longevity are not primarily the life-span of parents and grandparents, obesity, or the use of alcohol and tobacco. The evidence strongly suggests that emotional problems eventually produced physical illness in spite of clean living and good genes. Valliant notes that while habits and genes affect our health, mental attitude plays a surprisingly powerful role in what happens to our bodies.

Valliant concludes, "No matter what, the men who were better at loving, who had more satisfying personal relations, seem to avoid early aging, while the health of poor emotional copers was significantly more likely to deteriorate during middle age."[3]

Occasional anger is not harmful when expressed in healthy kinds of ways. In fact, learning how to express our anger in healthy ways can strengthen our health and increase our effectiveness. However, when anger is overexpressed (external anger) or under-expressed (internal anger) for long periods of time our bodies remain in a constant state of emergency. McKay notes in detail the dangerous physical consequences.

[Chronic or sustained anger] results in elevated levels of testosterone (for men), epinephrine, norepinephrine, and cortisol. Chronic high levels of testosterone and cortisol potentiate arthritis, the most common cause of coronary artery disease. Cortisol also depresses the immune system and reduces the body's ability to fight infection. Epinephrine and norepinephrine stimulate the sympathetic nervous system to shunt blood from the skin, liver, and digestive tract to the heart, lungs, and skeletal muscles. Blood pressure is elevated, and glucose is dumped into the blood system to provide energy for confrontation or escape. When blood is shunted away from the liver, the liver is less efficient in clearing the blood of cholesterol, thus contributing to the fatty deposits in the arteries. Elevated blood pressure also damages the arteries and the heart. Hypertension forces the heart to work harder and creates a large and less efficient heart muscle. Turbulence caused by the high pressure of the blood flow also damages the arteries. Tiny tears develop on the artery wall. Fatty deposits cover the tears, but these can eventually grow to fill the artery and stop the flow of blood.[1]

ANGER: FOR YOUR OWN GOOD

We need to continually remind ourselves that anger is energy and energy is neutral. While we may have minimal control over our feelings of anger, we can, with God's help, have total control over how we choose to express that anger. We can choose to harness and channel that anger-energy in healthy, positive ways. Anger is energy—we can choose to spend it or we can choose to invest it.

As you understand God's purpose in giving us the emotion of anger, as you become more aware of the many constructive and positive functions of anger, you will be able to experience why some consider anger one of their most valuable emotions. As you learn creative ways to invest your anger-energy, as you develop more effective anger management skills, you will find one of the most powerful sources of motivation available to mankind. What are some of the constructive and positive functions of anger? We conclude the chapter with four benefits of anger.

ANGER IS A SIGNAL

One of anger's most valuable services is that it can serve as a warning signal that I need to take a look at some aspect of my life. Anger tells me that something is wrong. It may be a problem that needs a solution. It can make me aware of an issue that needs my attention. It may be that I am in danger. It can increase my awareness of inequity and injustice. It may help me identify a difference between me and a family member.

God can use anger to get our attention and make us more aware of opportunities to learn, to grow, to deepen, to mature, to make significant changes for the good.

ANGER IS A MOTIVATOR

Anger is a powerful source of motivation. Abraham Lincoln felt great anger at the brutality and inhumanity of slavery. He chose to invest the energy of that anger to change his country's laws and emancipate the slaves and abolish slavery. Gandhi chose to invest the energy of his anger at the plight of his people and the nation of India was born.

The energy of anger, when wisely invested, can provide greater focus and intensity and lead to greater productivity. Martin Luther said, "When I am angry I can write, pray and preach well, for then my whole temperament is quickened, my understanding sharpened, and all mundane vexations and temptations gone."

Lee Iacocca, chairman of the Chrysler Corporation, provides us with an excellent example of the constructive motivational potential of anger. *The Wall Street Journal* in 1979 published a devastating editorial criticizing Chrysler's mismanagement and concluded that the nearly bankrupt company should be allowed to "die with dignity." When he read the editorial Iacocca got mad, but he realized that he was faced with three choices. He could either lash out in anger at the *Journal* and condemn and criticize them and thus do more damage to himself; he could ignore the criticism and hope it would just go away; or he could invest the energy of his anger and use that same criticism to motivate his people. In an excerpt from one of his speeches Iacocca tells his response:

I got mad; my colleagues in Highland Park got mad. Tens of thousands of Chrysler people all across America got mad. Our labor unions, our suppliers, and our lenders all got mad. We got so mad, we banded together, we talked things over, and working together, we fixed what was wrong at Chrysler. We doubled our productivity. We rejuvenated our factories. We cut our costs. We started building the highest quality cars and trucks made in America. In short, we turned things around. Now, we're selling cars and making lots of money.[5]

Anger motivates more than politicians, church leaders, and executives. Consider three fathers who were moved to constructive action though their anger. Joe Mangrum was raking leaves in his yard on a quiet afternoon. Stray bullets whizzed over his head, and he quickly dove for cover. When he finally got up and brushed himself off he was angry. James Walker is a father of three. When his children began finding syringes on the vacant lot next door he got angry. Gabe Moreno is a thirty-six-year-old father of two. When he saw drug dealers approach children on the streets of his neighborhood, tempting them to earn a quick pair of $125 Nikes by selling a fistful of rock cocaine, he got angry.

Mangrum, Walker, and Moreno are three dads who got good and angry. They determined to invest their anger-energy in helping to make their neighborhood a safe place. They are part of a group of about seventy men ranging in ages from twenty-eight to sixty-six who developed the Denver chapter of MAD DADS—Men Against Destruction Defending Against Drugs and Social Disorder. On a regular basis they patrol their northeast Denver neighborhood. In only a few months this group of angry men has put a major dent in the drug traffic and has made their neighborhood a much safe place for their families.

Wonderful things can happen when Americans get mad. I think some well-directed anger can cure most of what's wrong in America today.

ANGER GIVES STRENGTH

Several years ago I read about an eighty-five-year-old man who was touring New York City with his wife and her sister. They had just finished seeing a play and were getting into their car to leave. His wife and her sister sat in the front seat, and he sat in the back.

As his wife started the car two young men, one of them with a pistol in his hand, came up to the car, opened the door, and demanded that the women give them their jewelry and purses. At first they didn't see the old man sitting in the back seat. As they turned to take off with the loot they noticed the old man and started to open the back door and said, "Give me your money and your jewelry."

As one of the men opened the back door the elderly man turned towards the door, placed his feet against the door and pushed as hard as he could. The robber was caught by surprise, and the force of the door knocked him off balance; his gun flew from his hand. He recovered from his surprise, but both he and his accomplice fled, leaving the loot behind them.

One of the first questions reporters asked the elderly man was, "Why did you do it?"

"I don't know," he replied. "If I'd had time to think about it I probably wouldn't have done it." He said that he was first aware of feeling fear, but when he heard the fear in the quivering voices of his wife and sister-in-law he found himself getting angry. In what seemed to him like an automatic response he was able to harness the power of his anger to protect himself, those he loved, and their possessions.

When we harness the power of anger it can be a source of strength and provide protection. It can keep us from being a victim. It can help us break free from the immobilization of worry and fear and empower us for constructive action.

ANGER CONTRIBUTES TO CLOSER RELATIONSHIPS

Managed anger can lead us to more intimate relationships. What? Anger can help us become more intimate? That's right. During the past twenty years we have found that couples and families who have learned to identify their anger and take the time to express anger in healthy ways have several traits in common. They develop more effective communication skills, are better at problem-solving, and find it easier to trust and experience much deeper levels of intimacy and security.

Anger is a normal part of close relationships. Whenever two people begin a relationship, part of what attracts them are their similarities and another part of what attracts them are their differences. Opposites do attract, but not for long. It doesn't take very much time for differences to lead to disagreements. Disagreements may involve the emotions of fear, hurt, and frustration. Fear that our relationship is threatened and that we will never be understood. Hurt over what has been said to us and about us or over how it has been said. Frustration that we've had a similar disagreement before and this is the same song, twenty-second verse. Disagreements often involve anger and lead to conflict.

At that point we have a choice. We can choose to spend our anger-energy by dumping on our spouse or child, showing our victim where, once again, he is clearly wrong and we are right. Or we can throw up our hands in futility and stomp out of the room. By that act we communicate one of two things. Either the other person is not worth taking the time to work out the issue with, or communication between the two of us is impossible. Both choices lead to feelings of hopelessness and helplessness and set us up for more failure in the future.

However, there is another option. We can acknowledge our fear, hurt, or frustration and choose to invest our anger-energy by seizing this opportunity to better understand our loved one. One of the most practical ways to "bear all things, believe all things, hope all things and endure all things" (1 Corinthians 13:7) is to develop the habit of working through our differences. This takes time and involves listening, asking questions, listening, asking more questions, and finally reaching understanding.

When you know that someone loves you enough to take the time to work through a difference rather than taking a walk out the door you know that person really loves you, and not with a shallow, conditional love. You know that no matter what happens he/ she will not desert you. You know that you are loved and valued for who you are. You know that you can be secure in his or her love for you.

Our differences and disagreements provide a window of opportunity to better understand and thus appreciate the uniqueness of our spouse or child. They don't have to escalate to a quarrel, a fight, and abuse. Anger provides the energy to stay focused, stick with the issue, and bring it to a positive conclusion.

Take Action

1. If before you read this book you had been asked whether anger was a negative or a positive emotion how would you have answered? _____

2. Based on what you've read thus far, in the space below write out your own one sentence definition of anger: _____
   _____

3. Most of us learned about anger before we knew we were learning. As young children we observed our parents and other adults modeling various ways of expressing their anger toward each other. We also observed and experienced their expressions or anger towards us.

   (1) What is your very first memory of anger? _____
   _____

   (2) Picture yourself at that time. Where were you and how old were you? _____

   (3) What do you remember feeling when you became angry?
   _____

   (4) How did you respond? _____

4. List what you believe are the three most positive aspects of anger:
   _____
   _____
   _____

5. Remember, anger is a secondary emotion. Therefore, during your next experience of anger take time to begin to develop skills in identifying your primary emotions that may have activated the anger.

Notes

1. Dwight L. Carlson, *Overcoming Hurts and Anger* (Eugene, Oreg.: Harvest House, 1981), p. 28.

2. S.I. McMillen, *None of These Diseases* (Old Tappan, N.J.: Revell, 1984), p. 116.
3. George Valliant, *Adaptation to Life* (Boston: Little, Brown, 1977), n.p.
4. Matthew McKay, Peter D. Rogers, Judith McCoy, *When Anger Hurts* (Oakland, Calif.: New Harbinger, 1989), pp. 25-26.
5. As quoted in Allan Loy McGinnis, *Bringing Out the Best in People* (Minneapolis: Augsburg, 1985), pp. 132-33.

6

WHERE DID ALL THIS ANGER COME FROM?

If you were me you wouldn't come home either," Randy said emphatically. "Carla spends the day loading her gun, and as soon as I walk in the door it's open season on Randy!"

"That's because you rarely walk in the door before 8:00 or 8:30, and if I'm lucky I might get five minutes to talk to you," Carla responded sharply.

"Well, I'm getting sick and tired of you always dumping on me," Randy shot back.

"Well, I'm sick and tired of your insensitivity, your broken promises, your pity parties, your running away from problems— I'm sick and tired of you. Life would be a lot easier for all of us if you weren't around!"

Randy and Carla had replayed this same conversation hundreds of time. It would usually end with Carla raising her voice and hurling accusations and Randy gradually refusing to talk and withdrawing to another part of the house. Carla decided that she had had enough, and that's what brought them into my office.

Randy and Carla had been married for nine years and had three children. They met when he was in medical school and married shortly before his graduation. Whereas medical school had kept him busy, his residency kept him exhausted. Carla knew that this would be a difficult time, but her expectations of a normal life after residency kept her going. After completing his training Randy was able to enter practice with several other physicians.

Carla was optimistic. However, Randy, as the youngest member of the physicians' group, felt a need to prove himself, and so he began to work long hours: often ten or twelve hour days, six days a week. The pattern he had established during his years of training simply continued, and he had limited time with his wife.

Randy felt overworked and unappreciated. He was weary, frustrated, and discouraged. He said he loved Carla. He said that his marriage and his family were important to him. But from Carla's perspective his actions said just the opposite. "If I didn't care about you and the kids do you think I'd be doing as much as I do?" he told her. "There are a lot of women who would give anything to be married to someone who works as hard and provides for his family as well as I do."

Carla felt abandoned, unloved, unappreciated, and used. She was discouraged and frustrated. "I'm not important to you," she said to Randy with a bitter hurt in her voice. "You have an office manager at work and a family manager at home. The only difference is that you see your office manger more than you see me and she gets two paychecks a month."

Why was Carla so angry? What made Randy so angry? Two intelligent Christian people who professed to love each other stayed in this destructive dance for many years. Why? These are important questions for us to ask. Only when we are able to identify and understand the sources of our anger can we make that anger work for us rather than against us. Otherwise anger will destroy us and our relationships.

It's obvious several factors were contributing to Randy and Carla's anger. This is one of the most important things to remember when dealing with anger. Rarely is there only one source, or cause, of anger. It's also important to recall the truth of chapter 5: anger is a complex emotional reaction. Many factors influence, contribute to, and maintain anger.

We cannot say that Randy and Carla have an anger problem; anger is only a symptom. Lerner suggests that for most people the real problem isn't the fact that we have anger "but our inability to identify and understand that experience and then choose the healthiest and most effective way to express that anger."[1]

In anger workshops I have asked people to indicate the major causes of their anger. In a group of sixty-five people I often receive more than fifty different responses. Any number of situations can trigger an anger response; however, ten major factors contribute to the arousal of anger in most people.

Notice I said *contribute to* rather than *cause*. That is an important distinction. The exact same event can happen to five different people, and there can be five different emotional reactions. But a number of factors can increase the probability that a person will experience anger. In this chapter we will look at nine of the ten major contributors to anger. (We will investigate the number one cause in the next chapter.)

CHILDHOOD EXPERIENCES

Deuteronomy 6:4-9 contains some of Scripture's most specific insights on quality parenting. This passage makes clear that one of the most important aspects of parenting is being a model. We can tell children all kinds of things, but what they see and experience is much more powerful that what they hear. As a result, one of the most powerful factors that influences how we deal with our anger involves our experiences with this emotion when we were children.

These childhood experiences influenced us in several ways. Consider what you observed as a child. How did your parents communicate their anger to each other? How was anger communicated to you? Was anger negative and something to be avoided? Did anger often lead to physical violence? The positive and negative modeling in our family of origin has a profound influence on our own emotional patterns.

Numerous studies have demonstrated that children learn about dealing with their angry feelings by experience and by observing the success of others with aggressive behaviors. Several researchers carried out a comprehensive multi-year study on grade school children in New York state. The results of this study revealed that certain aspects of children's experiences at home —particularly their parents' behaviors—were associated with aggressiveness in the children.[2]

Another childhood influence is the ways in which our parents responded to our anger. How did your parents respond to you when you got angry? Was it OK for parents to be angry but wrong for children? Did they yell and scream? Were you simply ignored? Were you physically abused? Did your mom handle anger one way and your dad handle it another way? Did you learn that men and women have different ways of expressing anger? Did you discover that anger was a way to get what you wanted?

Twila has to pay attention when she wheels her three-year-old son Jimmy down the grocery aisles. The little guy loves to spring to action near one of the numerous candy displays. He points, leans, and tells Mom what he wants. If she refuses, Jimmy increases the volume of his communication. His blocked desire can lead to frustration, and his frustration can lead to anger that is expressed in a temper tantrum. When Twila becomes sufficiently embarrassed and exhausted by his dramatics, she usually gives in and buys him the candy.

But what has this child learned? He has learned that if he loses his temper and yells and screams long and loud enough he will get whatever he wants. When a child's temper tantrum is reinforced, the child learns quickly (and often unconsciously) that he can get what he wants or avoid what he doesn't want through an extreme expression of anger.

If this works as a preschooler, Jimmy will probably continue some form of this behavior in elementary school, middle school, high school, college, and into his adult years. He has learned that out-of-control anger can control people. He can get what he wants with it. He can remove obstacles and people by it.

PHYSIOLOGICAL FACTORS

When God created us He gave us body, soul, and spirit. Most Christians are aware of the importance of the spiritual dimension. They spend time going to church, reading and memorizing Scripture, and being involved in various ministries. Many Christians have become more aware of the importance of the soul, or personality—their mind, their will and their emotions.

However, it is surprising how many people still underestimate the importance of the physical. They seem almost unaware that the ways in which we treat our bodies can have a tremendous impact on how our mind, will, emotions, and spirit function.

Before Christ ascended to heaven, He promised that the Holy Spirit would reside in each of His followers. And Paul confirms that the Holy Spirit is within believers: "Your body is a temple of the Holy Spirit who is in you, whom you have received from God.

You are not your own"(1 Corinthians 6:19). Our body is the temple of God. God's Spirit dwells within us. I believe that just as God wanted His people Israel to care for the Tabernacle and Temple, He wants Christians to take care of their bodies. Certainly bodies are more important than buildings. As goes our health so goes our ability to process information, to think, to feel, and to have the energy to do.

When we are overworked we become tired and rushed. When we don't have adequate sleep, when we allow our nutrition to suffer by skipping meals or becoming junk food junkies, we become worn down. It is then easier for us to get thrown off our emotional stride and become vulnerable to the emotion of anger. It's not uncommon for poor health or extreme fatigue to produce a response that may look and sound a lot like anger. Sometimes it may be anger. When we are exhausted and weary, our guard is down and we are prone to let our emotions, including anger, to take control of us.

That's why one of the first things I do when working with an angry person is to take a lifestyle check. I've found that responsible habits, such as regular aerobic exercise, good nutrition, and adequate rest, can help someone move from being a victim of his anger to a victor. These are some of the questions I ask my counselees. How would you answer them?

1. How is your general health? When was the last time you had a physical?
2. Do you get aerobic exercise at least twenty minutes a day at least three times a week?
3. How is your nutrition? Do you eat a healthy breakfast?
4. How long do you sleep at night? Do you have problems going to sleep, staying asleep or waking up early and not being able to go back to sleep? In the past two years has the amount of your sleep increased or decreased?
5. How many hours a week do you work?
6. How much quantity time do you spend with your spouse and children on a regular basis?
7. When was the last time you and your spouse went away for a weekend without the kids or other friends?

Accumulated Stress from Normal Everyday Events

Normal everyday events are a major source of anger. The reason? They occur with such frequency. Over the years I've noticed that a common source of many marital conflicts is not major issues but a series of minor issues that were never identified and dealt with.

Most parents don't find their child stealing the family car or burning the house down. Typically anger rises when the bike is left out for the fifth time this week, the bedroom is left messy, the child borrows the car and loses the keys. The list of seemingly insignificant incidents goes on.

Remember that events that may seem at best insignificant can lead to irritation. Repeated irritations can lead to frustration, and continued frustration can lead to anger. How big do the irritations have to be? Not very big.

Even something as simple as a series of interruptions when you are concentrating on something important can cause anger, such as being interrupted when you're busy. Something important like writing a book on anger. Can you guess where that illustration came from? As I was writing this chapter I had several little interruptions. The first two were mildly irritating. The third and fourth were frustrating. On the fifth interruption I was aware that I was angry.

Suffice it to say, you must be aware of the "little" things in life that are potential sources of anger for you. What are some of the irritations that contribute to your anger? Consider these developments:

- You get into the car to go to an important appointment and find that your daughter brought it back with the gas gauge on empty.
- You discover that the last person in the bathroom didn't replace the toilet paper.
- You are late for an appointment, and a driver pulls in front of you going five miles below the speed limit.
- You finally get your kids down for a much needed afternoon nap and the doorbell rings—but the person got the wrong house.

- You've just scrubbed and mopped the floor when your precious little daughter opens the patio door and your dog runs through with muddy paws.
- You lie down to take a rare nap, and the neighborhood kids decide to play basketball under your window and tune their dirt bikes.

INJUSTICE

In the early chapters of the gospel of Mark we find the Pharisees looking for ways to find fault with Christ. Once Christ entered a synagogue and noticed a man with a withered hand. The Pharisees were watching His every move to see if He would heal him. Christ turned to the man and said, "Rise and come forward!" He turned to the Pharisees and asked, "Is it lawful on the Sabbath to do good or to do harm, to save a life or to kill?" They wouldn't answer Him (see Mark 3:1-5, NASB).

"After looking around at them with anger, grieved at their hardness of heart, He said to the man, 'Stretch out your hand.' And he stretched it out, and his hand was restored." Christ felt and expressed anger at the injustice of the Pharisees. He was frustrated by the fact that they held their rigid orthodoxy to man-made rules as more important than the suffering of a fellow man.

An injustice involves the violation of that which is moral or right, the rights of another, or your own personal rights. There are examples of acts of unfairness and injustice all around us.

Anger is a frequent and potentially healthy response to injustice. Abraham Lincoln, Gandhi, Martin Luther King, Jr., are all examples of men in whom injustice could trigger an angry response. They also provide examples of ways in which the energy from anger can be used for good. When our anger is channeled into righteous indignation it can help us identify the injustice. Then we can reach out in unselfish acts to the downtrodden and mistreated to right the wrong, to build up rather than tear down, to attack the problem and not the person.

LOW SELF-ESTEEM

Twelve-year-old Tim put his feelings in writing one day, and his note reflected his deep insecurities. "One day while I was in my room I finally realized that I was a nerd and that nobody appreciated me or wanted to be my friend. I need to try my best to do what I can and be the very best I can. Sometimes I wish I could crawl in a hole and stay there for the rest of my life. I am very different from other people. Sometimes I wish I was dead. At school I am a target to be made fun of. I don't even think my teachers like me or my work. At home I am a menace to my family. If I could I would lock myself in my room and never come out or let anyone in.

"Sometimes I think the work I do is useless, even a waste of my time and the teacher's. Sometimes my very best story is a piece of trash to my teacher. I even feel I am a useless piece of trash to everybody. I don't want to even go to school anymore. I think that I should run away. I will never be nothing but a failure. Nobody likes me. I wish I could hit them so hard."

Tim's long note is a classic example of how anger can both cause and be caused by low self-esteem. Dick and Carolyn brought their son's note into my office and expressed the concern that Tim might be suicidal. Tim was the oldest of three sons and had grown up in a home characterized by conflict. Dick had struggled with anger all of his life and at times referred to himself as a "rageaholic." Although Dick loved his boys and wanted to be a good dad he was crushed by his inability to change long-seated patterns.

Dick was a very gifted and intelligent man. He was a graduate of West Point and after leaving the military went on to be a good provider for his family. Although he had good performance skills, his ability to function interpersonally was limited. He had been raised in a home where there was little expression of affection or approval. Kids were to be seen and not heard. Enough was never enough. Love was conditional. He learned at a young age that his value and worth depended on his performance.

Several years earlier Dick had given his life to Christ. However, he had little idea of what it really meant to be made in God's image and now to be "in Christ."

Because of his biblically incomplete view of himself, the ordinary difficulties of life seemed life-threatening. His identity, value, and worth were always on the line, so it was difficult for him to accept criticism. There were times when Carolyn would ask for a simple clarification of what he had said. Dick's most frequent response would be to fly off the handle. It was obvious that the cause of his anger wasn't Carolyn's simple question. His insecurity led him to interpret her question as an attack. His automatic response was to defend himself by attacking her.

The scenario was the same with the kids, especially Tim. Dick's low self-esteem made him more vulnerable to the negative aspects of anger. His unhealthy expressions of anger to Tim contributed to his son's low self-esteem and were sowing the seeds for the same kind of anger response pattern in Tim.

How we view ourselves is important. Self-esteem is the value or worth we place on who God has made us to be. Biblically based self esteem is not some nauseating narcissism. It involves seeing ourselves from God's perspective, men and women created in His image. We acknowledge the reality of our sin nature, of our strengths and weaknesses; yet we see ourselves as worthy because of Christ's completed work for us on the cross. Self-esteem comes when we acknowledge that "we are partakers of the divine nature" (2 Peter 1:4) and are "becoming conformed to the image of His Son" (Romans 8:29)

WORRY

Some people find it difficult to admit that they worry. So they substitute the word *concern*. It sounds better to say, "I'm concerned," than, "I'm worried." However, worry and concern are different.

Concern is a constructive and healthy emotional activity. Concern consists of three phases. It begins with the awareness of a present or potential need or problem. Phase two involves a consideration of the available resources and solutions. Phase three usually involves taking some kind of action.

For most of us, the problem of worry usually begins in the second phase of being concerned. At the same time we consider the available solutions, we also tend to become more aware of all of the terrible, awful, horrible things that could take place. Then we start to feel as if all of those terrible, awful, and horrible things have already happened. We lose our problem-solving focus, our perspective becomes distorted. We get stuck in the rut of asking "What if . . ?" And, like the tires of a car stuck in the mud, our mind goes over and over and over the negative possibilities. Our concern has bogged down in the rut of worry.

Worry is a feeling of dread, apprehension, or uneasiness. It involves spending great amounts of time dwelling on a real or imagined problem. Almost always, the person assumes the worst about something that has not yet happened. When we allow ourselves to worry, we are trying to cross our bridges before we come to them, and we are assuming that they are all going to collapse while we are crossing them.

Worry tends to make us more impatient, and we want to take things into our own hands. Worry magnifies our problems and then distorts our perspective so we can't think logically or clearly about them. Then worry tends to paralyze us and hinder us from taking constructive action. The energy we have wasted on worry cannot be used to help us solve the legitimate problem that first attracted our concern.

When we worry we are focused on the negative, we become more critical, we are threatened more easily and can take offense at something that hasn't even happened. When we don't catch worry in the early stage we become more vulnerable to fear, depression, and anger. Things go from bad to worse.

CONFLICT

For many people *conflict* is almost as negative a word as *anger*. Most of us misunderstand the potential value of conflict and automatically interpret conflict as an attack. We view conflict as a rude interruption in our lives rather than a normal and necessary part of being in relationships.

Why is there conflict? Because we are all different. And we are different because God, in His infinite wisdom, chose to make each one of us different. In 1 Corinthians 12-14 and numerous other passages, it is clear that God designed differences. In fact the strength of a marriage and family is largely related to the diversity of the individuals that make up those relationships.

We are encouraged to "be of the same mind," to "accept one another," and to "admonish one another" (Romans 15). As we seek to become one in Christ, reflecting the unity Christ prayed for in John 17, we find that at times our differences produce problems. Differences can lead to disagreements that may result in conflict.

Relationships aren't destroyed by differences, however. They are destroyed by the immature, irresponsible, and unhealthy ways in which we view those differences and our unwillingness or inability to take them to God and allow Him to use them for His glory.

When you experience conflict it means that someone has a different value or opinion than you do. Most of us assume that our position is the correct one, and we try to convince the other person to see things as we do. Of course, the other person thinks exactly the same way. He invests an equal amount of energy trying to convince us to see things as he does.

Rather than working at listening and understanding, most of us attempt to change the other person. I've worked with many conflicting couples who weren't sure what the real issue was. But they were sure that whatever the issue, their position was the correct one. To add more muscle to their argument, they would say that their view was the more biblical one. Who would dare argue with that?

Some evangelicals believe that Christians who are mature will agree almost all of the time. Every decision made must reflect the unanimity of those involved. Conflict is viewed as a sign of immaturity and carnality. But in many ways the exact opposite is true. Those who believe that diversity always leads to division feel threatened by differences. In their fears—and immaturity—they tend to discourage individual uniqueness and creativity and urge individuals not to disagree. They mistakenly measure spirituality and maturity in part by the degree to which everyone thinks alike.

Yet someone once said that when two people always agree and think alike, one of them is totally unnecessary. They miss a crucial benefit of disagreeing. "Unity without diversity leads to uniformity," notes Bible teacher Warren Wiersbe.

There is a big difference between families with problems and problem families. All families experience stress and problems and have conflict. But healthy families value conflict and have the ability to handle problems in a constructive way. Families that don't face and deal with their problems become problem families. Healthy families understand that *conflict is a normal part of being in a healthy relationship*. In fact, conflict is essential for the development of understanding, intimacy, and unity.

FEAR

Tom had to run a few errands with his six-year-old daughter that morning. They had been a good team; she followed him closely and brought smiles to several clerks. On his last stop, with only one item to buy, Tom told Lisa to stay in the car. He had parked the van directly in front of the store so that he could see his daughter. "I'll be right back," Tom said, as he locked the doors.

When he returned from the store and looked at the front seat, he panicked. His daughter wasn't there. He hadn't been in the store much more than a minute. He ran over to the van and unlocked the door. He called her name but she didn't answer. He frantically looked all around the parking lot to see if she was wandering around or, worse yet, someone had taken her.

He returned to the van to see if he had missed something. When he opened the side door he saw little Lisa hunched down in the corner behind the driver's seat. When he had looked the first time from the driver's seat he couldn't see her. She jumped up and ran to him with a huge smile on her face.

"Hi, daddy!" she exclaimed. "Did I surprise you?"

Tom's reaction could be predicted. After a busy morning of trying to get many little things done, at the last stop his daughter has disappeared in less than a minute. If it were your child, you too would be upset, panicked, frantically wracking your brain for ideas on what to do next. When you learn your daughter is safe but also smiling at having surprised you (and anticipating your warm and enthusiastic response), your first response would be like Tom's —relief quickly followed by anger.

Tom gave his little girl a big hug and then in a calm but stern voice looked her straight in the eyes and said, "Honey, don't you ever, *ever* do that again." He explained that he thought someone had taken taken her and described the fear and terror he had felt. He told her that when she was at home she could surprise him all she wanted. "But when we are away from home please, please stay where you are supposed to be."

Many things can produce fear, including snakes, lightning, fire, sudden noises, crowds, driving, heights, being trapped, elevators, and new situations. Although we can encounter these and other physically threatening situations, most of us are much more likely to experience fear when we are threatened with rejection, humiliation, failure, put-downs, abandonment, being ignored, losing control, and the like.

Fear is an unpleasant and often strong emotion caused by anticipation or awareness of threat or danger. Fear is beyond a doubt one of our most uncomfortable emotions. Strong fear can consume our entire perspective and make it difficult for us to focus on anything else. Most people find it more comfortable to feel angry than anxious. It's easier to experience and express anger than fear. That's why anger and fear often go hand-in-hand. For many people anger is an automatic and unconscious response to the emotion of fear. As you uncover your hidden fears you may discover one of the major contributors to your anger.

HURT

More than ten years ago I had the privilege of counseling a delightful elderly woman. Sarah was in her mid-seventies, and she came to see me about her struggles with anger. It was soon clear that in Sarah's life the secondary emotion of anger was primarily in response to the primary emotion of hurt. As we discussed her story I asked her about her earliest memory of hurt. She responded immediately. "Well, I was raised on a farm, and our family was quite poor. When I started first grade at the local country school my parents couldn't afford to buy me dresses so my mother worked hard to make some dresses out of flour sacks. They looked nice, but all the other children knew where the material had come from. They made fun of me."

As she told the story of what had happened to her, tears came into her eyes. Sixty-five years later the pain of that humiliation was still there, and as vivid as if it had happened yesterday.

Hurt, like fear, is a very uncomfortable emotion. When we're hurt we are vulnerable; we're weak and drained; we feel hopeless and helpless. When the pain of hurt is denied and stuffed into the unconscious we may not think about it, but that doesn't mean it has magically disappeared. Out of mind does not mean out of memory. Eventually the layers of hurt, confusion, and misunderstanding make it more difficult to access the facts and interpretations that caused it. Second only to frustration in causing anger, hurt can remain repressed for years, its pain simmering inside us. If not dealt with, this hurt can suddenly boil to the surface, moving past the potentially positive emotion of anger to the damaging emotion of rage.

Hurt is emotionally draining, so we often turn to anger to find the energy to throw up walls to protect ourselves. At first the walls can keep people out and thus keep the hurt out. Anger can veil the hurt, fear, pain, and sense of loss that come from real or perceived rejection. *If no one gets close to me, then no one can hurt me*, we think.

Many people are surprised to learn that hurt and anger go together. People often assume that angry people are so insensitive they must be incapable of being hurt. In truth, the obnoxious person often has experienced deep hurt, typically in his childhood. Because we are more likely to be hurt by people who are important to us, we are more likely to feel anger toward those closest to us, especially our family.

It's important to learn how to distinguish between hurt and anger. Paul Welter suggests that for the most part hurt is the first emotion to be felt but the one that is least accessible to memory. Anger is the second emotion we experience and the one we are most aware of.[3] If we ignore the warning sign of our anger, it can easily turn into resentment and a desire for revenge. If we allow resentment to have its way, we will remain imprisoned in our past. Resentment will then poison our present and ravage our future.

In my work with someone who has a problem with anger one of the first questions I ask is, "Can you tell me the last time you experienced deep hurt?" Frequently people will pause and then tell a story. In many cases tears will come to their eyes. They may share situations from childhood when their brother or sister was favored. It is amazing that things that happened twenty or thirty years ago can cause a wound that can stick with us until we deal with it or until the day we die.

What is your most vivid memory of hurt? Were you wrongly accused? Were you betrayed by someone you trusted? Were you humiliated or treated unfairly? Was your honesty and integrity brought into question?

In this chapter we've looked at nine of the ten major factors that can contribute to our experience of anger. Because anger is a secondary emotion, we must learn to identify the situations and primary emotions that produce our anger. Remember Randy and Carla from the beginning of the chapter? Let's consider how the above causes may apply to their situation.

Randy and Carla had entered my office frustrated and fed up with the marriage. Carla was seriously considering divorce. They both stated that the other person had an anger problem.

Several factors contributed to Randy's passive-aggressive expression of anger. His *childhood experiences* were significant. Randy had grown up in a home where there was little modeling of healthy ways to express anger. Any expression of anger was punished. In terms of *physiological factors* Randy spent so much time at his medical practice that he didn't have time to exercise, to eat right, and since he was frequently "on call" he rarely got a good night's rest. His workaholism left him no time to develop hobbies or outside interests, develop healthy male relationships, or cultivate a meaningful relationship with Carla and the kids. Finally, while he wanted a healthy intimate relationship with Carla and wanted to be a great dad, Randy realized he had a lot of *fear*. He didn't have any idea how to be intimate or what it meant to be a success as a husband or a dad. He knew he could be successful as a physician. He had allowed his fear of failure to keep him from making a consistent quality effort.

Meanwhile, Carla's anger was mainly a response to her years of hiding her deep disappointment and hurt as well as her *fear* that things would never change. Randy's lack of thoughtfulness fed her already *low self-esteem*. She had been faithful through medical school and residency and even through the first couple years of Randy's establishing his practice. Eventually she decided that unless she turned up the heat nothing was going to change.

Randy and Carla learned that their anger was an asset and not a liability. It became clear to them that the secondary emotion of anger was not the problem. Other primary factors that were contributing to their anger had to be addressed. Because they were able to respond to the warning sign of their anger and took a close look at their relationship they began to experience constructive change and significant growth.

Their anger, used positively, helped to save their marriage. Your anger, used positively, can bring significant growth to your relationships.

TAKE ACTION

1. Which of the factors discussed in this chapter are most influential in your own experience of anger? Rate them on a scale of 1-10, with 1 being no influence on your feelings of anger and 10 being a major cause.

   My childhood experiences:
   1   2   3   4   5   6   7   8   9   10

   My physiological response:
   1   2   3   4   5   6   7   8   9   10

   My accumulated stress from normal everyday events:
   1   2   3   4   5   6   7   8   9   10

   My sense of an injustice:
   1   2   3   4   5   6   7   8   9   10

   My feelings of low self-esteem:
   1   2   3   4   5   6   7   8   9   10

   My worry:
   1   2   3   4   5   6   7   8   9   10

   Conflicts in my life:
   1   2   3   4   5   6   7   8   9   10

   My fear:
   1   2   3   4   5   6   7   8   9   10

   The hurt I feel:
   1   2   3   4   5   6   7   8   9   10

2. What are the top three factors that contribute to your experience of anger?

   (1) _____.

   (2) _____.

   (3) _____.

3. Were any of these a surprise? As you go through this coming week keep these factors in mind. Begin to train yourself to look for ways these factors influence how and when you experience the emotion of anger.

NOTES

1. Harriet Goldhor Lerner, *The Dance of Anger* (New York: Harper & Row, 1985), p. 1.
2. L. R. Huesmann, et al., "Stability of Aggression over Time and Generations," *Developmental Psychology* 20 (1984): 1120-34.
3. Paul Welter. *Family Problem and Predicaments: How to Respond* (Wheaton, Ill.: Tyndale House, 1977), p. 130.

7

FEEL THE FRUSTRATION

It festers like a splinter under your skin or a bleeding blister on the ball of your foot. Leaving the splinter buried or continuing to walk with that blister unattended intensifies the irritation and pain. In time its presence tends to dominate your thoughts and sidetracks your focus from the important issues of your life. The irritant's name? Frustration. It's the major cause of our anger.

Frustration is defined as a sense of insecurity or dissatisfaction arising from unresolved problems or unfulfilled needs.

When a hunter shoots a gun, he pull the trigger, and the firing pin ignites the gun powder in the shell. The powder explodes and propels the bullet toward its target. Remove the firing pin, and the hunter can still pull the trigger, but the gun won't go *bang* and nothing will get shot. Frustration is like the firing pin.

Frustration is the initial response in a three-step sequence that goes something like this: frustration, anger, and then wounding words. We tend to follow this destructive three-step path when people don't do as we ask, when something irritates us, or when someone fails to live up to our expectations.

Another person's attitude or behavior may pull your trigger. However, if you deal with your frustration before it ignites into anger, you can keep yourself from exploding with hurtful words or even violence. You may not always be able to prevent the irritant from occurring, but you can prevent the chain reaction that often results in an uncalled-for expression.

Here are four important truths about the frustration we all experience:

1. Frustration is a normal response. But you have a choice about how far your frustration will go and how you will deal with it.
2. Anger is also a normal response. God created us with the capacity to experience anger. But how you handle your anger at others is up to you, especially when it comes to communicating with them.
3. You will at times become irritated, disappointed, and frustrated with other people when they cause you problems, fail to fulfill your expectations, or uncover your unmet needs.
4. Accepting and recognizing your frustration and anger is healthy. Denying or repressing them can be disastrous.[1]

A common myth is that "frustration always has to upset us." That is not true. If another person is doing something that bothers you, you may be frustrated, but you can control both your inner and outward response. In your lifetime, hundreds of little annoyances can activate your frustration button. I've actually seen a man take his fishing pole and break it over the side of the boat because he lost a fish. I've known people to either bend a golf club around a tree or throw the entire golf bag in a pond. I've seen broken hands on clients who hit the wall because of their frustration.

Frustration need not result in an expression of anger. You can experience frustration without becoming upset and angry. Frustration is a matter of attitude, thought, and choice. Consider these words from a therapist who specializes in helping people deal with their frustrations:

> Millions of frustrations are far more easily tolerated than we usually think. Children not finishing their dinner is not an awful frustration, just the waste of a few cents. If a few cents bothers you, put the plate in the refrigerator until later. A person swerving in front of you in traffic is not doing something that calls for a nuclear explosion. It isn't awful to have someone honking his horn impolitely behind you—it's only slightly annoying. Not getting your raise can hurt your pocketbook, but not you—unless you let it. Frustrations are not usually earth-shaking to begin with; they can be toler-

ated quite nicely if we make the effort. Secondly, frustrations, even if they are severe, don't have to lead to disturbances unless we allow them to.[2]

Frustration doesn't have to lead to an angry reaction. You are free to decide how you will respond to it. Difficulties, disappointments, heartaches, and failures are an unavoidable part of life. Your response to them—either anger or joy—is your choice.

Two events during the 1976 Olympic games in Montreal illustrate the contrast between these two responses to frustration. In the two-man sailing event, the team from Britain came in fourteenth in a field of sixteen. The two British sailors were so frustrated by their performance that they set fire to their yacht and waded ashore while it went up in flames! Their response to frustration was destructive and costly.

Olneus Charles, a distance runner from Haiti, also experienced frustration in the Montreal Olympics. He was lapped nine time in the 10,000 meter race and came in dead last, five minutes behind everyone else. But he didn't become discouraged or quit. He chose not to let his frustrating experience get the best of him. He was glad to complete the race for his country.[3]

"I Expect It"

Three major culprits feed our frustration. One is our *expectations*. We all have them—for ourselves, our mate, our children, and even for our friends. Unfortunately, too many of these remain unspoken, and when they are not fulfilled they often turn into demands. And then they lead to frustration and ultimately anger. The higher our expectations and the more numerous our needs, the more often we invite frustration into our lives. Expectations undermine our moving ahead in life. They keep us focused upon what we are not getting and limit our options.

You need to determine your own set of expectations (see Take Action #1 at the end of the chapter). What expectations do you have for yourself? Where did they originate? Are they realistic? If you tend to be a perfectionist, you will probably have a more extensive list of expectations than other people. A perfectionist, however, has never fully succeeded at meeting his expectations.

What are your expectations for your spouse? (See Take Action #2 for determining such expectations.) Take that question and reword it for the other significant people in your life, and you may discover the source of much of your frustration. Identify how important each expectation is to you on a scale of 0-10 and then determine why it is so significant. You will discover that some expectations are reasonable, others are not. Reasonable expectations must be clearly stated for the person to change. You need to turn your expectations into requests.

Laura had not learned this approach, and the result was high frustration. Just two days before her appointment with me, she had spent six hours cleaning the house from corner to corner. She literally slaved over each room, making it spotless. She was hoping for some appreciation and response from her husband. Not only was she hoping, she was expecting it and felt that she deserved it. Unfortunately, he came home tired, hungry, and looking forward to the Monday night football game on TV.

"I didn't hear one word of appreciation, nor did he even seem to notice. In fact, in a half hour John had undone much of my work in the family room by spreading himself and his stuff all over the furniture."

We began talking about her thoughts that led up to the tirade and the big blow-up that lasted from 9:00 until 11:30 that night. Here are the thoughts she remembered: *He should have noticed all the work I did today. . . . He should have thanked me for what I did. I deserved it. . . . He shouldn't have been so insensitive and inconsiderate. . . . He has no class or sensitivity! . . . Look at him! He messes up all my work!*

The final thought she mentioned suggested the anger inside. *He'll probably want sex tonight. Just wait. He'll pay for this and sleep by himself!*

We then discussed each statement and how it made her feel. Soon Laura began to see how the statements created hurt, frustration, rejection, and then anger. The rest of the session was spent on developing some realistic responses to what had happened. As we brainstormed together about how to handle a disappointing experience, she began making a list. Here are some of the inner responses Laura could have used:

I wish he would have noticed all of my work.

I wonder why it is so important to have John notice the work and thank me for it? Did I do this for him or me or..?

Perhaps I could find a creative way to communicate to him what I did today. I could bring in the camera and ask him if he would like to take a picture of a fantastically clean house and the housekeeper who created this wonder!

We then formulated a summary statement that helped to put everything in perspective. It went like this: "I want John to notice the clean house that I've spent six hours slaving over today. But if he doesn't, that is all right, too. My happiness and sense of satisfaction does not depend on his response. I didn't clean it up just for his response. I cleaned it because it needed to be cleaned. I feel good about my effort and how it turned out. His appreciation would just be an added benefit."

John never did notice, but Laura did the right thing and was satisfied. In your own life a similar response could help you resolve that frustration. Perhaps there is a recent frustration that you could identify. Recall what you said to yourself and then formulate a new statement that would have lowered your frustration. It does work!

"I'M ENTITLED TO IT"

Another major cause of frustration has developed more and more during the past two decades. One of the main themes of the baby boomer generation is *entitlement*—the simple belief that if I want something very much, I ought to have it. "I'm entitled to it," they say.

I hear employers in their fifties complain about the younger employees they hire. They say these younger men and women come in demanding what they want for pay and benefits. They want to start at the same place as other employees who have been working for twenty years. They don't want to wait. I see this sometimes in young couples I counsel before marriage. They want to start out with the same style of living that their parents have, but they fail to remember how long it has taken their parents to arrive at that point.

Entitlement says the degree of your need justifies the demand that others supply that need. I've heard many say that if they want something so bad they are entitled to have it. This can include sex, emotional fulfillment, or a standard of living. Sometimes parents feel they are entitled to have some of their adolescent's time and attention because of all they provide for him.

Entitlement confuses desire with obligation. If the person wants something, then others have no right to say no. Unfortunately, this belief is saying that another person must give up his or her limits and boundaries for you. It denies the other person the freedom to choose. Strong entitlement feelings can overshadow care and concern for another person. And frustration is inevitable since entitlement is doomed to failure. We have a generation struggling with this issue at the present time.[4]

"It's Not Fair

The third culprit is the belief that *life should be fair*. We believe that relationships should be fair. We believe that if we do certain things, there will be prescribed results. However, fairness is subjective. It can be defined so that we can call anything either fair or unfair.

We use fairness to control the behavior of children. But as adults it is doomed to failure. Life is not a democracy. Life is not fair. That is a fact. When we use the word *fair* in interpersonal relationships it is a disguise for needs and wants. When we believe that fairness should prevail we set ourselves up to be victimized.

Time and time again people say, "Where was God when this happened? I can understand people not coming through, but God? Don't tell me He doesn't act fairly either!" Somewhere we developed the belief that God has to act as though life were a legal and contractual relationship. The difficulty is that we all have our own differing views of what is fair and unfair when it comes to God's dealings with us.

Our theology seems to come into play when we are disappointed by God. Perhaps we have focused just on the passages of hope and benefits without balancing them with the teaching that in life there will be pain, disappointment, and heartache. Frustration is just one step away from feeling that something is unfair. And the next step is anger.[5]

Handling Your Frustration

DEVELOP AN ACCOUNTABILITY RELATIONSHIP

One way of handling your frustration is to find someone with whom you can discuss your concerns and *develop an accountability relationship.* Select a person who will be willing to pray with you and check up on you regularly to see how you are doing. If you are working through these steps as a couple, ask another couple to keep you accountable. We all need the support and assistance of others.[6]

You also need to be honest and accountable to yourself and to your spouse about the changes you want to make. (See Take Action #3 for a project with your spouse or a prayer partner to plan changes.

INTERNALIZE GOD'S WORD

A key way to deal with frustration is to *internalize the guidelines from God's Word.* God inspired men to write the Scriptures, and He preserved them through the centuries for a major reason: God's guidelines for life are the best. Regardless of what you may have experienced or been taught in the past, God's plan works.

Here are three fundamental truths from Proverbs (TLB*):

Some people like to make cutting remarks, but the words of the wise soothe and heal. (12:18)

A wise man controls his temper. He knows that anger causes mistakes. (14:29)

It is better to be slow-tempered than famous; it is better to have self-control than to control an army. (16:32)

To help you internalize these biblical truths, write each verse on a separate index card. Add to these cards other Scriptures that you discover which discuss frustration and anger. Read the verses aloud morning and evening for one month, and they will be yours.

* *The Living Bible.*

PLAN YOUR RESPONSE

One smart tactic for handling frustration is to *plan your response to frustration in advance*. You will be able to change only if you plan to change. Your intentions may be good, but once the frustration-anger sequence kicks into gear, your ability to think clearly is limited.

Identify in advance what you want to say to the other person or situation when you begin to feel frustrated. Be specific. Write out your responses and read them aloud to yourself. In my counseling office I often have clients practice their new responses on me, and I attempt to respond as the other person. By practicing on me they are able to refine their statements, eliminate their anxiety or feelings of discomfort, and gain confidence for their new approach. Perhaps your spouse or a friend could assist you this way.

DELAY YOUR RESPONSE

Another important step is to learn to delay your response. Begin training yourself to delay your verbal and behavioral responses when you recognize that you are frustrated. The Proverbs repeatedly admonish us to be slow to anger. You must slow down your responses if you want to change any habits of hasty, verbal responses you have cultivated over the years. When we allow frustration and anger to be expressed unhindered, they are like a runaway locomotive. You need to catch them before they gather momentum so that you can switch the tracks and steer them in the right direction.[7]

One helpful way to change direction is to use a trigger word. Whenever you feel frustration and anger rising within you, remind yourself to slow down and gain control by saying something to yourself like "stop," "think," "control," and so on. Use a word that will help you switch gears and put your new plan into action. Accept the fact that everything will not always go your way.

ACCEPT THE FRUSTRATING SITUATION

One of the approaches I often suggest to diffuse a frustrating experience is this: mentally give permission for the frustrating experience to occur. The next time a family member does something that usually upsets you, say to yourself, "I don't know why she did that, but I'm not going to let it ruin my day. It's not the worst thing she could do. If she wants to do it, I give her permission to do so. I know there is a reason for it, and it's important for me to discover that reason. It will be a learning experience for both of us as we try to resolve this behavior."

The permission-giving approach defuses your frustration and gives you time to implement a level-headed plan. Most of us have run into the frustration of not having enough time. It happens at home, at work and often on the highway. You have an appointment and you're running late. You expect to make up time driving faster than the speed limit, but two miles onto the freeway traffic comes to a roaring halt. Nobody's moving. The time ticks by, and soon it's apparent that you won't make it.

Then your thoughts begin to feed the already present tension taking control of your body. *I can't be late. This is ridiculous. What's the problem up there? Probably some idiot who ran out of gas or road work again. Why can't they plan ahead?* The thoughts continue and feed the feelings of frustration and anger. You're out of control. You're at the mercy of the freeway. You can fight it all you want, and you'll just be more frustrated.

There is a solution, however. It may seem strange, but it works. Give yourself permission to be stuck in traffic and to be late. After all, that's the reality of what is happening. You can't change these two facts, so why not take control of them by giving yourself permission. Accept the situation, and you will begin to relax and calm down. Tell yourself, "It isn't what I expected and it's inconvenient, but I can handle it. I'm going to take three deep breaths and then use this time out to scan through these papers I have with me, or pray, or think of how I can greet my family in a loving manner tonight when I arrive home."

Sounds different, doesn't it? Once I explained this principle to a group of ministers at a conference; one of them had to leave at noon to conduct a funeral. He returned about 4 o'clock, pulled me aside and said, "Do you remember that odd suggestion about giving ourselves permission to be late? Well, it works! I'm amazed. I was due at the funeral home at 2:00, and at 1:53 I discovered I was late. I am never late. I am precise, punctual, and a bit compulsive. I started to get upset and tense and then remembered what you had said. I gave myself permission to be lost and late, I calmed down, retraced my steps and arrived at 2:10. No one even noticed that much. And here I am talking with you, and I am fairly calm about the matter. Norm, this is not the way I usually respond. Normally I would be frustrated and angry for twenty-four hours. But not today. Finally I found something that works!"

I have heard this time and time again. Much of our frustration can be eliminated. I heard of one man who carried in his car a small bottle of soapy water with a bubble wand inside. When he was stuck in traffic, he would take out the bottle, roll down the window, dip the wand in the soapy water, hold it out the window and blow. The bubbles that came floating out of it would rise and drift around his and others' cars, and in time the people around him were noticing, laughing, smiling—and their frustration and upset began to disappear.

I'm not suggesting that you emotionally give up and allow other people to do anything they want to do. Some behaviors, if allowed to continue, would be highly detrimental. But with every-day behaviors that are more frustrating than dangerous, challenge yourself to quit fighting and go with the flow. By doing so you may be able to skirt and solve the problem without wounding the person.

Many people are skeptical when I suggest the permission-giving strategy. But they often come back after trying it and report amazing results. One person said, "Norm, the first time I heard your suggestion, I thought you were crazy. But I tried it. I discovered that I was less frustrated, and I could think clearer and actually come up with a solution."

YOUR INNER CONVERSATIONS

Your inner conversation—also called self-talk—is where your frustrations are either tamed or inflamed. What you say to your family and friends and how you behave toward them is determined by how you talk to yourself about their behaviors and responses. In fact, your most powerful emotions—anger, depression, guilt, worry—as well as your self-esteem as a person and a parent are initiated and fed by your inner conversation. Changing your inner conversation is essential to keeping your frustrations from erupting into wounding words, or worse.[8]

Just before leaving for his Saturday morning golf game, Frank asked his eleven-year-old son to clean up his room and wash the family car. Jimmy said he would. But when Frank returned home, Jimmy was nowhere to be seen. His room was only half clean, and the car was still a mess. Listen in on Frank's inner conversation as he surveys the scene (perhaps you've had such a conversation with yourself):

"Where is that boy? He didn't follow my instructions. I can't believe he's so lazy and inconsiderate. I give him everything, and he doesn't even have the courtesy to do a little work. He never follows through. Wait till I see him. And he always leaves without writing a note telling me where he's going. I'll ground that kid for a month!" (Did you hear the three culprits? Expectations, entitlements, fairness.)

You may argue that Frank had a right to be frustrated and angry. Perhaps, but maybe not. Regardless, Frank was free to choose how he thought about the scene before him. And his inner conversation reveals that he chose to fuel his frustration with distorted thinking. He resorted to *labeling*, calling Jimmy lazy and inconsiderate. Labeling encourages frustration because it perpetuates a negative view. You begin to look for behaviors in another person that reinforce the labels you have attached to him. You tend to overlook the positives and look only for the worst. And it becomes a self-fulfilling prophecy.

Another evidence of Frank's distorted thinking is *magnification*. Words like *never, always,* and *every* magnify occasional misbehavior into lifetime habits. Magnifying the child's misbehavior only serves to intensify frustration. How frequently are these words a part of your vocabulary?

Frank's inner conversation was based on hasty, negative assumptions. Perhaps an emergency in the neighborhood called Jimmy away from his task. Perhaps an out-of-town relative arrived unexpectedly and took Jimmy to the mall for the afternoon. Perhaps a shut-in down the street called Jimmy to run an important errand. Maybe he left a note explaining his whereabouts, but Frank was so busy thinking the worst that he didn't look for it. You will save yourself a lot of frustration and anger if you learn to base your inner conversations on hard facts and positive assumptions. Wait until you know the reasons and then respond in a way that will bring about the change you want.

God's Word has much to say about how we think. If you have difficulty with negative inner conversations, I suggest that you write out the following Scriptures on index cards and begin reading them aloud to yourself every morning and evening: Isaiah 26:3; Romans 8:6-7; 2 Corinthians 10:5; 12:2; Ephesians 4:23; Philippians 4:6-9; and 1 Peter 1:13. Your thoughts can change if you choose to change them.

If you approach these steps thinking, "This will never work," you have set yourself up for failure. Instead, coach yourself to think, "I'm taking some positive steps toward resolving my frustration and anger. This will really make a difference in my relationship with others. I know my communication will improve as I take these steps of growth."

To help you to develop a positive attitude, take a minute to list the advantages of being frustrated and the advantages of not being frustrated. Compare the two lists. Which results do you want? You are more likely to achieve these results by following the steps above.

Advantages of Being Frustrated	Disadvantages of Being Frustrated
1. _____	1. _____
2. _____	2. _____
3. _____	3. _____
4. _____	4. _____

A RECORD OF PROGRESS

Keep a record of your progress by maintaining a frustration diary in a small notebook.[9] Keep your notebook handy at all times so that you can write down your responses to your daily frustrations. Later, read your entries with another person who is willing to support you in prayer.

The purpose of this diary is twofold. First, it will help you arrest your frustrations as they arise so that you can control them instead of allowing them to control you. Second, it will help you plan a healthy, controlled response to future frustrations.

Your frustration diary entries should include the date and time the frustration occurred and a rating of your level of frustration. Rate your frustration on a scale of 0 (none) to 10 (intense). Write, "On a scale of 0 to 10, my frustration was _____.

Here's a pattern for the rest of the entries regarding that particular frustration for the day:

1. My frustration was directed toward . . .
2. Inside I felt . . .
3. My inner conversation about this could be summarized:
4. My verbal response was . . .
5. Did I move from frustration to anger? If so, what was the intensity of my anger?
6. How did my response this time improve from the previous frustration experience?
7. What would I like to feel and say at the next incident of frustration?
8. What improvement will I make at the next incident of frustration?

Here's a fictitous example of how one man charted his progress in his frustration diary[10].

> *The date and time the frustration occurred:* Saturday, March 10, at 7:30 P.M., just after I got home.
> *The level of my frustration on a scale of 0 (none) to 10 (intense) was* . . . an 8!
> *My frustration was directed toward* . . . my 17-year-old son.
> *Inside I felt* . . . really irritated. In fact, I was ready to yell at him and take his car away for a week.
> *My inner conversation about him and his behavior could be summarized:* That kid is so irresponsible. He's so selfish, and he never listens to me. I wonder if he's ever going to change!
> *My verbal response to my son was:* "Ken, you're impossible. I gave you a simple task to do. How could you not remember? Don't you ever listen? Do you think you're entitled to a free ride here?"

Did I move from frustration to anger? If so, what was the intensity of my anger? I sure did. I was upset. My anger rose to about an 8 or 9.

How did my response this time improve from the previous frustration experience? I'm not sure it did. I was really upset. My words were louder—we were both shouting at each other. But I don't think it lasted as long this time; we got it settled in a half hour. So I guess I could call that an improvement.

What would I like to feel and say at the next incident of frustration? I don't want to feel irritated and angry. I don't want to yell. I guess I would like to talk to him in a firm, calm voice but also get him to be responsible.

What improvement will I make at the next incident of frustration? I need to figure that out more in detail now. If I don't have a plan, I'll react the same way. I'm going to memorize Proverbs 12:18; 14:29; and 16:32. Then I'm going to write out and practice exactly what I will say if Ken doesn't follow through. I'm also going to discuss and role-play the situation with my wife. We both can use some help.

I'm going to use the "conscious delay principle." I will stop for a few seconds and remember what I want to say and do. In fact, in my mind I'm going to say, "It's all right for this to be happening. Most of his misbehavior isn't dangerous or life-threatening, and it's not the end of the world for me."

Then I am going to go to Ken, sit down with him and ask him what I had asked him to do and what he will do now to get it done. I'll also ask him what he can do to remember the next time.

This approach may make a difference.

You can change your responses to the frustrations you face. Begin to believe you can change. God believes you can. And as believers in Jesus Christ, ask in prayer for His strength and guidance to bring about these changes. Also, allow others to help and support you along the way. With God's help, you can respond to frustration the right way.

TAKE ACTION

1. Evaluate the unspoken expectations you have for yourself. List two expectations. Then indicate where each expectation originated and whether it is realistic.

   (1) My expectation: _____
       Its origin: _____
       Is the expectation realistic? _____
   (2) My expectation: _____
       Its origin: _____
       Is the expectation realistic? _____

2. Evaluate the unspoken expectation for your spouse. List two expectations. Then indicate whether your mate knows the expectation and whether he/she has clarified which ones are realistic.

   (1) My expectation of my spouse: _____
       Is my spouse aware of this expectation? _____
       Have I asked my mate to clarify whether the expectation is realistic? _____
   (2) My expectation of my spouse: _____
       Is my spouse aware of this expectation? _____
       Have I asked my mate to clarify whether the expectation is realistic? _____

3. One way to handle frustration is to find someone with whom you can discuss your concerns and develop an accountability relationship. To be accountable to yourself and a spouse or other close friend about the changes you need, do the following exercise.[11] Take a sheet of paper and respond to the following questions.

   (1) How do you feel about becoming frustrated? Be specific.
   (2) How do you feel about getting angry? Some people enjoy their anger. It gives them an adrenaline rush and a feeling of power. Does this description fit you?
   (3) When you are frustrated, do you want to be in control of your response or be spontaneous? In other words, do you want to decide what to do or just let your feelings take you where they want to go?

(4) If you want to stay in control, how much time and energy are you willing to spend to make that happen? (for change to occur, the motivational level needs to remain constant and high.)

(5) When you are bothered by something that happens, how would you like to respond? What would you like to say at that time? Be specific?

Discuss your answers with your accountability partner. Have your partner help you be accountable for fulfilling number 5 (your desired response).

NOTES

1. H. Norman Wright, *The Power of a Parent's Words* (Ventura, Calif.: Regal, 1990), pp. 117-18, adapted.

2. Paul A. Hauck. *Overcoming Frustration and Anger*, (Philadelphia: Westminster, 1974), p. 65.

3. Wright, *The Power of a Parent's Words*, p. 120.

4. Matthew McKay, Peter D. Rogers, and Judith McKay, *When Anger Hurts* (Oakland, Calif.: New Harbinger, 1989) p. 85.

5. Ibid., pp. 86-87, adapted.

6. The section "Handling Your Frustration" is based on material appearing in Wright, *The Power of a Parent's Words*, pp.123-26, copyright 1990, Regal Books, Ventura, CA, 93003. Used by permission.

7. Neil Clark Warren, *Make Anger Your Ally* (Garden City, N.J.: Doubleday, 1983), p. 169, adapted.

8. The section "Change Your Inner Conversation" quotes from and is largely based on Wright, *The Power of A Parent's Words*, pp.126-28. Regal Books, Ventura, CA 93003. Used by permission.

9. The section "A Record of Progress" quotes from and is largely based on Wright, *The Power of a Parent's Words*, pp.129-30. Regal Books, Ventura, CA 93003. Used by permission.

10. Wright, *The Power of a Parent's Words*, pp.130-31, adapted.

11. Ibid., p. 125.

8

MEN AND ANGER

One of the oldest and most read stories is *The Iliad*. The first words of this epic are "An angry man." Homer tells us that he is about to tell a story of one angry man, Achilles.

According to the story, Achilles is the greatest warrior of the Greeks, who are in a major battle with the Trojans. Achilles becomes enraged with Agamemnon, the Greek king and commander. It's been suggested that *The Iliad* is one of the most painful stories in literature, because of the intensity of the anger. Here is how the story opens:

> An angry man—there is my story: the bitter rancor of Achilles, prince of the house of Peleus, which brought a thousand troubles upon the Achaian host. Many a strong soul it sent down to Hades, and left the heroes themselves a prey to dogs and carrion birds, while the will of God moved on to fulfillment.[1]

There are angry men such as this today.

Men and their emotions are a product of the physiological features that distinguish them from women and that are part of God's design. Men are also the product of cultural conditioning. How you act today as a man largely reflects how your culture—and family—trained you to respond. Many men today respond emotionally because of the way they were taught to respond, expected to respond, predisposed to respond, and are even physically capable of responding.

Have you ever considered some of the cultural expectations that we have for men? Think about it for a moment. Is a man expected to be in control or lose control? Is he expected to be a rock of confidence or to be fearful? Is a man expected to be more concerned with thinking or with feelings? Men are expected to be assertive, courageous, competitive, goal-oriented, able to handle stress without caving in, able to bear pain and, especially, able to express his anger. A man is supposed to do something, solve something, oppose something, or accomplish something. It is true that there are exceptions, and we have somewhat of a blurring of male-female expectations and characteristics today, but unique identifiable differences still exist between the sexes.[2]

It begins early. Parents have spoken and unspoken expectations. You don't have to talk about them for them to be felt. Traditionally parental expectations for their sons include:

- Boys are expected to have more strength than girls.
- Boys are expected to be more rational and less emotional and intuitive.
- Boys are expected to be more aggressive and impulsive.
- Boys are expected to be more alert and active.
- Boys are expected to be more self-reliant than girls.
- Boys are expected to play rough.
- Boys are expected to play games such as war and space-man, not house or feminine activities.

If these expectations are not verbalized, how do they become conveyed to the sons? Psychologists have observed a number of ways parents respond to their sons. Roughhouse games are played more with infant sons than with infant daughters. Mothers and fathers respond to their sons' attempts to grasp, walk, and crawl but pay less attention to their vocalizations than to the sounds their daughters make. Parents give their sons more latitude than they do their daughters in terms of letting them roam in the yard and the playground. Parents tend to push boys into activities that frighten them more than they would ever push their daughters.[3]

A MAN AND HIS FEELINGS

On occasion you may hear someone arguing that there are no distinctions between men and women when it comes to feelings. The speaker or writer may cite a number of exceptions to prove his point, but that is just what they are—exceptions. Men do not access or handle feelings in the same way that woman do. Most American men still feel uncomfortable when a man expresses his emotions, whether it is crying, raging, trembling in fear, or being out of control emotionally in any way. In spite of what a few are saying, the words of Herb Goldberg still reflect the man of the nineties.

> The autonomous male, the independent strong achiever who can be counted on to be always in control, is still essentially the preferred male image. Success in the working world is predicated on the repression of self and the display of a controlled, deliberate, calculated, manipulative responsiveness. To become a leader requires that one be totally goal-oriented, undistracted by personal factors, and able to tune out extraneous "noise" human or otherwise, which is unrelated to the end goal and which might impede forward motion. The man who "feels" becomes inefficient and ineffective because he gets emotionally involved and this inevitably slows him down and distracts him. His more dehumanized competitor will then surely pass him by.[4]

Why do the majority of men struggle with feelings? One reason is that many boys do not learn a feeling vocabulary. Girls develop their verbal skills at an earlier age and are fed a feeling vocabulary because they are girls. In contrast, boys lack men who will model a proper healthy verbal expression of feeling words and encourage boys to build a vocabulary. Thus they are at a disadvantage verbally. They struggle to describe those strange sensations within themselves. And unfortunately, many boys grow up unaware that these skills are lacking. As adults, they just think that the way they are is the way they should be.

Some boys have no incentive to learn to express their feelings. They weren't shown the value by role models and in many cases observed negative models instead. They witnessed plenty of feelings and emotions, but at such an intensity and decibel level that they vowed to keep what they felt bottled up forever.

Unfortunately, many boys were put down or ridiculed early in life for any expression of feelings. Their father may have been threatened by the sensitive caring side of the young boy. He didn't want his son to grow up being unable to take care of himself or to end up being unmanly. Crying was squelched. Too much playing or interaction with little girls was curtailed. Even the use of feeling words may have been discouraged, because it didn't sound appropriate for a boy to talk that way. Verbal sarcasm is difficult for any young boy to handle when the put-downs come from his father; thus the son learns to mask the tears outwardly and express them inwardly.

In his classic book *The Secrets Men Keep*, Ken Druck describes the dilemma men face:

> We got trapped at an early age in a set role. We were taught what is acceptable behavior for us, as little men, and what was unacceptable. We played hard at sports and fought for the right to be the king of the mountain. We learned that such traits as toughness, rationality, aggression, competitiveness, self-reliance, and control over our emotions were positive for men, whereas tenderness, emotional sensitivity, dependence, openness to experience, and vulnerability were negative.[5]

Men have been socialized to be emotionally stoic. Over the years we men have evolved a thousand and one clever ways to hide our feelings. We are masters at appearing emotionally unaffected and in control. Here are some of the common ploys we use:

— We rationalize a course of inaction by telling ourselves, "What good is it going to do to talk about it? That's not going to change anything!"
— We worry, worry, and worry, never facing what we really feel.
— We escape into new roles or hide behind old ones. ("Now wait just one minute—I'm the boss around here!")
— We take the attitude that "these feelings will pass" and shrug them off as unimportant.
— We keep busy.

— We change one feeling into another—by acting angry when we are really hurt, for example, we create a smoke screen, diverting attention away from our true feelings.

— We deny the feeling outright.

— We put our feelings on hold—compartmentalize them or put them in a back file.

— We dull or dilute our feelings with diversionary tactics (silence, indifference, tiredness, laughter) or with drugs or alcohol.

— We perform a "thinking bypass"—replacing our feelings with thought and logic, intellectualizing and rationalizing our way around the feelings.

— We tense our bodies, so that we do not feel anything.

— We let our women do our feeling for us—reinforce women for being emotional and showing their feelings, so that we will not have to feel.

— We avoid situations and people who elicit certain feelings in us.

— We get sick or behave carelessly and hurt ourselves so that we have a reason to justify our feelings.

— We go crazy, so that somebody else has to take responsibility for our feelings.[6]

Ronald Levant of Harvard Medical School verified man's tendency to escape his feelings in his remarks at the 1991 American Psychological Convention. Dr. Levant declared that men tend to distract themselves with daydreams or tasks when they feel uncomfortable or embarrassed in a situation.

Some men let their feelings build and then erupt. Men also take situations that produce uncomfortable feelings and block them, which leads to additional insensitivity to any feelings. As a result, men often express their unidentified feelings through body language. Even though their speech may be calm and friendly, their body language is angry.[7]

Men do tend to be less verbal (they are condensers) and less equipped verbally than women (who are amplifiers). Based on my counseling experience, I estimate that seven of every ten married men in our country are condensers, while their wives tend to be amplifiers. Neither style of communication is wrong, but it certainly can frustrate the other partner when the communication style is different.

WHEN THE ANGER COMES

A MAN'S WORDS

The lack of vocabulary and healthy models invades the emotion of anger as well as other feelings. The anger a man feels may then be expressed with limited but more powerful words. These could range from swearing to attacking and threatening words. The volume could be higher or the tone more tense. And as noted earlier, anger is more likely to be displayed as aggression if a person does not have the verbal skills to express it adequately.

Anger stored up against one person whether it be a boss, fellow worker, or family member is often released at the closest object around. And usually with damaging results. This happened to King Saul and his son Jonathan.

> Then Saul's anger was kindled against Jonathan, and he said to him, "You son of a perverse, rebellious woman, do not I know that you have chosen the son of Jesse to your own shame, and to the shame of your mother who bore you? For as long as the son of Jesse lives upon the earth you shall not be established or your kingdom. So now send and bring him to me, for he shall surely die."
>
> Jonathan answered Saul his father, "Why should he be killed? What has he done?"
>
> But Saul cast his spear at him to smite him, by which Jonathan knew that his father had determined to kill David.
>
> So Jonathan arose from the table in fierce anger and ate no food that second day of the month, for he grieved for David, because his father had disgraced him. (1 Samuel 20:30-34, Amp.)

The illustrations and admonitions of Scripture have clear implications for men concerning the proper control of anger. Proverbs, for instance, offers healthy guidelines for men dealing wth anger.

"An angry man stirs up dissension, and a hot-tempered one commits many sins" (29:22).

"Do not make friends with a hot-tempered man, do not associate with one easily angered, for you may learn his ways and get yourself easily ensnared" (22:24-25).

"A fool gives full vent to his anger, but a wise man keeps himself under control" (29:11).

In *The Man in the Mirror,* Patrick Morley describes a scenario that is familiar to many men.

> Anger resides behind the closed doors of most of our homes. Personally, I have never lost my temper at the office, I would never want my colleagues to think I couldn't control myself. But rarely a week goes by in which the sparks of family life don't provide good tinder for a roaring fire of anger.
>
> We put on a good show at the office and our social gatherings, but *how you are behind the closed doors of your own private castle is how you really are.* At the end of a long, hard day at the office, when you pull up the drawbridge to your own private castle, your family gets to live with the real you.
>
> Anger destroys the quality of our personal lives, our marriages, and our health. Angry words are like irretrievable arrows released from an archer's bow. Once released, traveling through the air toward their target, they cannot be withdrawn, their damage cannot be undone. Like the arrows of the archer, our angry words pierce like a jagged blade, ripping at the heart of their target.
>
> When anger pierces the soul of the home, the lifeblood of the family starts to drain away. You may notice that a secretary seems to find you attractive. You reflect on how your wife no longer appreciates you. It never occurs to you that it may be you, that if that secretary knew the real you—the angry you that lives secretly behind the closed doors of your home—she would find you about as desirable as a flat tire.[8]

A MAN'S AGGRESSION

Like women, men feel anger or aggression due to more than one cause. Much of it could come from a man's internal conflicts, which eventually turn into outer conflicts. However, boys learn at a young age to rehearse their anger. When boys are younger, they fight. They play war, space warriors, and a multitude of games involving overpowering others. When I was a young boy during World War II, the theme of our games, comic books, movies, and newsreels was fighting, killing, war, and aggression. The entire world was dominated by this theme.

Today, though no world war is in progress, boys still learn to fight in play and then as adults look for the real thing to take out their aggressions on others. Meanwhile, former soldiers often have difficulty adjusting to the calmness of peacetime since they were trained to be aggressive and violent.

Men can watch other men in various levels of combat on movies, television, and at sporting events. If you want to see angry, aggressive, violent men, watch "Wrestling Mania" on Saturday television. Look beyond the wrestlers' theatrics and observe the males in the audience. You can actually see their anger and aggression building. It makes you wonder what they do with all that energy and turmoil when the matches are over. Do their family members receive the brunt of these intense feelings?

Men sometimes use their aggression to rechannel their fears, sexual impulses, and dependency needs. The tension arising from these other feelings becomes diverted into anger or aggression. Men may suppress their reactions to daily frustrations, but eventually their holding tank overloads. All it takes is one fissure for the tank to break.

A MAN'S SELF-ESTEEM

With many men their anger is a direct result of the level of their self-esteem. Stoop and Arterburn point out the relationship between anger and low self-esteem.

> A man's low self-image is usually the result of threats of an interpersonal nature, such as insults or undue criticism. Studies show that men with a high sense of self-worth are much less affected by criticism.
>
> Insults and criticism are especially provocative of anger if the man already suffers from low self-esteem, instability relating to poor social adjustment, depression, anxiety, and low life satisfaction. These men usually did not receive the affirmation they craved from their fathers during childhood, and they get angry when they are not affirmed and appreciated as adults. No matter how hard he tries, the man with low self-worth never quite measures up to the idealized vision of what others expect him to be. He may appear to be quite confident and secure, but in reality he is insecure and highly sensitive to the criticism of others, positive or negative.
>
> A man's anger in response to his low self-worth serves a number of functions. It prompts him to express his displeasure at the affront he has suffered. It helps him defend himself against all his negative feelings. It encourages him to restore his wounded self-esteem and public self-image by going on the offensive. Yet in the

process of trying to save his own skin, he may bring pain to others, especially those closest to him."[9]

How do men react to stress, crisis, and turmoil in their lives? One counselor summarizes most men's response:

> A men's group counselor reflecting upon his experiences with men said, 'Men are very invested in not having fear, the kind that will debilitate them. So they need to surround themselves with supports from other men—that they are okay, they're powerful, omnipotent and nothing can destroy them. That is a very constant common denominator I see with men in general. Without that, they would not be able to fight wars or live life.
>
> Men are petrified, terrified of being helpless, out of control. If they acknowledge that they are helpless or terrified, they wouldn't be able to function."[10]

Men are expected to be in control, and they expect to be in control. As one man said, "I was so ashamed of that guy. He lost it. He couldn't control his feelings. He was an embarrassment to the rest of us guys." And if a man isn't in control, he is expected at least to get back in control.

The stresses of life affect everyone. But if you are a man, some silent or hidden stresses will influence you toward anger. One of them is changes in the routines of life. Even small changes can be stressful, such as the change of office space, a freeway exit suddenly closed for six weeks, a menu being changed at a favorite restaurant, or a change in a family member's schedule. The pressure comes knowing these small changes could be the start of some major changes. The changes eventually could interfere with a comforting routine that gives you security. They could also undermine both a sense of control and a sense of identity. When that happens frustration and anger are about to strike you.

WHO'S IN CHARGE?

Control seems to be at the heart of stress and anger for the majority of men. As a father, you will face a major adjustment in your child's developing independence—he no longer responds to your guidelines and opinions. A child's first date, career decisions, college selection, marriage, or a move thousands of miles away tend to worry fathers.[11] The struggle and drive for control manifests itself in so many simple ways. Consider the following situations. I have described these scenes to thousands of people in seminars, and their verbal and nonverbal reaction affirms that many couples have experienced these responses.

> Men are stressed when they are forced to be in the passenger seat rather than at the wheel of an automobile.
> Men are stressed when they must wait for a table at a restaurant, or in line for a movie, and they frequently choose to forgo the meal or movie to regain their sense of choice.
> Men become irate at gridlock, infuriated by road construction, and exasperated at "stupid" drivers who distract or detain them.
> Men dread funerals and psychotherapy, and sometimes equate the two as depressing reminders of life's uncertainties.
> Men postpone dental appointments and other procedures that require that they put themselves in other's hands.
> Men are terrified of illness or injury that may interfere with their ability to be in charge of their daily lives.
> Men prefer requests to demands, and free choice to requests —and they will demonstrate this by saying "no" to suggestions for things that they might have actually enjoyed.[12]

We even see this in a man's desire for control in the selection of pets. Most men prefer dogs over cats. There are a number of reasons, but one has to do with control. You can control a dog and rough it up and play hard with it, but it remains loyal and loving. Just try that with a cat. They are so independent! (I know. I have raised both for more than forty years.) As one person said, "You tell a dog to come to you, he responds and obeys. You tell a cat to come to you, the cat says, "Leave a message, I'll get back to you."

Both men and women want to control the outcome. And if nothing seems to work to bring a situation into control, frustration and anger spring forth. For the man, however, the issue may be more intense. Stoop and Arterburn describe the control issue for men in *The Angry Man*; they emphasize that the distinctives between sexes are still present.

> The macho masculine image is that of a man who is the captain of his own ship and the master of his fate. Most men want to be in complete control of all the elements of their lives. They want to

be the unchallenged boss at home, and they want an increasing measure of control over others at work. Many men break their backs to get to the top in their field or to own their own company, because it fulfills the masculine dream of being top dog.

But few men actually achieve total control of their lives. And those who crave control in an area where they can't achieve it are often angry men.[13]

The authors go on to ask wives several pointed questions:

Is your man especially controlling in your relationship, such as demanding that he sign all the checks or handle all the money? Does he often criticize his boss, claiming, "I could do a much better job of running the company than that bozo"? Is he critical of others in authority over him: his father, his pastor, the government, the police officer who pulled him over for speeding? If so, he's probably dealing with an undercurrent of anger from a lack of control.[14]

Have you ever considered the links between control, anger, aggression, and competitive behavior? How do men demonstrate that they are in control? By acting aggressively and competitively whether it be in sports, the office, a promotion, or in seeking recognition. If a man does not try to achieve in this way, often people think, *There's something wrong with him.* Our society has an image, even an expectation, that men are to be competitive. Business, sports, the armed services, and school are set up in this way. In America, the spirit of competition is apparent in most types of work. The frustration of losing or not moving ahead is the breeding ground for anger. After all, men have been taught few alternatives to competing.

THE AGGRESSIVE MAN

Some scientists believe that biological factors contribute to the aggressive behavior of men. Studies have shown that in all cultures, regardless of training and conditioning, men tend to be more aggressive then women. And it has been proven that increasing the amount of testosterone levels in men results in greater aggressive behavior.[15]

Our language and phrases reflect the aggressive tendencies. Listen to the conversations of men at work and at play. The statements reflect the importance of being in control and macho.

"I trampled him in that racquetball game."

"I leveled him when he came in to make that basket."

"I cut him off when he tried to oppose me in that meeting."

Why do men tend to be more aggressive? It is a way we men protect ourselves from being out of control, of feeling powerless. It's an act of protection, yet one that is often an overreaction. Whether the man has a real threat or one that is imagined within the mind, he responds to retain his power.

Consider just two settings. You believe that your wife or girlfriend is being unfair (even when she has your best interests at heart), and you will overreact. You are ready to buy a new car, and you believe that all car salesmen will try to push you toward a certain model—they'll try the ol' hard sell and be abrasive. In either case, whether the threat is real or imagined, you will try to change the other person, either the wife/girlfriend or the salesman. You may approach them with the attitude, "I know what you're going to try to do, and I am going to override you first." And if a man tends to be overly aggressive, he will perceive many more threats than would others. Many of the threats fall into that category discussed earlier—unmet frustrations or demands.

When a threat is perceived, most men quickly assume that the threat is major. And if we think that we might be overwhelmed by this threat or hurt, we react. Any time a man feels he is powerless to handle the threat, aggression is a possibility.

If you do not have the verbal skills to handle this threat, then anger is likely to emerge as aggression. Or if your anger has been allowed to build inside with no adequate release, aggression may come. Sometimes you may believe aggression is the only way to handle a threat. Or you may believe that the emotion of anger is in itself highly threatening or the consequences of letting the anger out too negative. In this case, you probably will turn the anger inward; the result is depression or passive behavior. Over time, that response can yield even more anger.

This cycle of perceived threat, decision-making, and response doesn't take two minutes or even thirty seconds to occur. It can happen instantaneously. Some of us are unaware of feeling threatened because we either believe we shouldn't be threatened or we feel bad for feeling threatened.

Certain beliefs can feed our tendency toward aggression.

"I must be in charge or on top to feel good about myself."

"If I don't come across strong and aggressive, they won't listen to me."

"We live in a tough world. Others are out to get me, and I have to be aggressive in order to survive. You can't give an inch, or others will take advantage of you."

"I have to influence others and get my way."

"Aggression is the only thing that has ever worked for me with some people."

"If I give up my anger and aggression, I give up my strength."

But these are not just beliefs, they are misbeliefs. They're reflected subtly in expressions and everyday phrases that men use: "I just told him to stuff it." "That guy is really cut off from his feelings."

Unfortunately, these beliefs become self-fulfilling prophecies. If a man believes any of these statements, he acts in accordance with that belief and sees people or situations accordingly. When you act aggressively you can activate exactly what you fear or believe will happen. You anticipate the worst, make assumptions, jump to conclusions, and create threats where they don't exist.

"I always assume that my seventeen-year-old is going to challenge any thing that I say," one father told me. "Or else he's going to get sarcastic and hostile when I ask him to do something. So I get him first. I cut his legs out from underneath him with my first comment and let him know who's in charge. And it's true. He always reacts the way I thought he would."

No wonder. The father set it up and created the scenario. And no wonder this son sees his father as an angry, unpleasant person. Aggressive people are not building their thinking on "whatever is true, whatever is worthy of reverence and is honorable and seemly, whatever is lovely and lovable, whatever is kind and winsome and gracious." Yet the Scripture indicates that when it comes to giving praise, a man should "think and weigh and take account of these things—fix your minds on them" (Phil 4:8, Amp.).

THE GRIEVING MAN

When a man experiences grief, anger often becomes the dominant emotion. And sometimes it turns into rage. He feels hurt; here is a situation he could not halt—the death of a friend or the loss of a relationship. The man wants to destroy the world around him that has hurt him so badly.

Jim, a hard worker in his midforties, had been dating a woman for six years. Finally he proposed, and Debbie accepted. Two days later she was struck and killed by a driver while crossing the street. Before and during the funeral service Jim's face was a mask, reflecting no emotional response. When he arrived home he took every picture and item that reminded him of his lost fiancée and tore or broke them into pieces. Neighbors could hear Jim raging and cursing for several hours.

No one saw him shed a tear, but for weeks following, Jim would snap at anyone for little reason. His facial expression became a constant scowl. If only he could have wept and felt the fulness of his lost. But, Jim thought, *Crying is not a way to get back at whatever has destroyed my life.*

Other men use the anger to consume their energy and create activities that help them function. Sometimes to cover the normal fear and anxiety of grief, a man will express anger since he is blocking out the other feelings.

HOW TO ATTACK AGGRESSION

Often we men recognize the need to rid ourselves of aggressive behavior. But giving up aggressive behavior isn't easy. We may realize that aggression creates personal stress and upset in others. We may know it alienates others and keeps others at a distance. But we are comfortable being able to control others. We have a sense of power. As agressors, we can let off steam; and besides, others may get the (false) impression that the aggressor is a person of power.[16]

How does a man come to want to forsake willingly his aggressive behavior? You will want to give up aggression when you discover that real power is not exercised through being aggressive and you are ready to reject several misbeliefs. You must feel secure about yourself, not needing to control others. That occurs when you discover your value and worth, which comes from God's perspective, not society's.

We also must learn to accept our imperfections and still feel good about our identity. We need to recognize we can never fully control our life or others' lives. The nonaggressive man is a true man—willing to become a risk-taker and discover new ways of relating to other people. His security comes through trusting the Person of Jesus Christ in his life, feeling secure in God's love shown through Christ.

TAKE ACTION

1. Complete the following control survey to measure how much you seek to be in control.

TAKING CONTROL

(1) When I am not in control I feel _____

(2) When someone else is controlling me I feel _____

(3) When someone else is controlling me I want to _____

(4) In order to stay in control I usually _____

(5) Others can tell I am out of control when I _____
_____

(6) I cover up my fear of being out of control by _____
_____

(7) An area of my life in which I need to relinquish control to another family member is _____

(8) An area of my life in which I need to relinquish control to God is _____

2. List three reasons you would be hesitant to give up responding aggressively. Then list some positive benefits of giving up your aggressive behavior.

Reasons:

(1) _____
(2) _____
(3) _____

Benefits:
_____
_____

3. List three things you build your personal security on:

    (1) _____   (2) _____   (3) _____

4. What are three weak areas of life you would like to see changed?

    (1) _____   (2) _____   (3) _____

5. Search out the following Scriptures and then write out how each one of these reflects how God views you:

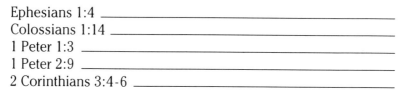

    Ephesians 1:4 _____
    Colossians 1:14 _____
    1 Peter 1:3 _____
    1 Peter 2:9 _____
    2 Corinthians 3:4-6 _____

6. If you felt totally loved and accepted by God, how would this change your way of responding to others? _____

    _____

NOTES

1. John Giles Milhaven, *Good Anger* (Kansas City: Sheed & Ward, 1989), p. 59, adapted.
2. Georgia Witkin-Lanoil, *The Male Stress Syndrome* (New York: Newmarket, 1986). pp. 12-13, adapted.
3. Ibid., p. 90.
4. Herb Goldberg, *The Hazards of Being Male* (New York, Signet, 1976), pp. 43-44
5. Ken Druck, *The Secrets Men Keep* (New York: Ballantine 1985), p.14.
6. Ibid., pp. 27-28.
7. "Treatment: Changing Roles and Male Relationship Problems," *Behavior Study Newsletter* 22, no. 98: n.p.
8. Patrick Morley, *The Man in the Mirror* (Brentwood, Tenn.: Wolgemuth and Hyatt, 1989), p. 214.
9. David Stoop and Stephen Arterburn, *The Angry Man* (Dallas: Word, 1991), pp. 58-59.
10. Carol Staudacher, *Men and Grief* (Oakland, Calif.: New Harbinger, 1991), p. 29.

11. Witkin-Lanoil. *The Male Stress Syndrome*, p. 123.
12. Ibid., p. 129.
13. Stoop and Arterburn, *The Angry Man*, p. 56.
14. Ibid., pp. 56-57.
15. Witkin-Lanoil. *The Male Stress Syndrome*, p. 38.
16. Patricia Jakubowske and Arthur J. Lange, *The Assertive Option* (Champaign, Ill.: Research Press, 1978), pp. 67-78, adapted.

9

WOMEN AND ANGER

Jean, a well-dressed professional woman in her mid-thirties, was undergoing a very difficult experience. Her husband, Steve, was involved with another woman, and now Steve was leaving home to live elsewhere. It appeared that he planned to eventually divorce Jean, and he had been telling her a number of lies for some time.

"I want to know why I'm not angry at my husband for what he has done to me," she demanded one day. "I know that I should be angry. It would be normal. I was never angry as a child. Or I was never allowed to show those feelings. I was cooperative, but as I reflect back, I just can't really think of a time when I was ever angry. My mother ruled the home with a firm hand, and perhaps I learned it was best to smile and comply.

"Is that why I can't get angry now?" Jean asked me. "Is there some connection between my upbringing and why I can't be angry at this time of my life?"

That's an important question and one that is fairly common among women. Now consider this exciting, potentially happy scene at a local hospital. One hour before, a couple arrived anxious and in a hurry. Tony's wife, nine months pregnant with the contractions just seconds apart, arrived fairly calm. Tony was anxious as he dressed in a sterile gown so that he could be with Gloria. Now his wife is rushed to the delivery room. Soon a baby girl is delivered, and the doctor, nurses, and Gloria beam. Even Tony breaks into a grin.

Wonderful! A girl, Tony thinks. *What a delight. And she'll be different than our three-year-old son. We'll encourage her to express her feelings and to say just what she feels . Of course, there are some expressions that we won't allow because they're unfeminine. We won't allow her to express her anger or be aggressive. She will learn to be cooperative. If she showed or expressed anger she would end up having problems when she is older.*

I'm sure fathers and mothers don't consciously think about their daughters in this way. Most of us didn't begin planning for our son's or daughter's life in this fashion. But there is a sad reality to the scenario just expressed. In fact, Jean's inability to show her anger may be due to such parental planning. From birth the parents' awareness of the child's gender does direct their response to the child's expressions of emotion. If a girl begins to express anger or aggression there is a negative response.

In spite of changes brought about by the feminist movement, angry expressions of feeling by women are still considered masculine and not at all feminine.

No Anger Allowed

Think about it. What have you heard about angry women? Are they accepted or condemned by others? Typically the silent but understood message is "Watch out. She's a libber. She is a controller. She's not 'feminine.'" As a result, in our society women tend to be overly inhibited in expressing their anger, and men not inhibited enough.[1]

Harriet Lerner sums up the attitudes toward angry women this way:

> Women, however, have long been discouraged from the awareness and forthright expression of anger. Sugar and spice are the ingredients from which we are made. We are the nurturers, the soothers, the peacemakers, and the steadiers of rocked boats. It is our job to please, protect, and placate the world. We may hold relationships in place as if our lives depended on it.
>
> Women who openly express anger at men are especially suspect. Even when society is sympathetic to our goals of equality, we all know that 'those angry women' turn everybody off. Unlike our

male heroes, who fight and even die for what they believe in, women may be condemned for waging a bloodless and humane revolution for their own rights. The direct expression of anger, especially at men, makes us unladylike, unfeminine, unmaternal, sexually unattractive, or more recently, "strident." Even our language condemns such women as "shrews", "witches", "bitches", "hags", "nags", [and] "man-haters". . . . They are unloving and unlovable. They are devoid of femininity. Certainly, you do not wish to become one of them. It is an interesting sidelight that our language—created and codified by men—does not have one unflattering term to describe men who vent their anger at women."[2]

ANGER AND HURT

How do women tend to handle their anger? Although there are variations and exceptions, many women tend to feel "hurt" rather than angry in many situations, whereas a normal and natural response would have been anger. In Chapter 6 we discussed hurt as a cause for our anger. But there is another connection between anger and hurt that we should recognize.

When you experience anger you also have feelings of being distanced and separate from the other person. You end up feeling isolated and alone even when you are in the same room. During an angry confrontation, you soon feel that you are standing up for what you believe, but standing alone. You don't feel connected to the other individual. An angry confrontation has been called a statement of differences between people that may tend to separate them. And when this angry confrontation occurs a woman may not feel much like the wife of a husband or the mother of a son or even the daughter of a mother. Anger causes a person to feel isolated and alone.

That's not a comfortable feeling, which is why many women, when expressing anger, also express tears, guilt, or sorrow. Tears, guilt, and sorrow can either contaminate the expressed anger, creating confusion, or negate its impact. Perhaps this is why a woman's anger often shifts into hurt. It protects her from feeling alone, and it's her way of saying that she does not want to be isolated and alone. Hurt can keep two people connected to each other and helps to draw them closer together. This is especially true of women who are dependent or who need to be caregivers. Feeling alone and cut off is very unnerving to them. For many women, being

independent and complete within themselves feels unreal and unnatural, and thus they turn their anger into hurt to continue being
close to another person.[3]

THE NICE LADY

Some women assume the "Nice Lady" syndrome of handling
anger, which means they don't express anger directly, they stay
silent. Silence can mean being self-critical or "hurt." In order to
avoid unpleasantness they keep their anger to themselves. But
most women do not realize the tremendous amount of energy this
consumes or the results. When a woman keeps her anger in she is
primarily trying to protect herself, the other person, and the relationship. But the cost of this is high. She loses touch with what she
really wants and who she is since she spends so much time trying
to keep everything on an even keel.

And the nicer she is, the more angry she becomes since the
anger does not go away. It builds and builds. And like a pressure
cooker, when there is too much the anger comes out fast and su-
perheated. The angry expression is so out of proportion to what
the situation warrants that it confirms to the woman that her anger
is irrational and destructive. Therefore she concludes it's better to
hold in that anger.

Nancy, an outgoing type, found herself becoming increasingly depressed. She couldn't understand why. What she had once
enjoyed doing had lost all its appeal. She felt unfulfilled but didn't
seem to have the drive to anything for herself anymore. After several weeks of counseling we discovered that a couple of supervisors
at work had taken advantage of others and treated them unfairly.
Nancy, a skilled member of the office publications staff, found herself not protesting, intimidated by the implied threats and innuen-
does of being replaced if anyone criticized the office policies.
Inside, however, she was seething.

Nancy wanted to say something. She wanted others to speak
up as well, but she didn't want to be seen as a troublemaker. Unfortunately the trouble arrived anyway, when one morning just before lunch she exploded. A coworker, Stephanie, suggested a new
way to format a report, and Nancy began yelling at her, telling
Stephanie, "You don't know what you are talking about! Can't you

see we're all behind? This is not the time for change." On and on she went, yelling at Stephanie in front of everyone, pouring out all the accumulated anger. Everyone was shocked by the intensity and overreaction.

Many women hold it in, like Nancy. Other women are expressors. They let the anger out and run the risk of being labeled by others with those uncomplimentary terms that Lerner described. If the anger is not expressed effectively, the disapproval that comes back only serves to increase the sense of anger and bitterness. A hysterical approach negates the purpose of the expression. Many fall into this trap because no one has taught women how to express their anger in a healthy way that will bring about some positive benefits.

GOOD ANGER

In chapter 5 we noted that anger is a signal, one both men and women need to listen to and heed. For some people the message is that other issues in their lives are not being addressed, that they are being violated or overrun in some way, or their needs are not being met. For some women anger's message is that they are giving too much or doing more than is comfortable or even proper. Anger may enable a woman to learn to say "no" and "yes" in healthier ways.

Anger also can be a means for constructive change. In fact, women who use their anger in a constructive way will be commended for it. Consider MADD, Mothers Against Drunk Drivers. Here the anger over the death of a family member has been directed in a positive way, the creation of an organization for women to push for tougher laws and enforcement against drunk drivers. And even though anger is the energy behind the movement, others say, "That's all right."

I have seen a number of angry women in counseling. Some of the reasons for their anger are legitimate. They needed to be angry and work toward a change in their lives. The problem was they often expressed it in such a way that it was virtually impossible for any change to occur. Some wives end up protecting their husbands and the relationship at the expense of their own growth.

Anger and Depression

This is unfortunate. Some wives compromise who they are without even being aware of it. And then they wonder why they are so angry! In any relationship the individual who sacrifices his or her own needs, desires, and wants the most ends up with the most repressed anger. And with no place to go with the anger, depression soon sets in. This often happens with the woman who typically surrenders her own desires for those of others.

The Caseys had visited me to better understand the tensions in their marriage. During one meeting June's anger began to emerge. During another session she spilled more of her anger, and Dwight became upset as she dumped on him. He was shocked. This was not the June he knew.

The problem, we discovered, was that June had been "underfunctioning" for years in their marriage. "June may appear weak, dependent, and vulnerable, Dwight, but in reality this is a cover for a high level of competence and personal strengths," I explained. Dwight didn't consciously realize that his wife's behavior and depression actually helped him look better in the relationship, so that he didn't have to show his own weaknesses or needs. His wife showed enough for both of them. June relinquished her own strength, which in turn helped her husband feel stronger. Do you know any relationships like this? If so, there is probably a husband who is oblivious to what is going on and a wife who is fuming inside.

Today's Angry Woman

Traditionally, women have been seen as more long suffering than their male counterparts. But more and more women are shedding this mantle and reacting. Some have said that women are different today. They are changing. But is that really the case? Are they different, or are they simply emerging and reflecting what has been hidden away for centuries?

Anger and aggression among women may seem more widespread simply because the hidden anger is come into the open.

Some of the repressed anger coming to the surface is over the way many women have been treated, slighted, and depicted. The reasons include such conditions as:

- Feeling compelled to adhere to male expectations that women be fragile, dependent, helpless, and willing to follow a man's dictates.
- Being harassed sexually by men at work or in social situations and being expected to accept this as a part of life. This can happen through comments, innuendos, off-color jokes, touching, and even being forced into sexual relations in order to keep their positions.
- Receiving rude and rejecting behavior from men simply because they are women. I have observed this many times in phone conversations and even at my office. A man will be curt and rude to one of our secretaries whereas he wouldn't think of talking to me in the same manner. Why is it that a man often gets more response or action when he calls and complains compared to when a woman calls?
- Not being taken seriously in meetings when voicing her opinion or being asked to take notes or get the coffee in a meeting because she is a woman.
- Being labeled hysterical when she is angry. She may even hear men suggest, "It's the PMS time of the month; that's why she's upset."

But many women are no longer passive reactors. As women are changing, the balance between men and women is undergoing a change, and this creates more anger in men as they have less control over women and are being faced with their anger.[4]

If as a woman you feel angry, it's likely the above situations or similar ones at home or office are making you frustrated. A lack of fulfillment can occur at any point in your adult years. Whereas men typically face a midlife crisis about their accomplishments and purposes, women face unexpected questions about their lives' purposes during their thirties. "Will my life change in any way? Time is running out," the woman concludes, and often panic and frustration set in. From this the anger grows.

Many women who chose to set aside certain dreams and aspirations years ago now are discovering that what they chose has not been fulfilling. They are asking, "Before I get any older and reach the point of no return, what options are left to me at this time in my life?" Perhaps their anger is not expressed as anger, but in many cases that emotion underlies their questions.

Perhaps you have asked some of these same questions, maybe not of another person but of yourself. When these questions are not addressed and investigated, or when it is too late to ask them, or when there is no fulfilling answer to them, anger may be the response. Consider some of the questions women are asking:

"What am I giving up for my marriage? If it can never be fulfilling, what else is there?"

"Why didn't I finish college when I had the chance?"

"Now that the children are gone, is my degree going to be any good?"

"Why did I have all these children and so close together?"

"I'm afraid that I waited too long to have a child. Is it still possible?"

"I wonder if I should go to work."

"I thought when I married I wouldn't have to work. Now with three kids I have to find a job."

"I like my career, but is this all there is? Maybe I'm missing out on some happiness by working so much."

"Am I in a rut? I feel it sometimes. Is it because I'm afraid to make any changes? Am I afraid to make waves?"[5]

If you the reader are a woman, what other questions of purpose do you think you might ask in the future? If you are a male reader, what questions might your wife be asking herself? Have you ever asked her to reveal them to you?

How Men Irritate Women

Some common issues between men and women generate anger in women. I have heard a number of them for years in the counseling office. One has to do with the feeling of betrayal. Perhaps one counselee's response sums it up for all of the others. "You know, before we were married he was kind, sensitive, open, and could communicate, even his feelings. But as soon as we were married, even during the honeymoon, he changed. He stopped being the way he was. I felt as though I had been betrayed. My trust had been violated, and I was angry." She isn't alone with her feelings.

Specific gender differences in communication also cause women to become angry with men. This can involve content, subject matter, style, or listening patterns. Over the years in our marriage renewal seminars we ask first the women and then the men to sit in a circle (with their spouse sitting behind them). The women in the circle (and later the men) discuss with the others the question, "What frustrates you about the way that the opposite sex communicates?" Invariably women would identify two major issues that frustrated them.

"Men do not share their feelings nor do they share sufficient details when they communicate." And as the women express these common themes, their anger begins to surface. The years of requests, pleas, and sometimes even demands had been met with a deaf ear. I've heard the same concern and complaint in my counseling office for the past twenty-five years as well.

Many women become weary of being an emotional pursuer —wanting closeness and intimacy with the special man in their life. The man often becomes an emotional distancer, and the couple plays a game of hide and seek throughout the years of their marriage. His logical and cognitive responses along with a desire to "fix" her problems are not met with the welcome reception he anticipated. She often pursues with a greater intensity, and he in time withdraws even more. Eventually the woman may turn her anger about this situation into a reactive distance. All this accomplishes is to continue filling the container of anger for its future eruption.

In my research for the book *Always Daddy's Girl,* I discovered that women who felt anger toward their fathers usually said the anger arose because their fathers were uninvolved and distant. Many women felt abandoned due to the divorce of their parents, the death of the father, or even worse—growing up with a father who was never there for them.

MOTHERS AND DAUGHTERS

Mothers tend to perpetuate the message that "women don't get angry." They teach their daughters to suppress their anger, sometimes subtly and sometimes overtly with messages such as "Nice girls don't get angry." In time, some daughters become tired of playing only the role of nurturer. They even begin to resent their mothers for their inability as grown-up daughters to defend themselves through anger when needed.

Sometimes the existence of anger becomes the issue between a mother and daughter because anger wasn't allowed or
accepted as a daughter grew up. The presence of these feelings
are uncomfortable to both mother and daughter. Paula Caplan, author of *Don't Blame Mother*, writes:

> Mother worries that a daughter who doesn't learn to suppress
> her anger is a sign that mother is a failure and that daughter will not
> do well in the world. A mother who has spent decades suppressing
> her own anger will be very unsettled to watch her daughters strug-
> gling to control similar feelings; daughter's expression of anger
> tempts mother to express her own anger. Unfortunately, we want to
> stay away from someone who elicits our forbidden feelings; we fear
> they'll bring out the worst in us.[6]

There is another major cause for mother/daughter anger.
When it comes to anger between a woman and her mother the
anger often originates over the mother's overinvolvement and inability to let go of her daughter.

Victoria Secunda writes, "No relationship is as highly
charged as that between mother and daughter, or as riddled with
expectations that could, like a land mine, detonate with a single
misstep, a solitary stray word that, without warning, wounds or
enrages. And no relationship is as bursting with possibilities of
goodwill and understanding."[7]

Kathy was thirty and single, living on her own but still struggling with her mother's attempting to run her life. Though her
mother lived on the opposite coast, Kathy told me that the 3,000
miles between them hadn't helped keep things calm. Her mother
called once a week, tried to find out all the details of her daughter's life, and then proceeded to make a value judgment for each
one.

"I know some of my standards are different than hers," Kathy
said. "I've told her straight out about them and that nothing she
says is going to change my mind. But it's like she doesn't even
hear me. She's got to try to rule my life. Christmas is coming up,
and this year I've decided not to go home to visit. I'm going skiing
with some friends, and it's free. I can't really afford to fly to the
East Coast. But I know if I said that, she would send a ticket and I

would pay for going the rest of my life. I wish it could be different, but we just don't get along."

It's true many mothers are healthy, balanced, loving, and act toward their grown daughters in a mature manner. Unfortunately, there are others who are unpleasable. No matter what is done, it is never right. Some mothers are like avenging angels; others are critical. They have the ability to toss out verbal hand grenades; when the grenades explode, the mother is the only one unscathed. Some mothers smother, and others avenge. Some mothers have no ability to connect with their own daughters, and they end up deserting the child in some way. They never link up emotionally. If any of these mother types were part of your heritage, there is probably a pool of accumulated anger.[8]

A woman can attempt to handle her anger over her relationship with her mother in one of three ways. First, she can angrily confront and tell her mother how she is wrong and try to change her. This is futile.

A second way is for the daughter to establish physical and emotional distance from her mother; the greater the distance, seemingly the better. This can bring some momentary relief but no resolution. The problem still exists and is activated any time the woman visits her mother. Sometimes the anger is expressed in a new relationship, such as with a spouse or close friend. In this second instance, the anger is just redirected.

The best alternative is to learn a different, constructive response. Assert your own position and act constructively regardless of what your mother does or how she responds. This is the one lasting solution.

This can involve viewing your mother in a different way, thinking about what type of a relationship you want rather than focusing on what it is now, rehearsing and practicing new responses instead of mulling over past scenarios again and again. It is possible to become independent without having to be emotionally distant.[9] (This procedure can be effective in any kind of relationship.)

Learning to express what you think, believe, feel, and desire in a nonblaming, unapologetic way can bring results in a relationship and will reduce your own anger. But it takes effort, learning new approaches and ways of responding, practice, prayer, and the support and prayers of others to help you in this endeavor.[10]

Inappropriate Source of Self-Esteem

This next cause for women's anger may surprise you; yet it affects many women. Building self-esteem on an inappropriate, unachievable basis leads to frustration and anger toward oneself and those around you. Women with inappropriate self-esteem build their worth on one of four faulty foundations. The first foundation is building your self-esteem upon what you do—in other words, falling into the performance trap. In her excellent book *Free to Be God's Woman*, Jan Congo summarizes the problem this way:

> The result of our misdirected energies is to create a monster —the superwoman. You've heard of her, haven't you? She can leap over tall buildings, solve any problem, overcome any enemy in her path. And she accomplishes all this within the confines of an immaculately kept house. How foolish she sounds to us, doesn't she? But many of us labor under the burden of being God's superwoman in our homes, our churches, and our communities. We try to be the best possible woman, wife, mother and career person—just to mention a few hats that we choose. We take self-improvement course after self-improvement course. Unfortunately, it ends up being self-enslavement rather than self-improvement. Why do we do this? It is because we have adopted the world's standard that our value comes as a direct result of what we do.[11]

Does this sound familiar to you? Have you ever felt irritated as you try to be the perfect woman?

A second faulty foundation is basing your worth on how much you possess. This can include all types of possessions. You may feel much more secure with a new wardrobe, better furniture, or one certain piece of jewelry. But this desire to have is misdirected, and in today's unstable society we end up being off balance perched on this shaky foothold.

Have you built your identity upon possessions? Has it ever irritated you, especially when you don't have what you want? Jesus had a better idea, which He stated in Matthew 6:19-21: "Don't store up treasures here on earth where they can erode away or may be stolen" (TLB).

Another faulty foundation is building your identity and self-esteem upon who you know. Do you spend many days, even years, comparing people and trying to earn recognition and affirmation from others? It may feel good for a while, but you cannot win this struggle. Someone will always have more, do more, or receive greater recognition.

The fourth faulty foundation is basing your self-esteem upon how you look. You probably already know how tenuous this can be, for there are days when, no matter what you do, you don't feel attractive. And this basis puts you at the mercy of others' admiring comments. Does this sound familiar to you? Have you ever felt irritated over this issue?

If your self-esteem is low, you may find a low-grade anger exists just like a low-grade fever. This anger could be against yourself as well as others. You may project your anger outward and blame others for the way you feel. (This section only highlights the dilemmas of this issue. For a helpful resource with a solid biblical base, we recommend Jan Congo's *Free to Be God's Woman*.)

ANGER AND CHILDREN

For most mothers, their children become a recurring source of anger. You love them, but their demands can lead to frustration and then anger. Some mothers overfunction with their children. They expect too much of themselves and their children. And when things don't go well with the child (as they often do) the questions "What's wrong with me? Why aren't I a good mother?" begin to emerge along with, "What is wrong with that child!" And the anger grows. With children, a mother experiences guilt along with her anger—guilt over the way the child is performing or responding and guilt over being so angry with her child.

Too many mothers hold to the myth that they should be able to control things and situations that are not realistically within their or anyone's control. This breeds frustration. And by now you know what frustration leads to.[12]

SOME SOLUTIONS

What can a woman do with her anger? First of all, accept your anger. It has a message for you, and it isn't to be denied. It's there for a reason.

Discover the reason for your anger. What is the real cause in each situation? You may want to return to chapters 6 and 7 to review the various causes. As you look at the situation or an encounter in which you are angry, ask yourself, "What is bothering me and what would I like to change?"

How are you reacting with your anger and to whom? Sometimes people respond differently to various individuals. You may argue with one individual, yell at another, use silent withdrawal from another, intensely go after another, and distance yourself physically and emotionally from someone else. Which do you do with whom and why?[13]

You can learn the difference between expressing your anger aggressively and assertively. Once you are able to express your anger without yelling, blaming, or attacking, you will feel better about what you are saying, and others will hear you more clearly. (See Take Action #5 at the end of the chapter for an exercise in expressing your anger assertively. Other chapters in this book will assist you in this process.)

When people express to others their hurt and disappointment in honest, controlled, and constructive ways, the other people are freed to be as honest with them. And growth in the relationship can occur. Remember, relationships can survive and even improve when disagreements occur and are handled properly. Expressing anger properly also has the effect of exposing us to criticism and challenge, and forces us to stop blaming others and consider our own responsibilities for change. Neither suppressed anger nor explosive tempers provide the advantage that constructive expression of anger does when it opens one up to a critical evaluation of one's own behavior. Suppression and rage are, by comparison, cowardly ways of dealing with anger.

Proper anger expression should represent a turning toward fruitful negotiation. Such negotiation becomes possible when the woman recognizes that she is angry and then tries as clearly as possible to present the problem to the other person. This is the wisdom behind Jesus' teaching in Matthew 5:23-24 and 18:15-18, which says, in brief, that when another has something against you, you go and be reconciled; and when you have something against your brother, you go and be reconciled. Either way, mature people work out the anger between themselves and others.[14]

Do not apologize for your anger. It's there. It's yours. As a woman, you need not be uncomfortable with the anger. Instead, see it as a messenger telling you about the cause. Then, with God's love and help, tackle the cause.

TAKE ACTION

1. Do you think showing anger as a women is unfeminine? _____ Have your parents, either directly or indirectly, told you that it's wrong to show your anger? _____

2. What is your attitude toward being accused of being angry? __
    _____

3. List the last time you felt really angry. _____

    What was the setting? _____
    What was the cause? _____
    How did you handle the anger? _____

4. You may have repressed anger and not know it. Ask your spouse or other close friend, "Do you think I am angry at times?" If the person says yes, ask him/her to describe the anger and your actions.

5. When we feel angry we can express the anger either assertively or aggressively. This exercise will help you assert your anger as you should. When you experience anger, before expressing it, write out what you would be comfortable in saying. Reflect upon it, then show it to a friend (or spouse, if he/she is not the object of your anger). When you are satisfied it contains what you want to say, practice saying it out loud until you feel comfortable making the statement. Then practice role-playing the situation with another person, so that you can gain the strength you need to express this response. This is exactly what we ask counselees to do in order to change their way of responding. It may even help to record on tape some of your practice sessions to hear your tone of voice.

NOTES

1. Harriet Goldhor Lerner, *Women in Therapy* (Northvale, N.J.: Jason Aronson, 1988), pp. 59-60, adapted.
2. Harriet Goldhor Lerner, *The Dance of Anger* (New York: Harper & Row, 1985), pp. 1-2.
3. Lerner, *Women in Therapy*, pp. 64-65.
4. Herb Goldberg, *The Hazards of Being Male* (New York: Signet, 1976), pp. 10-16, adapted.
5. Gail Sheehy, *Passages* (New York: E.P. Dutton, 1974), pp. 242-48, adapted.
6. Paula J. Caplan, *Don't Blame Mother* (New York: Harper & Row, 1989), p. 89.
7. Victoria Secunda, *When You and Your Mother Can't Be Friends* (New York: Delacorte, 1990), p. 5.
8. Ibid., pp. 159-60.
9. Lerner, *Women in Therapy*, pp. 67-87.
10. Some helpful reading would be chapter 4 of *The Dance of Anger*, by Harriet Lerner; *When I Say No, I Feel Guilty*, by Manuel Smith; and *When You and Your Mother Cannot Be Friends*, by Victoria Segunda.
11. Janet Congo, *Free to Be God's Woman* (Ventura, Calif.: Regal, 1985), pp. 18-19.
12. Lerner, *Women in Therapy*, pp. 147-48, adapted.
13. Ibid., pp. 4, 190.
14. Mark Cosgrove, *Counseling for Anger* (Waco, Tex: Word, 1988), p. 94.

10

ANGER IN MARRIAGE

An angry wife. An angry husband. An angry marriage! Is it common? Most of the anger we experience in life concerns relationships, so why should the marriage relationship be excluded? Believe me, it isn't. Marriage probably generates in couples more anger than they will experience in any other relationship. When two people live together constantly with vulnerability and closeness, the potential for hurt and misunderstanding is enormous. Learning to function in harmony without one overriding the other takes delicate skill and extended practice.

Anger and love can exist in the same relationship. But when anger is always smoldering it tends to diminish the quality of love, and in time resentment gains a foothold. Resentment is an eroding disease that feeds on lingering anger for its lifeblood. Resentment eats away at the relationship until the love is dead. Worse, if resentment continues it eventually can produce hate—and hate separates. It drives the other person away.

Sometimes love and hate coexist for a while. A husband may love his wife's involvement in church but hate her neglect of his concerns. A wife may love her husband's physical characteristics but hate his sarcastic tirades.

One man told me that his resentment took several years to develop. "I could never please my wife. I completed task after task that she asked me to do, and not once did I receive a compliment or a word of thanks. My resentment came from my anger which

159

was really intense." His final words revealed that his marriage had become a shell. "Now my resentment has subsided, and I have no feelings for her at all."

A wife told me about her anger over her husband's demands. "Every now and then I want to get back at him and make him pay for what he's said," she confided. "That frightens me since I know it's the beginning of anger."

Both of these people have been offended. Their anger is deep, and the results range from feelings of revenge to no feelings at all.

Expressions of anger in marriage vary from a harsh word, a bitter put-down, raised voices, a scowl, glare, flashing eyes, a slammed door, an openhanded slap, or a fist. These are the obvious direct expressions. But there are also less direct expressions of anger.

Sometimes anger is camouflaged by laughter that is forced. Angry and critical barbs are couched in "harmless" teasing.

In some marriages the anger goes underground and emerges as a passive expression such as using the car and leaving the gas tank empty; taking a long time in the shower and using all the hot water; spending the money the two of you have been saving on something just for you and depriving your partner; or leaving an important household item in a different place, causing your spouse extensive delays as he or she searches all over for it.

SEX AND ANGER

In marriage, sex and anger have a very close relationship. Sex should be used to give and receive enjoyment; however, a partner sometimes uses sex to punish, degrade, inflict pain, and express anger. Those who repress their anger are more likely to vent it sexually. One way is by being rough or excessively passionate or making insensitive demands. This could involve requests for sexual behavior that the partner finds degrading or repulsive, making negative comments about the partner's ability, or making no effort to please your partner sexually. This is commonly called sexual selfishness.

Another misuse of sex that is often tied into anger is withholding sex. But the manner in which this occurs can be subtle. Repressed anger can be channeled into the body in a variety of ways from developing a tension headache or back pain to having a lower interest level. Some people actually feel grateful for their symptoms. An underlying attitude might be, "Well, it just serves you right."

Another tactic that reflects a hostile intent is requesting or initiating sex when it's impossible for it to occur. It could be too late in the morning or evening or when you know your partner is too upset or exhausted or just before the kids are to return home.

Those who are most prone to let anger invade their sex life are those who do not express their anger when it's appropriate to do so, who always give in to others, who believe that it's wrong to become angry, and who are fearful of asking for what they want.[1]

On the positive side, sometimes sex is used by a couple to draw close together again after they have been distanced by anger toward one another. Sometimes following an angry interchange and the bestowing of forgiveness, a couple engages in intensely aggressive and highly fulfilling sex. Their energy level is high and they draw close. Every couple varies, but it is very helpful to learn how your anger affects your sexual thoughts and responses.

Admitting Anger

Anger doesn't have to kill a marriage. Anger can actually show that we still care about our partner and the relationship. Anger can be a sign that we are alive and well and wanting to have something better in the relationship. It's better to admit to the anger, face it, and learn to use its energy in a constructive manner than to bury it. Battered spouses and destroyed marriages are often the result of repressed anger. Acknowledged anger helps us identify what is really bothering each partner.

However, we must both acknowledge the anger and be willing to forgive. If resentment remains, true forgiveness has not occurred.

> Altercations, differences and offenses frequently occur between individuals, families and even nations. Apologies, clarification of issues, truces, and peace treaties make it possible for individuals and nations to live their lives unhindered and unaffected by conflict. But does peace really occur? Does a resolution of differences really take place? Or is superficial peace and harmony tainted by lingering inner resentment?

Nations often agree to stop their hostilities and sign peace treaties. But peacemaking formalities do not necessarily change warlike attitudes. Years after the end of World War I seething resentment eventually fanned the flames of World War II.

Your spouse may apologize and even give you a gift to show his or her good intentions. And you say, "Oh, that's all right. Let's just forget it happened." But inwardly you still feel cold and unforgiving. And the iceberg of resentment freezes both intimacy and romance![2]

David Mace, a pioneer in the field of marriage enrichment, has described the proper place of anger in marriage:

This does not mean you do not have a right to be angry. In an appropriate situation, your anger could be a lifesaver. Anger enables us to assert ourselves in situations where we should. Anger exposes antisocial behavior in others. Anger gets wrongs righted. In a loving marriage, however, these measures are not necessary.

My wife is not my enemy. She is my best friend; and it does not help either of us if I treat her as an enemy. So I say, "I'm angry with you. But I don't like myself in this condition. I don't want to strike you. I'd rather stroke you." This renouncing of anger on one side prevents the rush of retaliatory anger on the other side, and the resulting tendency to drift into what I call the "artillery duel." If I present my state of anger against my wife as a problem I have, she is not motivated to respond angrily. Instead of a challenge to fight, it is an invitation to negotiate.[3]

Ask your partner for help. This step is the clincher. Without it, not much progress can be made. The anger may die down, but that is not enough. Both of you need to find out the reason one got mad at the other. If you do not, it could happen again and again and again. Your request for help is not likely to be turned down. It is in the other person's best interest to find out what is going on and to correct it so that a loving relationship can be maintained.

POWER STRUGGLES

What creates so much anger in marriages? Unfulfilled expectations, unfulfilled needs, and problems of accepting differences in tastes. But these three often are lesser aspects of one of the major causes of anger and frustration in marriage—power struggles. Such problems as money, sex, communication, and in-laws often are only symptoms of a greater issue—power and control.

One definition of *power* is "the possession of control, authority, or influence over others." And *authority*, according to *The Oxford English Dictionary*, is "power or right to enforce obedience . . . the right to command or give an ultimate decision." Therefore, in a marital relationship when one partner has most of the power or authority, he or she has most of the control and makes most of the decisions. The person on the other side ends up feeling dependent, abused, neglected, and downtrodden. As a result, he or she fills with attitudes of dejection, anger, and resentment.

A power struggle is like two puppies each tugging on the end of a rope and neither will give in to save their lives. Power struggles only exist when two people play the game. Husbands want control, and wives want control. Most men and most women have strong drives to have more power and control. Perhaps part of this desire for control is generated by the fear of vulnerability and being dominated by the other partner.

Underlying most of the specific issues in which anger is involved in marriage may be a power struggle. Honoring Christ by submitting to each other (Ephesians 5:21) is not the norm today in marriage. And yet it is the answer. And the issue may not be profound. What power struggles do you see in the marriages around you? In your own marriage?

FIVE POWER LEVERS

Control is the core of the power struggles in a relationship. If the control is obvious and active it takes place by establishing dominance in the marital relationship. But if it is passive the partner will withhold something—typically attention, affection, sex, money, or approval. These five are called power levers. Have you ever seen them used in your family of origin or the family of a relative? Perhaps they operate in your own marriage. And of the five levers mentioned, sex and money are the most powerful. The more these two are used for the purpose of establishing control in the relationship, the greater the distance between the couple and the greater the potential for anger.[4]

HOW POWER ISSUES DEVELOP

Phil and Kim have a number of power struggles in their marriage, but a recurring one is his clothing. Kim is very uncomfortable with Phil's choice of wardrobe. She actually feels embarrassed by the cheap, out-of-style clothes that he continues to wear year after year. Money is not the problem, as they make a very comfortable living. Often Kim will buy him some sharp, up-to-date items, but in a short time Phil reverts to wearing his old clothes. She has confronted him about his dressing habits and usually says something like, "You know how much I hate that ridiculous shirt. Do you have to insist on wearing it? It's out of style, doesn't fit, and it's not even your color. Could you please wear the new one I gave you for your birthday?"

Kim really wants Phil to look better, and inwardly he knows that what she is saying is right. But what does he say to her? "You're always telling me what to do. I can dress myself. Why do you have this terrible desire to control me? You even want me to change my hairstyle each year. I like my clothes. They're me! And I'm angry!" A difference of opinion or style can end up as a power issue.

In most conflict-filled marriages, the partners are unaware of how much power each one has and emotionally feels the partner has far more power than he or she deserves. Power in the family involves the ability of one spouse to influence or change the behavior of the other. The one with the greater power is usually the one who somehow controls the actions of the other person.

DEPENDENCY

An overlooked arena for marital authority struggles is emotional power. This can be even more serious than the other problems mentioned. When a person is told what to do most of the time, when decisions are made for that person, or when he or she looks to the other person as the authority, we have emotional dependency. Some couples are comfortable with this style. Many others are quite frustrated.

"I wish I had some say in what we do or where we go," a wife once told me. "But my husband always overrides me, and I end up thinking that he is right. His ideas do make sense, and he is able to decide so quickly. It takes me longer, and I tend to waver back and forth with my decisions. But sometimes I just wish I could have some say—I guess I've been angry at him for a long time."

Not everyone who holds the power is content with that style of relationship. A husband reflected, "I wish she wasn't so dependent on me. I would like her to make some decisions, stick with them, and carry them out. There are times I get so frustrated with having to make decisions that are so simple and ridiculous. Why can't she make up her mind? I even get phone calls at work about simple decisions. I feel like a parent, and I'm ticked at her!"

In a healthy marriage relationship, each person leans on the other from time to time. But because of our culture, *dependency* has become a problem word. We are taught to be independent and self-sufficient. We put little value on being dependent, so who wants to admit he *is* dependent? We all struggle with problems that we can't solve by ourselves. We need the help of another person. Some emotional needs cannot be satisfied alone. A marital relationship can provide the most intense and enduring support. And when this happens, anger is minimal.

There are times in a marriage when each spouse parents the other by giving assistance and comfort. That's all right if the roles switch back and forth and each person maintains his or her own identity.

In marriage, many power issues and conflicts are tied into the differences between what "he wants" and "she wants," what "he needs" and "she needs," what "she expects" and "he expects." Other power struggles occur not over the need to control but because of the fear of being controlled. The possession and use of power determines how and when decisions are made in a marriage.

RESOLVING POWER STRUGGLES

Whenever a couple engages in an out-and-out power struggle, they face four choices.

1. They can agree that one person is right or correct in his perspective and the other is wrong.
2. They can agree that both spouses are wrong.
3. They can agree that both are right.
4. They can discover a better way of resolving the issue.

The first three don't usually work because part of the reason for the power struggle in the first place is the issue of who is right and who is wrong. When you are willing to resolve a disagreement without its being anyone's fault, each taking full responsibility for bringing about the problem, solutions occur. Making a commitment to live out Ephesians 5:21 as mentioned earlier and 2 Corinthians 13:11 "be of the same (agreeable) mind with another; live in peace" (Amp.) will lessen the power struggles in a marriage.

RESPONDING TO YOUR ANGER

In any expression of anger between two people, you are responsible for your own anger, and the other person is responsible for his.

You can project the anger onto your partner and hold him or her responsible for the way you feel and act. But that demands that your partner be the one to change. Holding the other person responsible is a protective response on your part. It says, "I have been victimized by you." But if you focus on yourself and take responsibility for the way you feel, there is a greater chance of resolving an issue.

Instead of saying, "You made me angry," tell your spouse "You acted in this way, and *I felt* angry because of the way you behaved."

As your own anger begins to escalate, use the interruption approach on yourself. Remember earlier in this book we identified the three basic causes of anger as fear, hurt, and frustration. Anger is the secondary response to any of these three.

If anger is a problem for you, keep a 3x5 card with you. On one side print the word *Stop!* in large letters. On the other side print the following three questions:

Am I experiencing hurt over something right now?
Am I in some way afraid?
Am I frustrated over something at this time?

The minute you begin to experience your anger rising, take out the card, read the word *Stop!* (out loud if it's appropriate) and then turn the card over. Read and respond to the three questions. Slowing down your anger response and identifying the cause will help you resolve the issue. You can still assume responsibility for choosing to respond in a way that will help defuse the other person rather than fuel the interchange.

RESPONDING TO ANOTHER'S ANGER

It's important for you to clarify in your own mind why you want to reduce the amount of anger in your spouse. You may simply find anger distasteful or be afraid that it may get out of hand. You may feel that it prolongs disagreements rather than resolves them. *Know why you are uncomfortable with your spouse's anger*, and at a calm time explain your position to him or her.

Second, as you respond to your spouse's anger, *remember that the anger is not the true emotion*. Regardless of how intense and destructive your mate's anger is, it is still an expression of his or her fear, hurt, or frustration. Unfortunately, the anger camouflages this and doesn't clearly identify the problem for you. If you can give your spouse permission in your own heart and mind to be angry, it will be easier for you not to respond with anger of your own. Then you can concentrate on the real issue between the two of you as well as the underlying cause of the anger. When you can learn to avoid responding to your spouse's anger with your own, you have taken a giant step.

There are several ways you can help to diffuse the anger of your spouse. One way is for you to heed a "prior agreement." When couples are aware of the intrusive influence of anger in solving disagreements, they can create an agreement or covenant on how they will act during their disagreements. The first step is for you to adhere to the covenant-agreement. Here are two points from an agreement that one couple developed in order to improve their communication and problem resolving skills.

1. We will not exaggerate or attack the other person during the course of a disagreement.
    (a) I will stick with the specific issue.
    (b) I will take several seconds to formulate words so that I can be accurate.
    (c) I will consider the consequences of what I say before I say it.
    (d) I will not use the words *always, all the time, everyone, nothing,* etc.

2. We will attempt to control the emotional level and intensity of
arguments. (No yelling, uncontrollable anger, hurtful remarks.)

(a) We will take time-outs for calming down if either of us feels
that our own anger is starting to elevate too much. The mini-
mum amount of time for a time-out will be one minute and
the maximum ten minutes. The person who needs a greater
amount of time in order to calm down will be the one to set
the time limit. During the time-out each person, individually
and in writing, will first of all define the problem that is being discussed. This will include, first, identifying the specific cause for my anger. Second, the areas of agreement in the
problem will be listed. Third, the areas of disagreement will
be listed, and fourth, three alternate solutions to this problem will be listed. When we come back together the person
who has been the most upset will express to the other individual, "I'm interested in what you've written during our
time-out. Will you share yours with me?"

(b) Before I say anything I will decide if I would want this same
statement said to me with the same words and tone of
voice.[5]

It is helpful for couples to come to the place where they can
ask one another, "When you are angry, how do you want me to
respond? Should I say nothing, leave the room, hold you, reflect
back what I hear you saying, ask questions, or get angry at you?"
After your partner has identified which way to respond then ask,
"What can I do to make that happen? What suggestions do you
have?" This way both of you are involved in the process of helping.

But if a couple has not agreed upon guidelines, what can one
person do by himself? One approach is to reduce your spouse's
level of anger by stating that his anger is hindering you from understanding what he is really feeling and wants. I've heard many
examples and variations of these over the years. One such conversation went like this:

FRANK: *(his voice stern, loud, and angry)* I'm getting tired of all
this hassle we have. You don't ever listen to me. I ask you
to do things and you never come through. What's wrong
with you, anyway?

JEAN: *(calm and not angry or loud)* I understand you're angry,
Frank, but I don't know exactly what you're angry at when

FRANK: you raise your voice. Let's talk about it and I'll listen to your specific concerns.

FRANK: We've talked about this for years. I'm sick of this. I want you to change. I want to be able to count on you, for pete's sake!

JEAN: Frank, I understand you're angry and frustrated, but its difficult for me to understand you when you're so angry. Please tell me exactly what you would like me to do without the anger. I can hear you and understand you better when you don't raise your voice.

FRANK: I'm raising my voice to make sure you do hear me! Anyone would be angry with you!

JEAN: I want to hear you. I don't want to short circuit your anger either. Please lower your voice, and I'll show you how well I hear you. I want to know the real cause for your anger.

FRANK: (*pause*) All right. Give me a minute to collect my thoughts. I hope this will work. Nothing else has seemed to, so I guess I don't have anything else to lose. I am frustrated. You're right when you say that. Here's the reason why . . . (The conversation continued.)[6]

Perhaps it was apparent to you who was in control and exhibited the most strength in this conversation. Anger and volume do not mean strength or control. Sometimes we perceive people like this as being powerful. But their reaction is more of a sign of lack of control or weakness. The person in a discussion who guides the people and the conversation toward resolving the problem is the one with the power or strength. In this case it wasn't Frank, but Jean.

In any disagreement or difference between a couple the purpose of the discussion is generally to resolve a problem. But when one begins to blame and the other responds to the blame the result is rarely resolution. But if the one blamed has spent time considering the results of retaliation, devised a new way of responding to his or her spouse and has mentally rehearsed that new response, he/she will be able to focus on problem-solving rather than a counter-attack and the escalation of anger. By doing this you are showing strength and control and are no longer a victim of your emotions and the other person's attack. When you are blamed, use questions to help the other person focus on the problem rather than making statements back to their attack.

AIRING THE ANGER

Some couples have found it beneficial to schedule and structure "anger ventilation sessions." Why would anyone ever want to purposely plan to air their anger? Actually, to plan a session to ventilate your anger will allow both individuals a greater sense of control. And if the subject is so intense and the anger is there and needs to be expressed, why not be in charge of it? Some individuals have difficulty bringing up some issues unless they are angry. If a ventilation session has been planned, the couple can also exercise more control in the way the anger is expressed as well.

Beck proposes several guidelines to make such sessions effective:

- Establish a specific time and place where both can talk but not be overheard by anyone else.
- Set a time limit for each session, such as fifteen to twenty minutes.
- Allow no interruptions, and, to eliminate controlling the time, a person can talk for no more than two minutes and then must allow the other to speak.
- Include some provision for time-outs in advance.

Avoid the following in any comments to your spouse: condemning the person; insulting the person; mentioning or picking on any vulnerable areas; recounting any past issues unless they pertain directly to the issue at hand; and stating that your partner made you angry. It is far better to say, "I felt angry," than, "You made me angry."[7]

The purpose of these sessions is to stay in control, release and reduce anger, and resolve the issues. When you stay in control in this way, your spouse has the opportunity to discover the inappropriateness of his or her response and perhaps follow your example.

ZONES OF ANGER

Some people like to use a stress reduction card to measure their excitement. A small square, sensitive to heat and moisture, measures a person's level of stress. You place your thumb on the square for ten seconds, and your level of stress will turn the square either black, red, green, or blue, depending upon how tense or excited you are. The green or blue color zone reflects calm, with little or no stress.[8]

There are proper zones to stay in with anger as well. Beck indicates that couples often move out of the temperate (green or blue) zone of anger into a red zone. Temperate is being objective and logical, and red is intense, irrational anger. In between, in what is called a yellow zone, the person feels anger toward the other person but is able to exert control over his thoughts and actions. He can still let his partner know that he is angry and needs to express it, but not at the expense of the relationship.

When a person moves from the yellow to the red zone all the symptoms of the yellow zone have been intensified. This "red" anger is characterized by attacking the person rather then the problem, being irrational, hurling accusations, demeaning your spouse's character, and believing that your partner deserves everything you're dishing out. This is where lasting damage can occur. The blue zone is characterized by calm presentations and listening.[9]

It is possible to learn to identify which zone you are in, let your partner know, and also identify which zone you are working toward. As one husband said, "I'm hovering between the yellow and red, and I don't like either. I want to get rid of how I am feeling and get into the blue zone. Please listen to me."

Some couples make little flags of each color and pin them up in a predesignated spot to denote the level of their anger. (Some have made this a family project in which everyone has their own set of flags. Each keeps his set of flags with him during a discussion or disagreement and holds the appropriate one to let others know his anger level.) When a person has chosen to use the flags to convey a message about his anger, he does have some control over his emotions.

TALK OR WRITE?

In this process of defusing yourself and your spouse, it may be helpful to ask, "What would be best for us right now? To *talk* about our anger or to *write* it out?" For those who have difficultly verbalizing, writing may help them release feelings that they tend to carry inside. And for the highly verbal, writing may keep them from saying too much at the wrong time. In addition, writing often helps us to see the issues much clearer than talking about them. You can decide whether to reveal what you have written or keep that just for your own expression. When you write you can simply list your feelings and identify the cause of your anger. You can say what you would never say directly to the other person, or you can write an angry (nonmailed) letter, which you might read aloud in an empty room and then burn or destroy. Once the letter is destroyed go back to your spouse and discuss the problem.

At the conclusion of this chapter, Take Action offers guidelines for writing your anger and for evaluating the effectiveness of expressing that anger after you have written about it. The next time you feel intense anger, go to your desk or some quiet spot and prepare a list or letter according to the guidelines in Take Action #1.

Anger Under Control

How can you keep anger from escalating in your marriage? David Viscott gives ten practical steps that many couples have successfully used. These guidelines can work for you, but you must be willing to implement them regardless of what your partner does. Your behavior is not dependent upon your partner's action. If it is, you've chosen to fall under his or her control. Remember, practice these steps even if your partner does not.

1. Don't wait for your feelings to accumulate. Express your hurt, fear, or frustration as soon as you become aware of it.
2. Be sure to share in the language style of your partner. If your mate uses few words (a condenser) in his/her communication style, keep it brief. If he/she likes to expand and explain (an amplifier), offer details and sufficient information.
3. The longer you wait to express your feelings, the longer it will take to resolve them. Therefore, you decide whether you want a long discussion or one that is brief. You do have a choice in the matter.
4. Don't imply or even hint that your spouse has ulterior motives or isn't trustworthy. He/she will turn you off if you do.

5. Any attempts to make your partner feel guilty will come back to haunt you. Your purpose is to resolve.

6. Choose an attitude that says you *will* resolve the issue and there will be a positive result eventually.

7. If your partner makes attacking personal comments, don't invest your time and energy in responding to them. Let them slide and keep on target.

8. If you make a generalization or embellish the facts (lie a bit), stop at once and correct yourself. Use statements such as, "I'm sorry, what I really meant to say and what is more factual is . . . " Whenever you realize that your statements are not what is best, correct yourself and admit to what you have done. It's all right to say, "I was wrong in what I said," "I was trying to get back at you because . . ," "I admit I was trying to hurt you, and I am sorry," "I was upset at something else, and I took it out on you."

9. Don't give ultimatums during your discussion. Even if one is given this is not the best time, and it reflects a control issue or power struggle. Rarely does it work.

10. Now it's up to you to list three other guidelines that you feel would be positive and helpful. If you want this list of guidelines to work, read it out loud everyday for three weeks, and you will find yourself changing.[10]

The wise king Solomon reminds us that controlling our anger makes good sense: "Good sense makes a man restrain his anger, and it is his glory to overlook a transgression or an offense" (Proverbs 19:11, Amp.).

TAKE ACTION

1. When you feel strong anger toward your spouse, sit down and write a list of your feelings. Write honestly, passionately—just as you feel. Exclamation points and underlining are allowed. At the end of the list write the reason for your anger. Identify the cause.

   If you prefer, write an angry letter to your mate. Again, be honest about your feelings. You may read the letter aloud in an empty room. Then destroy the letter.

2. Once you have reviewed the list (or destroyed the letter), set up a meeting time for an anger ventilation session with your spouse. Then discuss the causes of your anger. Be sure to follow the session guidelines on p. 170.

3. After your spouse and you hold an anger ventilation session, complete the anger expression form below. This form can be used following your expression of anger with any person to help you identify the positive and negative effects. This will be your own perceptions and thus could be different from the perception of the other person.

EVALUATE YOUR ANGER EXPRESSION

Place a check by those statements you believe are true:

POSITIVE RESULTS

_____ 1. My spouse responded better after I expressed my anger.
_____ 2. I felt better after expressing my anger.
_____ 3. I feel my spouse felt better after the interchange. (It would be helpful if you asked him or her about this.)
_____ 4. Becoming angry protected me when my spouse became upset.
_____ 5. My spouse gained a clearer understanding of my position because of my anger.
_____ 6. I feel closer to my spouse because of expressing my anger.
_____ 7. Becoming angry helped solve the problem so we won't need to experience it again.
_____ 8. We felt more loving toward one another because of expressing anger.
_____ 9. My expression of anger involved more constructive statements than provocative.
_____ 10. We learned from this experience so that our next disagreement should be better.

NEGATIVE RESULTS

_____ 1. In expressing my anger, I was so upset that I didn't clarify my position well.

_____ 2. I made statements or behaved in a way that I now regret.

_____ 3. My spouse did not accept what I said.

_____ 4. My spouse had difficulty hearing me because of my anger.

_____ 5. My spouse became upset because of my anger and became very emotional.

_____ 6. My spouse was hurt by my anger.

_____ 7. My spouse is still recovering from my anger.

_____ 8. My anger prolonged the disagreement and hindered us from finding a solution.

_____ 9. Our next disagreement will probably be more difficult because of my anger. We really didn't learn from this experience.[11]

NOTES

1. Frank Hajcak and Patricia Garwood, *Hidden Bedroom Partners* (San Diego: Libra Publishers, 1987), pp. 74-79, adapted.

2. H. Norman Wright, *Romancing Your Marriage* (Ventura, Calif.: Regal, 1987), p. 130.

3. David Mace, "Marital Intimacy and the Deadly Love-Anger Circle," *Journal of Marriage and Family Counseling,* April 1976, p. 136.

4. Philip J. Guerin, Jr, "The Stages of Marital Conflict," *The Family Journal,* 10:22, adapted.

5. H. Norman Wright, *So You're Getting Married* (Ventura, Calif.: Regal, 1985), pp. 180-81, adapted.

6. Aaron T. Beck, *Love Is Never Enough* (New York: Harper & Row, 1988); Idea adapted from pp. 269-70 and communication experiments over several years of counseling with couples.

7. Ibid., pp.272-74, adapted.

8. Ibid., pp. 270-74, adapted.

9. Ibid., pp. 274-76, adapted.

10. David Viscott, *I Love You Let's Work It Out* (New York: Simon and Schuster, 1987), pp. 177-78, adapted.

11. Beck. *Love Is Never Enough,* p. 267, adapted.

11

ANGRY PARENTS, ANGRY CHILDREN

F or many families, home is a battleground, filled with constant bickering, shouting matches, and exhausting power struggles," Nancy Samalin writes. In *Love and Anger: The Parental Dilemma*, she describes a parent's plight, perhaps your plight.

> Parents are amazed that they can go from relative calm to utter frustration in a few seconds. An uneaten egg or spilled juice at breakfast can turn a calm morning into a free-for-all. In spite of parents' best intentions, bedtime becomes wartime, meals end with children in tears and food barely touched, and car rides deteriorate into stress-filled shouting matches. . . . Whatever its source, we often experience parental anger as a horrifying encounter with our worst selves. I never even knew I had a temper until I had children. It was very frightening that these children I loved so much, for whom I had sacrificed so much, could arouse such intense feelings of rage in me, their mother, whose primary responsibility was to nurture and protect them."[1]

Samalin's description mirrors my own experience and those of hundreds of parents I counsel. In the arena of parenting we can readily see our need for growth in understanding the God-given emotion of anger. In no area of life are the consequences of not dealing with our anger more evident than in relationship to our children.

It should not be surprising that the greater your love for someone, the greater your capacity to experience a wide range of emotions. That includes emotions such as irritation, resentment, anger, and even rage. It doesn't matter whether it's your own parents, your spouse, or your children.

Two of the most common questions parents ask me at parenting workshops and family enrichment seminars are about the emotion of anger. The first question is, "How can I more effectively deal with my anger towards my children?" The second question is, "What are some specific ways I can teach my children to deal with their anger?" That second question is very important. If children can learn to value the emotion of anger, if they can learn how to become assertive-responders, they will have access to a strength and intensity that can help them throughout their lifetime.

Dealing with Your Anger

Let's start with the first question. "How can I more effectively deal with my anger towards my children?" When most parents ask this question they want to know how they can deal with their anger once they are already angry. But as we've seen in previous chapters, the best time to deal with our anger is before it rises within us. If we plan ahead we can create an environment in which it will be much easier to experience and express difficult emotions.

REMEMBER YOUR MISSION

The first step in planning is to remind yourself that a healthy home environment is important. Childhood is an influential time. One of the greatest sources of influence on the developing personalities of our children is what they hear and see at home.

Your mission is both a challenge and a great opportunity—to mold the minds and hearts of future adults. God's purpose for parents is to provide love, guidance, and protection for their children. It's through watching their parents that children learn who they are, if they have any value and worth, how to love, how to communicate and deal with conflict, how to understand and express emotions. They learn what it means to be a boy or a girl, who God is, and how relevant He is for their lives. A healthy home provides a nonthreatening environment that is supportive, nurturing, and flexible, one that encourages the uniqueness of each individual.

In an unhealthy home the environment is rigid, restrictive, and demanding. Love is conditional, and children learn to ignore who they are and are forced to shape their behavior to meet the needs of their parents. Instead of developing their real selves, by discovering what it means to be made in God's image and who God designed them to be, they develop false selves. The false self learns how to "read" the environment, including Mom's and Dad's moods, to get the love and approval it desperately needs.

When children grow up in unhealthy homes, they become emotionally, psychologically, and spiritually damaged. Their normal development is at best hindered and at worst arrested. Over the years we've worked with hundreds of men and women who were chronologically in their thirties and forties but emotional and psychological adolescents.

Since modeling is such an important need, it follows that we can't give our kids what we don't have. If we want them to have healthy emotional development, they need to see us deal with our emotions in healthy ways. If we want them to learn constructive ways to deal with anger, they will learn that best from what they see us do. This means that we need to grow in our ability to deal with our own anger toward them.

KEEP AN ANGER LOG

One simple way to deal with your anger is to keep an Anger Log (see chapter 14) that deals only with your anger toward your children. What is the frequency, intensity, and duration of your anger with your kids? When are you most likely to lose it? When I looked at my own Anger Log I discovered that one of the times I was most vulnerable was when I came home from work. I love my sons, but at the end of an exhausting day I did not relish coming home to three delightful but jumping bundles of boyhood, each with his own unique needs and wants. They all had one common want, however: each wanted a piece of Dad. Meanwhile, I'm torn among my love for my sons, my desire to help my wife, my need to catch my breath, and my sons' need for my attention.

By identifying this point of vulnerability in my Anger Log, I was able to make some changes in my preparation for coming home. That eliminated most of the problem. Just being aware of the problem was a part of the solution. Someone once said that "a problem defined is a problem half solved." That was true in this situation. Once I became aware that I am physically and emotionally vulnerable, I became more sensitive to my potential responses.

I told my wife, Carrie, about my concern, and together we prayed about the problem. We developed several specific strategies that God has used to help produce change. The first is that I work harder at not being so frazzled when I come home. This involves being more aware of my schedule, using the "N" word—no! —with greater frequency, and making sure I am getting adequate aerobic exercise. I also make it a regular habit to call home for a "weather report" on my boys before leaving the office. If it has been a particularly stormy day, I will spend extra time at the office before coming home to prayerfully commit the burdens and concerns of the day as well as my evening with my family to Him. I've found that prayer refreshes me, relaxes me, and renews my perspective. I'm able to go home and be there in spirit and not just in body. You can also use your Anger Log to identify some of the situations that are most likely to trigger your anger. Here are a list of triggers given by parents at a parenting workshop. You probably have encountered several of these situations yourself. Put a check by the actions that are most likely to trigger your anger.

- ☐ When they won't do what I say
- ☐ When they won't take no for an answer
- ☐ When they defy me
- ☐ When they "hang" their clothes on the floor
- ☐ When they won't clean up their room
- ☐ When I see them making the same mistakes I made
- ☐ When they act like helpless babies
- ☐ When they don't do their homework
- ☐ When they whine or argue in "that voice"
- ☐ When they tune me out or ignore me, and become "parent deaf"
- ☐ When they embarrass me or throw tantrums in public
- ☐ When they won't take responsibility for their belongings
- ☐ When they won't share with their friends or siblings
- ☐ When they try to boss me around
- ☐ When they don't show appreciation for the things I do for them
- ☐ When they fight and bicker with one another
- ☐ When they give me that "attitude"
- ☐ When they talk back and say things that hurt or insult me

☐ When they say, "I hate you," or, "You're mean"
☐ When they don't eat what I've prepared
☐ When they dawdle when I'm in a hurry
☐ When they won't go to or stay in bed[2]

STUDY YOUR CHILD

You will also be more successful in dealing with anger toward your children if you understand them. It is so easy to hold our children to adult standards and expectations. By their very nature, children offer their parents frustration, contradictions, aggravation, and at times, chaos. But they also bring us surprise, delight, wonder, joy, humor, vulnerability, creativity, and boundless energy.

Study your child. Be aware of his or her uniqueness. How is each one similar to and different from other members of the family? Become aware of their differences. Try not to compare one child with another. See each one of your children as a unique individual created in the image of God. Ask God to help you discover that uniqueness.

Ask yourself what he or she is capable of learning at this age? What kinds of concepts is his little mind capable of grasping? Try to learn about the behaviors you can expect for his/her age. This anonymous poem expresses well the challenges of dealing with younger children and is a good reminder of what might be realistic expectations for the preschool child.

WHAT TO EXPECT OF YOUR TODDLER

He will reach into every closet,
Every door, every cupboard in the house.

He will indiscriminately
Taste, touch, smell, pull on, lick, jerk, bite,
And swallow every particle he can reach—
And he can reach them all.

He will not be afraid of water
Even if it's 3000 feet deep.

He will not know the potentials of fire
Even if it's 3000 degrees hot.

He will not be afraid of autos and tractors
Even if they are 3000 pounds heavy.
He will resent, ignore
And crawl away from all your warnings
But wiggle into your heart.[3]

This little poem illustrates the limitations, frustrations, and joys of raising a toddler. Keeping in mind the age-appropriate characteristics of the toddler allows you to have more realistic expectations of this young explorer. If you anticipate his curiosity, you probably will experience less unnecessary frustration, and your anger will decrease.

Sometimes it's easy to read adult motives and intentions into our children. At times what seems real to them seems very silly to us. But remember this is a child! Remember that his little mind does not work as yours does. Fears and concerns that may seem silly to an adult can be real to a child. Recently I came across an anonymous poem that was a powerful reminder of this distinction.

WHATIF

Last night, while I lay thinking here,
Some Whatifs crawled inside my ear
And pranced and partied all night long
And sang their same old Whatif song:
Whatif I'm dumb in school?
Whatif they've closed the swimming pool?
Whatif I get beat up?
Whatif there's poison in my cup?
Whatif I flunk that test?
Whatif green hair grows on my chest?
Whatif nobody likes me?
Whatif a bolt of lightening strikes me?
Whatif I don't grow taller?
Whatif my head starts getting smaller?
Whatif the wind tears up my kite?
Whatif they start a war?
Whatif my parents get divorced?
Whatif the bus is late?
Whatif my teeth don't grow in straight?
Whatif I tear my pants?
Whatif I never learn to dance?

Everything seems swell, and then
The nighttime Whatifs strike again!
(Source Unknown)[4]

WATCH OUT FOR DUMPING

As we become more aware of the anger we experience toward our children we will be able to clarify what that anger is about. Frequently our anger isn't caused by our children. It's caused by some other factors. At times its easier to *displace our anger and dump on our kids* instead of on our boss or our spouse. Displacement occurs when we take out our anger on those who are not the true reason for the anger.

Lynn's day at work had gone about as bad as possible. In the morning her car wouldn't start, so she had to ask a neighbor for help. She was late for an important meeting at work and didn't have time to prepare the expected handout for her brief presentation. When the computer shut down for two hours, she fell further behind in her work. Before leaving for home her husband, Dan, called to let her know he would be late for dinner.

On her drive home she anticipated walking in the door and having a few minutes to relax and unwind. But when she entered the house, the front room looked like a testing ground for nuclear weapons. She immediately stormed out into the backyard and yelled at her kids.

"You know how hard I work!" She brought her children inside and then began to rant loud and long. "I'm sick and tired of doing all the work. How thoughtless you are, too. You never think of anyone else—you certainly don't appreciate my efforts to give you nice things. Are you going to spend your entire lives being selfish and irresponsible?"

For a brief moment Lynn felt better, but when her sanity—and blood pressure—settled back, she realized that not only had she not solved her problem, she had created another problem.

Yes, the house was a mess. Yes, the kids could have picked things up a bit. Yes, there were times when her kids didn't appreciate her. But her anger wasn't really about the messy home. Her anger was about her frustrating and disappointing day *at work*. It was about the selfishness, lack of appreciation, and unrealistic expectations of *her boss at work*.

Learn to ask yourself the question, "What is my anger about?" Is it about my children, is it about things in my past, my present, or a combination of all three? As parents we bring emotions from our own childhood into our experiences as parents. At times we can replay unresolved anger from our childhood into our current relationships. This is especially likely to occur when one of our children reaches the same age we were when a traumatic event or crisis occurred. It is a fact that one of the major problems in dealing with our children's anger is dealing with the angry feelings it stirs up in us. If you've had a hard day, if you've been frustrated by something that didn't go as planned, if you've been hurt by a friend's comment, you are at risk.

EXPRESS YOUR ANGER POSITIVELY

When you find yourself getting angry at your children, consider these seven ways to express your anger. These approaches will heal rather than hurt relationships, encourage rather than discourage.

1. *Don't overreact.* Neither minimize or maximize the situation. Don't assume you know what the problem is. The most important issue isn't what you think of the problem but how your child thinks and feels about the problem. So listen, and then ask questions. If there is more than one person involved, hear all sides of the story. Give your children time to explain their perspective.

Anger involves strong feelings that shouldn't be ignored or denied. An angry outburst or a temper tantrum is not necessarily the sign of a major problem. When parents overreact to their child's anger the covert message is "Anger is bad. When you get angry you are bad, and you are wrong."

Like adults, children have flashes of anger. (How to deal with a child's anger is discussed beginning on page 187. However, children's anger is unlike adult anger in one very important way. Children do not usually carry grudges. They don't harbor resentment. They don't plan ways to get revenge. Because of their limited perspective on life and short attention span, most children easily forgive and forget. They tend to take life as it comes and then let it go. Each day is fresh and new to the child.[5]

Often conflict among young children will not need adult intervention. One study found that among toddlers, conflict involved overt aggression less than 25 percent of the time. In six- and seven-year-olds, physical attack occurred only 5 percent of the time, and verbal attack took place 40 percent of the time. The majority of conflicts among preschoolers were settled without adult intervention, and play resumed 75 percent of the time with little or no upset.[6]

2. *Use the first-person singular pronoun* when you confront your children. Clearly identify your own feelings with "I" statements rather than "you" statements. When you begin with "you," your statements will often come across as demeaning, demanding, and accusatory. By making "I" statements you can make your point with greater clarity and with less probability of damaging their sense of value and worth. Consider these examples of healthy "I" statements:

"I am very angry right now."
"I need to take a time out to think and pray about what I am feeling before I decide what I'm going to do."
"It's hard for me to concentrate on my driving when you are yelling and throwing things."
"I'd like you to be quiet."
"I'm disappointed and hurt that you lied to me."
"I'm exhausted, and I need some peace and quiet now."
"I'll be glad to help you with it after dinner."
"I don't like it when you talk to me like that."

3. *Stay in the present.* Don't dredge up all of the past failures. One of the mistakes that I struggled with when communicating my anger to one of my children was to give a list of all his recent transgressions. Over time I noticed that instead of adding more power to my point my kids felt overwhelmed and discouraged. They got more frustrated or simply turned me off. In addition, consider what happens when you scold the child by recalling mistake after mistake—the child will turn you off. What happens when you know he is ignoring you? That's right, it tends to increase your frustration and can lead to more anger. That's a lose-lose situation.

4. *Keep it short and simple.* Have you ever been in a situation where a parent, spouse, or boss was correcting you and he or she seemed to go on and on *ad nauseaum*? Do you remember

what that felt like? Do you remember what you would have liked to have said to the person? Did it increase your motivation to listen? Did it encourage you? Probably not.

All of us have a limited attention span. The people who make television commercials know that and they structure their expensive messages accordingly. The attention span of children is much more limited than that of adults. If you as an adult have a difficult time handling a tirade, how much more difficult will it be for a child? The shorter and simpler your message, the greater the probability that your child will be able to receive it.

5. *Be specific.* Focus on the essential. Make the expression of your anger descriptive, accurate, and to the point; not several points but one point. What's the bottom line? What's negotiable and nonnegotiable? Do you know? Do your children know? Furthermore, keep consistent your rules, standards, and expectations; changes only confuse.

6. *Ask yourself, "What's my motive?"* What do I want to accomplish? How can I use this situation to communicate my love and concern, draw us closer together, strengthen the bonds of trust, and help them learn? Your goal should be to communicate your anger in such a way that your children know that they are still valuable and important. Parents who react aggressively to their children's anger are more likely to make negative and critical statements that communicate to their children that they are unworthy and unlovable. Before responding ask yourself, "How can I acknowledge my child's rights, values, and concerns? How can I respond in a way that will encourage him? How can I help him become more responsible?"

7. *Follow the seven steps described in chapter 14.* As you read those steps, recognize that you must follow them *before* anger hits home. That way you will have a plan of attack to confront your anger constructively. There are few situations that demand an immediate response. When you have followed those seven steps, you will be able to teach your children what it means to "be slow to anger" in the best way—letting them see a slow, measured, response in you. If you don't say or do the wrong thing you won't have to go back later and try to undo it.

Perhaps you've been concerned about your anger toward your children. Is it too strong or excessive? In its most aggressive form, anger results in physical or sexual abuse. Abusive behavior and its causes are discussed in detail in the next chapter. For now, let's consider the signs that suggest you may want professional help to learn to respond to your children with restraint. Don West-gate, executive director of For Kid's Sake, an organization dedicated to preventing child abuse, has developed this quiz to help you discover whether you should seek help for your anger.

1. Do you feel inadequate as a parent and about knowing child development?
2. Do you have low self-esteem?
3. Are you getting angry more and more often?
4. Have some people indicated your disciplinary reactions are unreasonable?
5. Do you feel your child seldom meets your expectations or wonder if your expectations are too high?
6. Do you feel isolated or depressed?
7. Have you ever left a mark on your child?
8. Were you abused as a child?
9. Do you envision any sexual fantasies about your child?
10. Do you visualize hurting your child and think it would feel good to do so?

If you place check marks by one or two of the questions it doesn't necessarily mean your anger is out of control. But if you checked more than two, or if you checked any of numbers 7-10, it would be wise for you to talk with your pastor or a professional Christian therapist. Doing so will help you deal more effectively with your anger.[5]

Dealing with Your Child's Anger

Let's turn to the second question parents have regarding anger. That is, "How can I help my child deal with his or her anger? With some slight modifications the same seven steps that work for adults have also proven to be very effective with children.

1. *Help your child identify his or her anger pattern.* The most effective way to teach this is for your child to have seen how you've identified your own anger pattern. I remember well the first

time my son at age five came up to me and announced, "Dad, I'm angry."

"That's great!" I answered. "I bet it feels good to understand what you are feeling." After he talked about the situation for a while he told me he was going outside to play. That was the end of it.

You may keep an Anger Log for your young child, or your older children can keep logs themselves. This will make it easier to help them identify their anger. Look for the typical symptoms that can include withdrawal, difficulty concentrating, nail-biting, loss of sleep, change in appetite, bedwetting, nightmares, stuttering, throwing toys, breaking things, and picking on other children.

Calmly acknowledge their behavior. "Honey, I can see you are very upset. Do you know what's bothering you? Do you want to talk about it now or later?" Where possible, link their behavior with the secondary emotion of anger. Then over time you can move to linking the emotion of anger with the primary emotion such as fear, hurt, or frustration.

2. *Help your child admit his anger and accept responsibility for it.* Adults aren't the only ones who like to hurl the responsibility for an action on someone else. What started with Adam and Eve is alive and well in us and in our children. Kids love to blame. Especially if it is their brother or sister.

When your child blames someone, you can acknowledge the reality of what the other person did. But then present the idea that he or she had some other ways they could have responded. "Yes, David took your toy, and that wasn't very nice. But you didn't have to hit him. What are some other ways you could have expressed your anger?"

Don't dwell on what they did wrong. Focus on what their choices were and what they can learn from this situation to help them next time. Show them that you accept their feelings while suggesting other ways to express those feelings. You might say, "Let me tell you what some other children might have done in this situation."

3. *Help your child decide who or what will have control.* It will take some time and patience, but kids can learn to distinguish between feeling their anger and how they choose to express it. They can learn the concept of taking time to respond, especially if we parents model it. They can begin to understand that thinking,

feeling, and doing aren't the same thing. They can know that they have the freedom to choose how they will respond.

4. *Help your child identify and define the cause or source of the anger*. This is a difficult yet not impossible task for children. Obviously children don't understand the difference between a primary and secondary emotion. All they know is that what they feel isn't good. Avoid the temptation to explain things to them. Start by helping them understand what they are feeling by asking questions.

Kids have anger for many of the same reasons we do. But they have had fewer years to see the consequences of the unhealthy expressions of their anger. They don't have the abstraction skills of adults. It's hard for them to stand back and look at the situation from another perspective. Yet most children may express anger when they feel sad, depressed, hurt, fearful, frustrated, anxious, or rejected.

When you are angry, let your child hear you think out loud about your anger. Tell him or her the primary emotion that led to your anger. As you discuss your child's emotions with him/her, it will become fairly easy for your child to identify the emotion of anger. In time he will be able to identify the emotion that led to his own anger.

5. *Help your child choose his response*. Like adults, a child is likely to say things that hurt when he doesn't have a plan to deal with his anger. One way we can help our children is to guide them to alternative responses for their anger based on what has or hasn't worked in the past.

Abby stormed into the house, slammed the front door, stomped up the stairs, and slammed her bedroom door, as only an angry eight-year-old can. Her mother, Karen, went into Abby's room and asked her what was wrong.

"Emily said she's not going to invite me to her birthday party, and I invited her to mine. I hate her, and I never want to see her again."

Karen waited a minute to see if Abby wanted to add anything else and then said, "It sounds as if you are really hurt by what Emily said. I know four different ways you can handle this hurt and some of them may work. If you want to hear them, let me know." Karen gave her a hug and left the room.

A few minutes later Abby came back asking what they were. "Do you really want to know?" Karen asked. Abby mumbled, "Yes." "Well," she said, "here they are. Some of them might be better than others, but you can decide." She sat down with her and offered Abby four options.

"Abby, you can choose one of four approaches. I'll give each a letter.

"A. You could set the timer on a clock for thirty minutes and go into your room and kick and scream and pound on the floor until the timer goes off.

"B. You could call three of your friends and tell them what a terrible, awful, horrible person Emily is.

"C. You could write a letter to God and tell Him how sad and hurt you are and then read it to a friend.

"D. You could tell Mom how sad and hurt you are and then maybe we could pray and talk about how you can choose to respond."

Abby decided to choose option D, and she and her mother had an interesting and profitable discussion. Abby chose a healthy response and felt good about "her" decision.

6. *Help your children develop their own solution.* My seven-year-old son, Matt, became angry at his nine-year-old brother for teasing him. After asking Nathan to quit several times, Matt took off his snow boot and threw it at him. When it bounced off his head, Nathan bounded down the steps yelling, "Matt hit me with his boot."

What's the best way to respond? I could have become upset at both of them, or said, "You really shouldn't get mad," or, "There's no excuse for that." My dilemma was how to honor the feelings and concerns of both kids and yet help them deal with the real issue. Once such a situation has occurred, it's best to ask the question, "How can I help them solve their problem in such a way that the next time they will be able to solve it by themselves?" That's what I did.

Now I turned to them both and said, "It's probably frustrating to be teased, and I know it hurts to have boots bounced off your head. Nathan, do you know what it feels like to be teased? Have you ever been teased? Did you like it?"

"Matt, did Nathan's teasing you make it right for you to throw your boot at him? What were some other choices you had? What else could you have done?

"I want you to go to your room and discuss what your choices are. What do you need to say to each other? What can you learn from this situation? How can you respond differently if this happens again? When you've come up with a solution let me know. I'm sure you guys can work this out." Nathan and Matt went off and discussed the situation and resolved it.

Will this situation or something similar happen again? Probably. If that's true then what was accomplished? A lot! This was another opportunity to help them recognize the reality of their emotions while at the same time being aware of the emotions of another person. They had another chance to see that with the experience of anger there were choices for how it can be expressed. Another seed was planted, another truth was reinforced, another healthy example was modeled.

7. *Help the child review his response to the anger*. Remember that this is a process. It takes time. It involves trial and error. How long has it taken you as an adult to learn to become an assertive-responder? Remember that the product is worth the process. When the child takes even the slightest step in the right direction congratulate and praise him on a job well done. Ask him what he learned from this situation and how he can be more effective next time.

Temper Tantrums

In only a matter of minutes John's irritation, like a runaway train, had roared past frustration and anger and moved into rage. He was out-of-control and running full speed ahead into a temper tantrum.

Few things are as dramatic as a full-blown temper tantrum. The child runs around shouting and screaming, or he holds his breath, jumps up and down, kicks wildly, bangs his fist or his head, throws himself or other objects on the floor or at you, and rolls around. Tantrums leave both participants and observers exhausted.

They are most likely to happen when your kids are frustrated by someone or something or when you have set some boundaries by saying, "No!" Children want to be grown up, independent, in control, and able to do whatever Mom and Dad do. Yet they are still small, dependent, not in control, and limited in what they can do. This is a perfect recipe for frustration.

Carol Tavris has observed that temper tantrums first appear during a child's second year, peak between the ages of two and three, and decrease by age four. At this age the child is forming a sense of self: the toddler is old enough to have a sense of "me" and "my wants" but is too young to get what he wants when he wants it. Although some tantrums result from organic disturbances or allergies, most are caused by the combination of high energy and low self-control.

Most children throw tantrums only in a particular place and with a particular person. They usually last as long as it takes to get what they want or until they realize it's not going to work.

> The immediate fate of the temper tantrum depends on the child's level of energy and the parent's level of patience. Because a tantrum is rarely an expression of real anger, but rather a desire to stay up later, have a cookie, not put on shoes, and endure the many frustrations of being only two and a half, then every time the parent yields, the child learns that tantrums work.[8]

When your child has a temper tantrum don't rule out a physiological cause. But also ask yourself, "Is it a power struggle?" "Is it a result of my setting some boundaries?" "Is he ready to learn a lesson in impulse control?"

Your child wants some candy at the supermarket. You have said no. If she starts the tantrum pick her up, hold her firmly, and say, "I love you, and you can't have the candy." Don't give in to the theatrics. Your response to your child is much more important than what anyone in the grocery store might think of you. Seneca said that "the child should gain no request by anger; when he is quiet let him be offered what was refused when he wept." That's still good advice. It still works.

Take Action

1. Many parents have asked the question, "How do I know if my child needs help with his/her anger?" One way is to identify the way he or she responds to feelings of anger. To find out his/her anger response, take the Capable Kid Test below.

THE CAPABLE KID TEST

STEP 1: Think of a situation in which your child has experienced anger. It could be not getting his way, not wanting to share with a brother or sister, being embarrassed, being rejected by friends at school, and so on.

STEP 2: Think about how he dealt with that anger. He may have said nothing, holding the anger in. This suggests he is a *passive reactor*. Or he may have exhibited selfish behavior by attacking others physically or verbally. The child who typically responds to frustrations by attacking others is an *aggressive reactor*. If the child usually shows a reasoned response, he will honestly explain he is angry, tell why he feels that way, and seek to bring about a solution with the other person. This child is what we call an *assertive responder*. Identify which type of response your child typically has to his anger.

My child responds to his feelings of anger as (circle one):

(1) A Passive Reactor.
(2) An Aggressive Reactor.
(3) An Assertive Responder.

STEP 3: Choose one statement from the following list that best describes your child's reactions. Put a check mark in front of the one that strikes you as accurate.

☐ 1. "I never get what I want. Nobody cares about me." (May become belligerent and verbally abusive.)
☐ 2. He starts going through a list of people to blame.
☐ 3. "Things like this always happen to me. I guess I deserve it."
☐ 4. "Wow, that really hurt!" Then a few seconds later, he says (or thinks), "I'm going to tell him how that felt and ask him not to do that again.")
☐ 5. "I shouldn't be surprised. I knew something cruddy would happen." (He then becomes withdrawn and preoccupied.)
☐ 6. "That really makes me angry. But maybe I was unkind. I wonder if there is anything I can do about it now?"

☐ 7. "That's not fair! It just not fair. I never get what I want." (He then begins a temper tantrum.)

☐ 8. Doesn't visibly react, pretends everything is normal, but just withdraws. Won't talk about it and tends to isolate himself.

STEP 4: Now, find the corresponding number below. Read the description of your child's behavior Remember, the statement you have selected should be your child's *typical* way of dealing with anger.

#4 or #6: This is a capable child. He handles anger well and shows characteristics of an assertive-responder. This child has developed some skills in distinguishing between the experience and the expression of anger. He tends to control his anger rather than letting the anger control him.

#1, #2, or #7: This child shows characteristics of an aggressive-reactor. There is a tendency to overgeneralize, overreact, and hurl blame at someone or something else. Is it possible that one or both parents have modeled this pattern?

#3, #5, or #8: This child shows characteristics of a passive-reactor. There is a tendency to hide his emotions, take on too much responsibility, pretend things are fine and let others walk all over him.[9]

2. These three ways, or "styles," of reacting to anger are discussed in detail in chapter 13. (Of course, styles influence adults as well as children.) The earlier you are able to identify any unhealthy tendencies in your children's response to anger the sooner you can begin to help them move toward healthy anger skills. If not identified and dealt with, the pattern may become more automatic and deeply entrenched and will probably carry over into adulthood.

Meditate on Proverbs 22:6a: "Train up a child in the way he should go." That's our parental duty. But a word of encouragement. Training takes time. It proceeds by trial and error. You cannot expect a child to quickly learn the right response to his anger. Especially for a child, change occurs gradually. It's somewhat like helping your daughter work on a jigsaw puzzle.

You encourage her to discover as many pieces as she can, you point out a few of the pieces, and then you work together at putting the pieces together.

NOTES

1. Nancy Samalin, *Love and Anger: The Parental Dilemma* (New York: Viking Penguin, 1991), p. 5
2. Ibid., pp. 5-6, adapted.
3. As quoted in Samalin, *Love and Anger,* p. 35.
4. As quoted in H. Norman Wright, *Helping Children Handle Stress* (San Bernardino, Calif.: Here's Life, 1987), p.29.
5. Mark P. Cosgrove, *Counseling for Anger* (Dallas: Word, 1988), p. 120.
6. Carolyn Uhlinger, "Conflicts Between Children," *Child Development* 58 (1987): 283-305.
7. Brochure from For Kid's Sake, n.p.; P.O. Box 313, Lake Elsinore, CA 92331 714-244-9001.
8. Carol Tavris, *Anger: The Misunderstood Emotion* (New York: Simon and Schuster, 1982), pp. 136-37.
9. Mary Susan Miller, *Childstress* (Garden City, N.Y.: Doubleday, 1982), pp. 42-53, adapted.

12

WHEN ANGER CROSSES THE LINE

L ess than six feet away, traveling in the opposite direction, vehicles are passing you at 65 miles an hour. Sometimes the
wind from their speed shakes your car a bit, more so when a
semi-truck flies by. You aren't bothered by these vehicles streaking
by, however, as you continue to your destination. Why should you
be? You're safe—as long as you stay in your lane and they stay in
theirs.

All our highways are set up in this manner. Cars in one lane
roar in one direction, and vehicles on the other side zip in the
opposite direction. A crucial center line divides the two lanes. You
are completely safe—that is until someone crosses the line. And
then you're dead.

It happens every day. Someone falls asleep, doesn't pay attention, loses control, drives under the influence, or a tire blows,
and then he crosses the line right in front of an innocent driver.
Both cars are destroyed along with the occupants. That's what
happens when the line is crossed.

When lines are crossed in other settings, there are dire results as well. In baseball when a batter hits the ball it's in play
unless the ball crosses the foul line. In the 1991 World Series an
Atlanta Braves player hit a tremendous drive to right field. The
crowd began to cheer as the ball headed out of the field and into
the stands. At the last moment the ball curled across the foul line

by a mere twelve inches. Instead of being a home run, the grand swing cost him a strike.

Crossing the line or boundary in football, basketball, or hockey is a violation. In baseball, the act earns the umpire's bark, "Foul!" In freeway driving, the act can have fatal consequences. When anger crosses the line of appropriate expression and becomes abusive it too is a violation. Abuse is not a pleasant subject to talk about. It's not a pleasant word to consider. And many reading this book may want to shy away from this chapter because they feel it doesn't apply to them. But in many forms abuse thrives in the living rooms of America.

Consider the facts. An estimated one of every two families in our country experiences some form of domestic violence every year. And one family in five experiences this on a consistent basis.[1] Unfortunately, many Christians believe that it doesn't happen in "Christian homes." But that type of thinking only covers up the incidents. Some Christians tend to deny and hide their problems, others seek counsel; but in both instances, their home is the setting for abusive behavior.

The signs of the victims are often hidden, but they exist. A child or adolescent begs not to change into his or her gym clothes because of the fear that others will discover the bruises. A woman comes to church with long sleeves and high collars to hide the black and blue bruises. A husband uses makeup to hide the bruise and dent in the side of his cheek where his wife hit him with a frying pan. I have met these people and others. And each of these situations took place in Christian families.

Eve was the mother of three young children. While at a Christian family camp she made an appointment and seemed quite upset. "I was so shocked this morning," she began. "One of the other families here at the conference came to me and accused me of abusing my children. I couldn't believe it. They claimed that I abused them every day. I don't even spank them. How could I abuse them? They need to be controlled, and I may come on strong with what I say, but abuse? Not me. I couldn't be guilty of that!" But in continuing a discussion with her, I discovered that she really was abusing her children. She was like so many who are unaware of what they are doing because they have never fully understood the term.

Abuse—what is it? The term needs a careful and specific definition. I've heard it used to describe situations that in reality are not abuse. But I've also heard an individual describe an abusive situation and then fail to recognize the act was abusive.

THE NATURE OF ABUSE

Abuse can be defined as any behavior that is designed to control and/or subjugate another human through the use of fear, humiliation, and verbal or physical assaults. In a sense it is the systematic persecution of one family member by another.[2]

When congress passed the Child Abuse Prevention and Treatment Act in 1974, the act identified four types of abuse: physical, neglect, emotional, and sexual. Neglect occurs more than we realize and includes abandonment, neglecting needed medical treatment, inadequate supervision, disregard of health hazards in the home, and inadequate provisions for the child's basic physical and educational needs.

Physical abuse usually refers to brutal physical contact rather than accidental. This can include any behavior that either intends to inflict or actually does inflict physical harm. It consists of pushing, grabbing, shoving, slapping, kicking, biting, choking, punching, hitting with an object, or attacking with a knife or a gun.

Emotional abuse has a multitude of expressions. Scare tactics, insults, yelling, temper tantrums, name calling, and continuous criticism fall into this classification. Threatened violence is a form of emotional abuse, too. Holding up a weapon, swinging a fist near the person's face, destroying property, or kicking a child's pet falls in this category. Withholding privileges or affection or constantly blaming one family member for the family's difficulties is abuse.

I've heard some people defend their shouting pattern of behavior as normal. They say, "That's just the way we did it in our family. Everyone shouted, and we accepted it. That isn't abuse." But in their new family it may become abuse because of the sensitivity of the other family members. Shouting can become terrifying if it is consistent, intense, and very loud. Grace Ketterman, a Christian psychiatrist, writes, "Almost all children experience screaming as verbal abuse, sometimes even more painful than physical abuse."[3] Criticism that is relentless and fault-finding has an ongoing eroding effect. I have seen hundreds of adults who came from "fine" Christian homes who were damaged by this form of abuse.[4] Ketterman notes the tragic irony of this situation:

> The family is supposed to be a haven, a place of safety in a heartless and increasingly frightening world. Yet all too commonly, home has become a private world of horror—the safe place to explode one's frustrations, shredding the emotions of those unfortunate enough to be there. Few relationships absorb as much chronic abuse as marriage.
>
> Verbal abuse is in part an expression of personal inadequacy. In the stressful arena of one's job, only a few individuals have much power. Employees take abuse from others in order to keep their jobs and maintain the appearance of strength. But at home, these same victims can displace their fears and inflict the accompanying anger upon those who have even less power than they do. Doing so usually produces a feeling of power. And when family members react in fear and trembling, that false power is exaggerated. So the vicious cycle is established.[5]

One form of abuse that has recently come to light is abuse of the elderly. An estimated 4 percent of the elderly are abused in some way, and one in ten who lives with a family member is abused. The rate could be much higher than this; such abuse is not as likely to be reported as is child abuse.[6]

Why does violence occur? We live in a violent society. Keep track of the violent acts that you and your family watch each week on television. Count the number of violent acts you read about each day in the newspaper. You may have come close to verbal or physical violence in an encounter when driving your car. Think about it. Have you ever muttered or shouted threats at another driver?

Abuse Through the Generations

Our socialization process breeds a tendency for violence in men, who are told that a "real man " must be strong and tough. Family factors enter in to both the continuance of this problem and its increase in our society. God warned His people that generational influences are responsible for "visiting the iniquity of fathers on the children and on the grandchildren to the third and fourth generations" (Exodus 34:7).

Research confirms that violent patterns of behavior are transmitted from one generation to another. A child's role models are his or her parents. If the child observes abuse, the action serves as a model for adult behavior, even though the child detested the experience and the results. A young boy observing abuse may conclude that the best way to express anger is in violence; he learns violence works in controlling or dominating another person.

However, some boys who observe violence identify with their mothers and develop negative feelings toward their fathers because of the abuse. Sometimes a boy will try to intervene. As he grows older he may begin to take on the role of helper and confidant for his mother, which is actually the father's role. What often happens is a wide distance between the father and son and an overly close relationship between the son and mother.

But in adolescence something different begins to occur. As the boy tries to break away from his mother, he may begin to identify with his father and start to become abusive. He could become physical toward his girlfriends or siblings, and then his mother has two problem people on her hands.[7]

In contrast, a young girl may conclude that it is her lot in life to be abused. (There are some who eventually take on the abuser role as well.) Sometimes a girl whose mother is abused will tend to take on child-rearing responsibilities for the younger children in the family because her mother is so overwhelmed and distraught. But some girls coming from abusive families end up rebelling in various ways as adolescents. Daughters may use drugs, run away to get away from their present abusive home, or marry early. Their dream, of course, is to have a happy home, and they'll do anything to get away from the present situation. Unfortunately, their marriages years later end up a replica of their childhood home. As a result, their own children typically will undergo the same abuse.

One mother described the tragic legacy of the verbal abuse she endured as a child:

> When I was a child, I repeatedly vowed that I would never scream at my children. And I rarely did. But I can, with horrifying clarity, recall a number of times when I behaved in exactly the way I so firmly determined I would never do. On those unfortunate occasions, I did indeed yell ugly words at my children.

I would give almost anything if I could reverse those home movies in my memory and take back those harsh words. The tragedy of verbal abuse lies in that very fact—it can never be erased. Forgiveness and healing can be achieved, thankfully, but the scars are there for life!

With such an absolutely firm commitment, if I could abuse those dear to me, so could you.[8]

If you experienced abuse as a child, this abuse affects how you view yourself even as an adult. Unfortunately, many children end up believing that they deserved what happened to them. They end up feeling that they are not worthwhile people. And these feelings lay them open to further abuse as they move through adolescence and adulthood.

You may doubt abuse is very prevalent. Yet think for a moment: Who do you know that experienced abuse in your immediate or extended family? Which of your friends experienced abuse? Who do you know in your church that is in an abusive situation? Often both home and church deny the presence of abuse; church leaders rarely address the subject. But the abuse still exists!

A CLIMATE FOR ABUSE

During recent years researchers have been able to answer most of our questions about the circumstances leading to and involving abuse in marriage.[9]

Where does most marital violence occur? Usually in the home and most often the living room or the bedroom.

Is there a safe place within the home? Strange as it seems, the bathroom becomes the safe place where family members take refuge. It's usually the only room that has a lock on the door.

Are there certain times for violence to occur? Most couples become involved in abuse between 6:00 P.M. and midnight. Other common times are weekends, Christmas, and New Year's Eve and Day.

The evening meal can create an abusive climate because of family tensions. During the dinner, family members often tend to complain about their day. Many of the conflicts begin over the control of the children, with money matters running second.

Does abusive behavior become more severe over time? A very serious finding is that as the frequency of abusive episodes increases, the more severe the episodes become.

A couple's working pattern seems to contribute to the likelihood of abuse. Abuse is more common when the spouses works on different rotating shifts or when both are unemployed. Abuse is also more likely to happen when the wife is pregnant.

THE PATTERN OF ABUSE

There is a distinct pattern to abuse and especially marital abuse.[10] Many of the abusive couples display a high degree of mutual dependency. They rely upon each other almost exclusively for the satisfaction of all of their needs, including emotional. But this in itself helps to create the conditions for frustration, for when there are no outside sources for need fulfillment, having your needs left unfulfilled by your spouse becomes much more serious. Even little irritations, such as the favorite shirt not being ironed or dinner being delayed, lead to the tension-building phase.

Some of the irritations may be expressed but most are usually held inside, where the tension builds more and more. At this time each person in his or her own way may attempt to force the other person to meet his/her needs. This leads only to more frustration. The wife may make some attempts to control her husband's angry responses, but these do not solve the problem, so she may withdraw from him in order to keep the problem from intensifying. But her withdrawing angers him even more.

The next phase happens when the abuser believes that he can no longer endure the situation. He believes he has done everything that he can, and now his anger erupts and he becomes violent. This is the phase when injuries occur. When the abuse is over, there is a release of tension and, unfortunately, what has taken place has set the stage for a later recurrence. Why? Because what the abuser did worked for him. It stopped whatever was creating his stress, and he is further convinced that this is the way to eliminate frustration.

In some couples just prior to the onset of the abuse the husband will withdraw and refuse to communicate. He may even let his wife know in some fashion that he is about to explode, and he tells her to stop what she is doing. Unfortunately, she may persist in her efforts to get through to him by continuing to talk even louder, move closer to him, or attempt to prevent him from leaving or withdrawing. And for him this is the last straw. This is often why husbands then blame their wives for creating the incident.

The final stage following the abuse is remorse or repentance. The tension is gone. The abuser often apologizes, swears that it will never happen again, brings gifts, is attentive and is even kind. This is prompted by his guilt and fear that he may lose her. And often the man feels that he never will abuse his wife again. And she is willing to believe him. This is almost like a honeymoon phase and can actually reinforce the cycle of violence. This is a relief to the wife, and it may be the only time in the relationship when he is attentive and kind and she feels loved. For some wives it is almost worth the experience to receive these benefits.

During this period alone, the relationship tends to shift, and the victim moves from being powerless to having power. There is a role reversal, and the wife may even be protective of her husband now because of the good attention she is receiving. She may protect him from authorities or the children. But, unfortunately, this shift in power sets the stage for the repetition of the abuse. In time, when the husband's guilt has diminished and he realizes that she will stay with him, or when the stress beings to build again, he resents his loss of power—and the cycle beings all over again. And each time it erupts the potential for even greater damage occurs.

TRAITS OF THE ABUSER

Can your spouse become an abuser? What can cause *you* to cross the line and turn your irritation and anger into damaging abuse? Abusers are not confined to any age, race, or religious belief. In fact, studies show that those who are abusive span all socioeconomic and educational levels. But there are some personality characteristics that abusers have in common. Our focus here will be with men since they are the ones most often being the abuser within the family. To a lesser extent, women may display some of these traits.

FAMILY BACKGROUND

Once again the family background provides the breeding ground for future abuse. Those who came from a home in which they experienced a violent and abusive childhood are more likely to abuse their mate or children. Abusers typically were abused personally, or they witnessed abuses on their mother or father. When verbal or physical abuse is the pattern for settling disputes and conflict within the family, the children are limited in their opportunity to learn alternative ways of expressing their anger. Why shouldn't they continue the pattern?

Even if only one person within a family is subjected to abuse, everyone is victimized by that abuse. The greater the frequency of abuse within the home the greater the possibility the victim will repeat this pattern as an adult. That is a bit frightening, isn't it? That's why those who work with children and youth should attempt to discover who are the victims of abuse. Though this could be a difficult task, such discovery and helping abuse victims could break the cycle of uncontrolled anger. The future generation could then be given a better chance for healthy relationships.

INABILITY TO EXPRESS FEELINGS

Another characteristic of those who abuse is a difficulty in expressing their feelings with words. Much is said about the inexpressive male in our society; indeed, this is a common problem. Those who abuse have difficulty not only in expressing their feelings but in identifying and dealing with them when they occur. And too often, whether the feeling is fear, frustration, anxiety, or even affection, the only way the man can let it out is through anger.

In some families the man uses inexpressiveness as a power tool to dominate the family. When a person is silent, who knows what he is thinking? And who is willing to shatter the calm by rocking the boat? So the family members will go along with what he wants rather than risk unleashing what may be inside of the man. If his inexpressiveness isn't working, he can use abuse to control and vent the inner rage.

LOW SELF-ESTEEM

Numerous studies indicate that abusive men are usually non-assertive away from home and struggle with low self-esteem. Their behavior within the home reflects this. In feeling poorly about themselves and not living up to our society's portrayal of what a man should be, they exceed what is normal behavior and become abusive.[11]

It is unfortunate for both the abuser and the abused person that the abuse seems to work. The abuser then has no reason to give it up and learn healthy ways of relating. Nor does he see any need to come to grips with his own insecurities.

PHYSICAL ABUSE

Both husbands and wives engage in physical and psychological abuse, and the number of abusing wives is on the increase. But much of the marital violence inflicted by wives is in self-defense. Women overall are the primary victims. Husbands use more physical violence, and wives suffer more physical injuries.[13]

June's husband was a prominent, respected member of the community, and at one time she loved him deeply. But in recent years fear had replaced the love. At first June lived with emotional abuse. Then one day David crossed the line. As his anger welled up, he raised his hand; it descended as a slap across the face.

Later David told me with an angry scowl, "She deserved it." Eventually the slaps turned into closed fists, usually delivered in a place where no one could see the bruises.

When the fists came, June began to live in terror, which grew each afternoon as the time approached for her husband to come home.

"I even planned what I would say and do so I wouldn't set him off," she told me privately. "But I can never know when his anger might erupt. It just doesn't make sense."

The abuse continued year after year. No one knew—until the day she went to the hospital with three broken ribs. And then everyone knew. But many had difficulty believing it. How could the senior pastor of the leading evangelical church in town abuse his wife? That abuse had ruined their marriage and self-esteem.

A DESIRE TO DOMINATE

The inflexibility of abusive men is seen in their rigid beliefs about the role and responsibility of husbands and wives. They want to dominate every area of their spouse's life. Often the wife becomes socially isolated; then she becomes dependent upon her abusive husband for emotional support.

The abuser has a belief system about what a husband should be like—the absolute, autocratic leader in the home. Unfortunately, I have encountered Christian men who misinterpret and misuse Scripture to substantiate this belief. This view of a man's role also includes that he never appear to be weak, doesn't ask others for help, makes all family decisions, is "honored and respected" in all ways by his family, and is always in control of his emotions. He expects his wife to be both submissive and inferior in all areas.[13] In other words, he has a distorted view of what a man is and what Scripture teaches.

One last characteristic is not surprising. Many abusers have difficulty with substance and alcohol abuse and especially the latter.[14]

TRAITS OF THE ABUSED

Who are the victims of spouse abuse? What are they like? Realize that there are exceptions to the following profile. Many women will not tolerate this behavior and either intervene in a successful way or immediately terminate the relationship. Now try to imagine a woman who is the victim of physical abuse. Compare your image with the following composite of an abused wife.

SIMILAR TRAITS

Like the abuser, the abused often come from abusive family backgrounds and have a poor self-image. Some of the women accept the abuse as normal behavior because they are likely to have been raised in an abusive home. Unfortunately, a number of women tend to blame themselves, thinking, *If only I had responded differently he wouldn't have been physically abusive.*

Women who are abused tend to have low self-esteem, and this feeling makes them easy prey to their husband's abuse. The emotional abuse of threats, ridicule, put-downs, and criticism is devastating and feeds their feelings of low self-esteem. Anyone hearing this repetitive tirade begins to believe the statements. Many end up believing that they don't deserve anything better. They become "pleasers" attempting to meet the needs of everyone in the family except themselves.

UNREALISTIC HOPE OF CHANGE

An abused spouse clings to an unrealistic hope. She believes that in time if she is patient and faithful her husband will change; she accepts every promise that he gives. The times when abuse is absent are good, so she has a taste of what she has always hoped for.

Tina had been coming to counseling for several weeks. One day she arrived and said, "I'm not sure that I need to come for counseling anymore. Jim has done such a dramatic turn around and seems to be living up to his promise of not abusing me any more. I think he really means it this time. And when he isn't abusive the relationship is so wonderful."

My reply was a twofold question. "Tina, how long has it been since he was abusive toward you, and how many other times has he said he wouldn't do it again?" I already knew the answer from our previous discussions, and when I asked, the smile left her face as she too remembered the litany of broken promises. It had been only ten days since the last abuse occurred.

ISOLATION AND DEPENDENCY

An abused wife tends to isolate herself over a period of time. She will begin to isolate herself socially because of her own fear that others will discover her plight and because her husband prefers that she be at his beck and call. In time she is so cut off that she is unaware that she has any other alternative and becomes more enmeshed in this abusive pattern.

Dependency, both emotional and economic, keep her locked into this relationship. If she has little education or work skills she may fear being left destitute. If she does work, her husband probably controls her money too.

One of the tragedies in this situation is the loss of healthy boundaries. Many women lose the sense of objectivity to make the determination that they are in any danger. The abuse becomes so common that even blood, bruises, and pain do not signal her that her personal boundaries have been invaded by an enemy. But what might cause such a woman to go for help? Her children. If they are in danger, or experience abuse, she then takes action.

UNWILLING TO CONFRONT THE MARRIAGE

One final characteristic is the adherence to a traditional role in marriage. This is not wrong in itself, but she will allow her husband to remain at home even if he is a threat to her and the children, in order to save the marriage. She is unwilling to consider separation for her own safety. She believes wives should be tolerant of such transgressions in order to be patient, loving, submissive, and giving. If the marriage isn't working, the wife believes that it's her task to fix it. And since her self-worth is tied up in the success of her marriage, it is easy to see why she is under so much bondage to fix it.

Divorce is a sign of her failure, and that, coupled with cultural, Christian values and perhaps coming from a divorced home, all act to keep her where she is.[15] Sometimes, though, a temporary separation of residence is needed to convince the spouse that he is harming both the marriage and his family (see Step 4, page 210).

HOW TO RESPOND

What can be done now? Please realize there is hope for anyone who came from an abusive background or who is currently in one. Consider the following steps:

Step 1. If you grew up with abuse, either receiving abuse or observing it in another person, take steps to *become a transition person and break the pattern.* Don't assume that you will be different just by vowing you will never repeat the pattern. This is what you know best.

Read books, take classes, memorize Scriptures that describe the way God has called us to respond. In prayer ask for the Holy Spirit to guide your thoughts and responses. Write out in detail how you want to respond to your children and spouse. Practice and role-play the new responses so that you have an alternative approach. Believe that you can become a different person. I would encourage every spouse and parent to read the book *Verbal Abuse*, by Grace Ketterman (Servant).

Step 2. If you find yourself with thoughts or a borderline response that is ready to cross the line, do all of the above but *ask someone else to stand by you and assist you*. Make yourself accountable to a wise person who will help you, listen to you, guide you, and pray for you. This could be a good friend, church staff member, minister, or a support group of people struggling with anger on the verge of being out of control.

Step 3. If you are already abusing others, either emotionally or physically, *go for professional help*. You need to confront the issues and reasons for your behavior and to learn new responses.

This includes verbal abuse as well, which is prevalent in Christian homes. Our guide is the Word of God, and our pattern for speaking to others includes the following:

"Therefore encourage one another and and build each other up, just as in fact you are doing" (1 Thessalonians 5:11).

"When words are many, sin is not absent, but he who holds his tongue is wise" (Proverbs 10:19).

"Reckless words pierce like a sword, but the tongue of the wise brings healing" (Proverbs 12:18).

"He who is slow to anger has great understanding, but he who is hasty of spirit exposes and exalts his folly" (Proverbs 14:29, Amp.).

"Pleasant words are a honeycomb, sweet to the soul and healing to the bones" (Proverbs 16:24).

If you or a family member is being verbally and/or emotionally abused, take healthy confrontational steps to change this pattern. If your partner is open to hearing you and changing, have him/her follow steps 1-3. It would probably be helpful for both of you to have some sessions of counseling and allow someone else to help you change. But if this does not work, continue to step 4.

Step 4. If you are currently being physically abused (or your child is by your spouse), take the necessary steps to *remove yourself from the setting where you are being victimized*. (This is assuming that you have tried on your own through proper confrontation or even using a family and friend's intervention program and nothing has changed.) Remember that you are a valuable, chosen person and your body is a temple of the Holy Spirit. Don't let others mistreat you; no one deserves abuse. If you are in a church that tells you to stay in an abusive environment, find another church.

Go immediately for professional help. The person or agency can assist you with the following steps. Find out what the laws are about abuse and what legal steps you can take. You need to know your legal status and options, spouse abuse or child abuse laws, police procedures and victim options. Devise a safety plan for you or the other abused person. This should include a safe environment—one that is accepting, nonthreatening, and protective. Develop a plan to get to the safe environment including the best timing, transportation, money, clothes, and so on. Develop a network of other people to rely on and who can support you.[16]

After removing yourself from the threat, focus on changing your life so being a victim does not occur again. This will take courage, but any change in our lives happens when we allow the Holy Spirit to give us strength and courage.

TAKE ACTION

1. Please complete the following sentences.

    (1) The times when I've felt emotionally abused were _____

    _____

    (2) A time when I ended up emotionally abusing someone was

    _____

    (3) If I see someone emotionally abusing another person, I will

    _____

    (4) To make sure I will never abuse another person, I can ___

    _____

    (5) If an abused person came to me for help I would suggest

    _____

2. If you are a victim of physical abuse, there are steps you can take the next time—or immediately—to prevent the abuse from continuing. However, you must be willing to act. Below are specific things (from Step 4, page 210) you can do. Put a check mark before each action step you are *ready to consider* to stop the abuse. Then act on at least one of those steps.

    _____ (1) Seek professional help with an agency or trained professional.

_____ (2) Find out about the abuse laws to determine what legal steps you can take.

_____ (3) Devise a safety plan for you or the other abused person. This includes a place to go for protection and a way to get there.

_____ (4) Find a church (your present one or another) that will offer support to escape an abusive environment.

3. What could your church do to deal with the problem of abuse? Approach your church leadership, asking them to take these or similar steps.

(1) _____

(2) _____

(3) _____

4. Write out a prayer below for an abused person you know; also write a prayer for the one doing the abuse. Then pray on their behalf.

_____
_____
_____
_____
_____
_____

NOTES

1. Matthew McKay, Peter D. Rogers, and Judith McKay, *When Anger Hurts* (Oakland, Calif.: New Harbinger Publication, 1989), p. 270, adapted.

2. Susan Forward and Joan Torres, *Men Who Hate Women and the Women Who Love Them* (New York: Bantam, 1986), p. 43.

3. Grace Ketterman, *Verbal Abuse* (Ann Arbor, Mich.: Servant, 1992), p. 163.

4. For assistance in this area see *The Power of a Parent's Words*, by H. Norman Wright, Regal Books.

5. Ketterman, *Verbal Abuse*, p. 18.

6. Grant L. Martin, *Counseling for Family Violence and Abuse* (Dallas: Word, 1987), p. 243.

7. Matthew McKay, *et al.*, *When Anger Hurts*, pp. 274-75, adapted; and Martin, *Counseling for Family Violence and Abuse*, pp. 26-27, adapted.

8. Ketterman, *Verbal Abuse*, p. 203.

9. Martin, *Counseling for Family Violence and Abuse*, pp. 30-31.

10. This pattern, expressed as phases, is described in McKay, *et al., When Anger Hurts*, pp. 272-3, adapted; and Martin, *Counseling for Family Violence and Abuse*, pp. 43-45, adapted.

11. Howard J. Parad and Libbie G. Parad, eds. *Crisis Intervention, Book 2* (Milwaukee: Family Service America, 1990) p. 161.

12. Ibid., p. 162.

13. Kathleen H. Hofeller, *Battered Women, Shattered Lives*, (Palo Alto, Calif.: R & E Associates, 1983, n.p.

14. Martin, *Counseling for Family Violence and Abuse*, p. 36.

15. Parad and Parad, *Crisis Intervention*, p. 163, adapted.

16. Ibid., p. 167.

13

YOUR ANGER STYLE

Whenever one of my boys wants to put down his brother or a friend he will say, in a very whiney tone, "Grow up!" I hear the expression at least once a week. It's usually used in an attempt to manipulate the other person to stop some activity or to do something he doesn't want to do. The real meaning of this expression is "You're acting like a baby." Of course, no self-respecting boy of elementary school age wants to be accused of that.

God also exhorts us to "grow up!" However, He doesn't say it in a sarcastic kind of way. He doesn't say it to humiliate us or to manipulate us. He says it because He loves us. Several years ago I heard Leighton Ford say, "God loves us just the way we are, but He loves us too much to leave us that way."

In numerous passages He urges and encourages us to "grow up!" and become Christlike men and women. The writer of Hebrews expresses concern over his readers' lack of growth (5:11) and exhorts them to "press on to maturity" (6:1). Paul writes, "But speaking the truth in love, we are to grow up in all aspects into him, who is the head, even Christ" (Ephesians 4:15; NASB).

As children we all experienced events that elicited the anger reaction. What might have started out as a conscious reaction over time and with many repetitions became an unconscious reaction. Because it is so automatic it seems it's part of who we are, rather than a pattern that has been learned, and thus a pattern that with

God's help can be changed. True maturity, however, is measured by the degree to which we are "becoming conformed to the image of His Son" (Romans 8:29; NASB), the degree to which there is change and growth in our deep-seated patterns of thinking, choosing, and feeling.

YOUR STYLE OF ANGER

For most of us the emotion of anger is an unidentified, undeveloped, or underutilized source of power. You may have recognized in chapter 3 your own anger myths that have kept you stuck in the rut of an unhealthy anger style. That rut will keep you from making your anger work for you. Perhaps at this point you've identified how your family background has contributed to the unhealthy ways you experience and express the emotion of anger. Perhaps you've decided that you want to allow God to help you "grow up" in this important area of your emotional life. If so, you need to identify your anger style and, if appropriate, change it.

Many men and women have told me, "You've helped me see that anger is a God-given emotion and I don't have to be afraid of it. I believe that anger is a gift from God that can help me grow and be more effective in my personal life and in my relationships. The only problem is, I'm not sure how to begin to change my automatic and unconscious ways of responding. Where do I start?" That's an important question.

HOW TO IDENTIFY YOUR STYLE

The first step in changing your anger style is to identify what your predominant style is. What is the typical way you feel and express anger? Throughout the book we've seen that the causes and expressions of anger can come packaged in many different shapes and sizes, all the way from withdrawal to abuse. Over our lifetime each one of us has developed his or her own unique reaction pattern or style of dealing with anger.

Anger can parade through our lives in many different ways. Not long ago I filled two sheets of paper with some of the words and phrases people use to describe the experience and expression of anger. Here are some of the words I came up with:

aggravated	agitated	annoyed	animosity
aroused	begrudge	bitter	bristle
burned up	catty	criticize	cool
cranky	cross	despise	disdain
disgusted	enraged	exasperated	frustrated
fume	furious	grieved	grumpy
grouchy	hateful	hostile	hot
huffy	hurt	irked	incensed
ill-tempered	ill-will	irritated	infuriated
inflamed	jealous	mad	mean
miffed	moody	offended	provoked
repulsed	resentful	riled	sarcastic
scorned	spiteful	steamed	touchy
vexed	vicious	wounded	wrath

Some of the most common phrases include:

flew into a rage	hot under the collar
did a slow burn	boiling mad
blew up	swallow your anger
storming mad	get it off your chest
blow off steam	let it all hang out
fired up	bad blood
raised his hackles	went ballistic
rant and rave	totally lost it

As I looked at these lists I asked myself, "What do these have in common? Is there any pattern? Are there any significant differentiating factors?" After staring at the list for almost one-half hour it hit me. I quickly turned to Genesis 3 and the record of the temptation and the Fall of man, to consider sin's ongoing impact on humanity. Here I noticed two specific reactions to sin that relate specifically to how we deal with anger.

THE PATTERN OF ADAM AND EVE

We find the first reaction pattern in verse 7. Adam and Eve chose to hide. They made a covering of fig leaves so they could hide their bodies from each other. Not only did they try to hide from each other, but they also hid from God (v. 8). This tendency to cover, to hide, to repress, suppress, deny, or ignore aspects of who we are is an outcome of the Fall, a part of the human nature. We hide from God, we hide from ourselves, we hide from those we love. Though we don't hide all of the time, we hide whenever we can. Sometimes hiding has become such an automatic part of who we are that we aren't even consciously aware we are doing it.

The second pattern is in verses 12 and 13. When God confronts Eve with her awareness of her nakedness, she places the blame somewhere else. "The serpent deceived me, and I ate." When God confronts Adam he first hurls the blame at "the woman you put here with me," thus blaming Eve and, in a bold addition, God Himself. J. Grant Howard suggests every person can be a "hurler," casting blame on others in a variety of ways.

> We act as judge and jury and condemn others. We project our problems on those who live with us. We ridicule. We dominate. We are dogmatic. We are sarcastic, obnoxious, overbearing. We pronounce the final word, when we have no reason nor right to. We cut a person down neatly with a word or criticism. To his face. Or behind his back. We nitpick at someone else's behavior patterns and often fail to acknowledge our own weaknesses. We say, "You never do anything right. You always forget." "Never" and "always" are the hurler's communication quiver. We blame God. We blame others. We even blame ourselves.[1]

The tendency to react by hiding and hurling is bound up in each of us, yet most people have a tendency toward one response or the other. The person whose predominant style is hiding tends to be more of a passive person who reacts to anger by keeping it inside. The hurler is usually someone who is more aggressive and reacts to anger by trying to get rid of it. Most of the unhealthy ways in which anger can be expressed fall into one of these two patterns, or styles. Let's take a look at these two unhealthy reaction patterns—passive and aggressive—and then we'll look at a third and healthy alternative.

THE PASSIVE STYLE

One of my family's favorite drives is between Estes Park and Loveland in Colorado. The scenic drive passes the steep granite walls of the Big Thompson Canyon. We enjoy stopping along the way to see the views and hear the relaxing sound of the Big Thompson River winding its way down the mountain. For generations people have enjoyed camping, fishing, and just driving through this scenic canyon.

However, on one lovely summer day in 1976 the soothing serenity of this mountain scene became a nightmare. On August first, an unprecedented flash flood ravaged this popular tourist spot. It began in the evening when a torrent of water overran the deceptively named Dry Gulch. In only a few hours a deluge of rain dumped 11 ½ inches of water into the canyon river and its tributaries. At its crest the water achieved a volume four times that of any previously recorded flood.

Hundreds of campers, hikers, and sightseers were caught totally by surprise. Terrified refugees who had managed to climb high enough on the canyon walls to escape harm watched helplessly as camp trailers, houses, cars, exploding propane tanks, and human bodies rushed by in the torrent. By morning 144 persons were presumed to be dead and property damage was more than $80 million.[2]

Over the years I've met many people who are like the Big Thompson River. Most of the time they are passive, controlled, and stable. They are a joy to be around. However, when they experience a deluge of discouragements, a downpour of disappointments, or their emotional dam bursts, there can be an emotional flood with devastating effects.

REPRESS AND SUPPRESS

What's the passive reactor like? When provoked, the passive reactor will often say nothing. Instead of overflowing in his expression of anger, he contains the churning waters within. His immediate response to even the slightest hint of anger is to repress it or suppress it.

What's the difference between repress and suppress? *Repress* means to hold in, to put down by force, to prevent the natural or normal expression, activity, or development of an emotion. When I repress my anger I'm aware of it but through a lot of practice I'm able to keep it down. Few people are even aware that I'm angry. If over a period of time I continue to repress my anger, it is likely that my anger will become suppressed. When I suppress my anger it is kept from consciousness; I'm not even aware of it.

The passive reactor rarely feels in control of his life, will often submit to unfair circumstances, sacrifices his own growth to bolster and protect someone else, feels powerless and helpless, and often turns his anger into tears.[3]

Typical behaviors of the passive reactor include:

resentment	forgetting
anger turned in	apathy
procrastination	stubbornness
unhealthy shame	forgetfulness
dependent	guilt-prone
overresponsible	self-condemnation
avoiding the problem	denial
using the silent treatment	self-pity
conflict-avoider	subtle sarcasm

FAMILY BACKGROUND

The passive reactor is often someone who grew up in what many call a dysfunctional family. All families fall somewhere on a line between fully healthy, or functional, and unhealthy, or dysfunctional. Healthy families are not perfect; in fact, all families have problems. However, healthy families learn to identify and admit their problems and grow from them. Dysfunctional families don't identify or won't admit their problems. Thus they are unable to grow from them. They cease being a family with problems and become problem families.

In a dysfunctional family the members are spiritually, emotionally, and relationally undernourished. This malnutrition leads to many devastating effects. Children raised in this environment are much more likely to experience difficulty or even an inability to form long-term relationships. They have a hard time trusting and forming strong commitments and are afraid of intimacy. They pretend everything is fine when it isn't. They struggle with emotional stability, communicating clearly, effective conflict-resolution, as well as difficulty with believing in and trusting God.

In these families it's not OK to talk about problems, feelings are not to be openly expressed, communication is often blocked or is at best indirect, and the expectations are unrealistic. The parents discourage independence in favor of dependence, and they undermine healthy self-esteem with an unhealthy shame. Guilt and fear become the primary sources of motivation. Since the children have never seen healthy problem-solving skills modeled, they learn to stuff, repress, suppress, deny or ignore their emotions. Conflict is either constant, or it is totally avoided.[4]

Children raised in these kinds of families are surrounded by rules: Don't make any waves, peace at any price, don't trust anyone, and whatever you do, don't allow yourself to feel—it's too painful. This type of background can cause children to experience the kind of shame that leads them to label themselves as defective and worthless.

FEELINGS OF SHAME

God designed the emotion of shame to lead us to Himself. Healthy shame says, "God loves me. I have been made in His image. I have value and worth. But I am also a sinner. I am not perfect. I have made and will make mistakes. I need God." Healthy shame leads us to acknowledge both the fact that we are image-bearers and the reality of our sinful humanity. That reality drives us to the cross.

But when shame becomes the basis for our identity, the shame that God intended for good can become toxic. A shame-based person is one who focuses on his shame to the exclusion of Christ's completed work for him on the cross. At this point shame becomes hazardous to one's emotional and spiritual health.

Christians who are shame-based either ignore or are unaware of the reality of who they are in Christ and of what He has accomplished for them at the cross. They are unaware of their legitimate needs, and they have little sense of their value and worth. They have given up on the possibility of experiencing the abundant life. With feelings of hopelessness and helplessness, they often abandon their opportunities to grow and to become all that God would have them to be.

If you are a passive reactor, you probably have ignored your own feelings and needs. Eventually you can (or have) become numb to those feelings. Most passive people achieve harmony with others by abandoning appropriate personal goals. The price for this peace is often your own God-given uniqueness, individuality, and identity. And as you ignore your own happiness you are prone to assume responsibility for the happiness of others. At times you may even take the blame for something you haven't done.

RESENTMENT

In time passive reactors become bitter and resentful. Resentment is an insidious disease. It can actually destroy us and, in time, other people as well. "Resentment is like a poison we carry around inside us with the hope that when we get the chance we can deposit it where it will harm another who has injured us. The fact is that we carry this poison at extreme risk to ourselves."[5]

THE CONSEQUENCES

Reacting passively to your anger means making repression and suppression of pain a fundamental part of your life. Most passive reactors seek out activities or substances to numb their emotional senses so that they don't feel the pain in their lives. This is the first step on the road to addiction to a substance, a person, or an activity. The passive reactor is attracted to anything that can keep him from acknowledging and dealing with the real issues of life. The attraction can quickly become addictive.

There is increasing medical evidence that being a passive reactor can be hazardous to your health. We can repress, suppress, deny, and ignore our anger for a while. But if on a long-term basis we attempt to bury our anger it's possible that, in time, the effects of our mishandled anger will bury us. Like the flash flood in the Big Thompson Canyon, at some point the accumulation of fears and hurts and frustrations are likely to rush out of us.

When the anger does flow, it may be in the form of violence. Research has demonstrated that people usually kill someone they know quite well. Ironically, their history is one of *not* getting "angry." They tend to have rigid inhibitions against the expression of any form of anger.

However, when the instigation is great enough they may act out in an extremely aggressive manner. Often the most aggressive acts are committed by the overcontrolled passive-reactor.[6]

As I was writing this chapter, a Denver-area newspaper published the story of a man who got involved in an argument and ended up killing two men and wounding a woman. He was a quiet man who tended to keep to himself. Friends said that they had never seen him mad. In fact a close friend told the police, "Last night was the only time I'd seen him explode." But that's all it took, one time.

Repressed anger can also come out in the form of physical illness. After years of medical studies cancer researchers have developed a profile of traits that appear more consistent in people who get cancer than in those who don't. They have called this the "typical cancer personality." The four major components of the profile are (1) a poor self-image; (2) an inability to form or maintain long-term relationships: (3) the tendency to self-pity and to hold resentment and (4) an inability to forgive.[7]

According to Leo Madow, professor and chairman of the department of psychiatry and neurology at the medical school of the University of Pennsylvania, chronic high blood pressure (hypertension) and strokes are related to repressed anger and "have a strong emotional component."[8] Such anger may have caused Nabal's death, recorded in 1 Samuel 25. David had sent some of his soldiers to the wealthy businessman Nabal to get some food. Nabal, however, rebuked them and sent them away. When David heard this he gathered his men together to fight Nabal. Nabal's wife, Abigail, went to David with a large amount of food and gave it to David and his men in hopes of appeasing them. When Nabal heard what Abigail had done "his heart died within him, and he became [paralyzed, helpless as] a stone" (1 Samuel 25:37; Amp.). The text suggests that Nabal "blew his top." In the original language the phrase "his heart died within him" implies he suffered a stroke or a heart attack.

THE AGGRESSIVE STYLE

At the opposite extreme is the aggressive reactor. Whereas the passive reactor doesn't give adequate attention to legitimate personal needs, the aggressive reactor doesn't give adequate attention to the needs and rights of others. He becomes preoccupied with himself and displays selfish behavior. In contrast to the typically implosive anger of the passive reactor, the anger of the aggressive reactor is most often explosive.

When provoked, the aggressive reactor is likely to attack, label, put down, and humiliate others. He often communicates in ways that violate the dignity and rights of other people. In Philippians 2:3 we are exhorted to "consider others as better than yourselves." In 1 Peter 4:15 we read, "If you suffer, it should not be as a murderer or theft . . . or even as a meddler." The aggressive reactor ignores these principles.

The disciples James and John were aggressive-reactors. In Mark 3:17 we read that Jesus nicknamed these two brothers Boanerges, which means "Sons of Thunder." Their response to the Samaritans' lack of hospitality was to ask Jesus to call down fire from heaven and destroy them (Luke 9:51-66).

RAGE

People who make a habit of dumping their anger on others tend to get more angry more often. When we choose to deal with our anger by an aggressive reaction pattern it is easy for the anger to become rage. It doesn't take much for us to reach the boiling point and become steaming mad. King Saul, a classic aggressive reactor, "hurled his spear at [Jonathan] to kill him"(see 1 Samuel 30-34). Saul's frustration had moved past anger to rage. With his rage in charge, Saul was out-of-control—so much so that he tried to kill his own son, Jonathan.

It is important to note that rage is different from anger. The emotion of rage is more powerful and more volatile and much harder to control. Mismanaged anger leads to hostility, which leads to rage. Rage easily leads to a desire for revenge that can result in verbal or physical attacks or even in murder. When rage runs rampant it can destroy other people and eventually it will destroy us. John Lee, founder of the Austin Men's Center, gives a graphic description of rage's devastation:

> Rage is the ugliest and meanest human emotion. Rage is the father throwing his infant child against the wall and killing her. Rage is the mother scalding her child with boiling water to teach a lesson. Rage is the husband choking the family dog because it sneaked into the house. Rage is the driver who tailgates you for 10 miles blowing his horn because you cut him off by mistake. . . . Rage is awful and has no decent place in normal human relationships. Not at home. Not at work. Not in public."[9]

Remember that anger is one of the most powerful of all the emotions. When we experience anger a dose of adrenaline is pumped into our system. In comparison, hostility and rage are like taking a triple dose of adrenaline. Over time people can become addicted to the adrenaline rush they get from being enraged and can become rageaholics. According to Proverbs 22:24 this is the type of person we are to at all costs avoid.

Is there is a difference between people who get angry and angry people? Yes! From time to time everyone experiences anger. However, when our expression of anger dominates our lives and becomes a dominant feature of our personality we have shifted from being a person with anger to an angry person. Angry people are individuals who have developed a hostile personality. They are candidates for hostile behavior, and even rage.

OTHER SYMPTOMS

In *Treating Type A Behavior and Your Heart*, Friedman and Ulmer identified certain behaviors that, based on research, may be indicators of a hostile personality. According to Dr. Friedman, if even one descriptor fits you, it may be time to contend with your tendency toward hostility.

1. You become irritated or angry at relatively minor mistakes of family members, friends, acquaintances or even complete strangers, or find such mistakes hard to overlook.
2. You frequently find yourself critically examining a situation in order to find something that is wrong or might go wrong.
3. You find yourself scowling and unwilling or unable to laugh at things your friends laugh at.
4. You are overly proud of your ideas and enjoy telling others about them.
5. You frequently find yourself thinking or saying that most people cannot be trusted.
6. You find yourself regarding even one person with contempt.
7. You have a regular tendency to shift the subject of a conversation to the errors of large corporations, of various departments and offices of the federal government, or of the younger generation.
8. You frequently use obscenities in your speech.

9. You find it difficult to compliment or congratulate other people with honest enthusiasm.[10]

Most aggressive reactors believe that venting their hostility and rage helps them achieve their goals. Unfortunately just the opposite is true. As David Augsburger has written:

> Explosive anger is powerless to effect change in relationships. It dissipates needed energies, stimulates increased negative feelings, irritates the other persons in the transaction and offers nothing but momentary discharge. Vented anger may ventilate feelings and provide instant though temporary release for tortured emotions, but it does little for relationships.[11]

In addition to his rage and hostile attitude, the aggressive reactor typically displays the following characteristics: blatant sarcasm, teasing, concern for self, obnoxious behavior, loudness, quickness to blame, and drivenness. In his relationships, the aggressive reactor is shallow, with few intimate friends, suspicious, punitive, combative, and overcompetitive. The aggressive reactor also is prone to violence and has a desensitized conscience.

FAMILY BACKGROUND

Frequently aggressive reactors came from homes in which they suffered parental rejection, hostility, and rage. There were no models of healthy anger. What they learned is that aggression can be an effective way to keep people at a distance to avoid being hurt. They believe aggression is a good way to pay back those who have hurt them. However, if you can get past the rough exterior you will almost always find the aggressive reactor has a lot of hurt and fear.

It is easier to become an aggressive reactor than you may think. You need only to cultivate several of the following ten attitudes.

1. Few people can be trusted. Therefore always be suspicious. Assume the worst about everyone.
2. Material possessions are more important than relationships. Learn to love things and use people.

3. I am usually right. It isn't necessary to waste much time listening to another person's point of view.
4. Everything should be taken seriously.
5. There is always enough time to do at least one more thing.
6. I can never forgive and never forget. That's for suckers and fools. Besides, I probably will get hurt if I do.
7. I am always right. It's easier, it feels better, and if you come on strong others will tend to doubt themselves and give in to you.
8. One does not need to think before speaking. I'm probably right the first time.
9. I will have no compassion for people who are suffering. The weak deserve what they get.
10. Every silver lining has a cloud. Nothing is ever as good as it seems. If I look hard enough I will always find something to be critical about or worry about.

THE ASSERTIVE STYLE

Most people's primary anger style is that of the passive or the aggressive reactor. Notice I wrote *reactor*—both styles involve what is usually an automatic and unconscious *reaction to* some real or perceived problem or threat. Both styles are unhealthy. Both styles fall short of God's purpose in giving us the gift of anger.

One of the reasons the passive and aggressive styles don't work is that they involve a denial of our real selves. When we stuff and dump or hide and hurl our anger, we are ignoring anger's potentially important message. We have lost touch with the primary emotion that triggered our anger. Passive and aggressive people deny their grief and pain. Resentment and rage keep us from dealing with legitimate fears and hurts, and they limit God's ability to bring recovery and restoration. If we refuse to allow God to help us face the issues of our lives, how can we understand, forgive ourselves, and forgive others? How can we grow?

Fortunately there is a third option: the assertive response. This style is not an automatic reaction but involves a reasoned response. It is a way of responding that allows us to "be angry and sin not," as the Scripture commands (Ephesians 4:26).

INDIGNATION

If the passive reactor is characterized by resentment and the aggressive reactor is characterized by rage, then the assertive responder can be characterized by indignation. Indignation is a healthy response to anger. E.K. Simpson in his Bible commentary has noted that "a man totally destitute of indignation is a maimed sample of humanity."[12]

Indignation is a form of anger that is aroused by something that is unfair and unjust. This unfairness and injustice may affect you or someone else. Indignation is an activating emotion that stirs us to constructive and loving actions to change injustice and to protect ourselves and others.

How does indignation differ from rage and resentment? Author Richard Walters compares the effects of all three emotions: rage, resentment, and indignation:

> Rage seeks to do wrong, resentment seeks to hide wrong, indignation seeks to correct wrongs.
>
> Rage and resentment seek to destroy people, indignation seeks to destroy evil.
>
> Rage and resentment seek vengeance, indignation seeks justice.
>
> Rage is guided by selfishness, resentment is guided by cowardice, indignation is guided by mercy.
>
> Rage uses open warfare, resentment is a guerrilla fighter, indignation is an honest and fearless and forceful defender of truth.
>
> Rage defends itself, resentment defends the status quo, indignation defends the other person.
>
> Rage and resentment are forbidden by the Bible, indignation is required.[13]

> Rage blows up bridges people need [in order] to reach each other, and resentment sends people scurrying behind barriers to hide from each other and to hurt each other indirectly. Indignation is constructive: it seeks to heal hurts and to bring people together. Its purpose is to rebuild the bridges and pull down the barriers, yet it is like rage and resentment in that the feeling of anger remains.[14]

The assertive response is a style of responding to anger that enriches relationships. Here are are some characteristics of an assertive responder:

- responsive
- indignant
- has healthy shame
- responsible
- proactive
- motivated by love
- firm
- direct communication
- listens
- careful
- trusting
- communicates anger
- warm
- interdependent
- unselfish
- I win/you win
- caring
- constructive

HONESTY

The assertive responder is free to "speak the truth in love." The passive reactor will often speak in love, yet due to his over-concern for others he may not speak the whole truth. He does not want to hurt someone's feelings or have tensions, so he may say only as much as he thinks the other person wants to hear; he fears provoking the person. Meanwhile, the aggressive reactor is not usually concerned with what others think or feel; therefore he typically will speak the truth as he sees it, usually without love. The aggressive reactor is much more likely to dump and run.

DISCIPLINE AND THOUGHT

When provoked, the assertive responder is less likely to immediately react without thinking; instead he responds in a way that reflects some discipline and thought. He has learned the value of anger. He has learned to be aware of and choose his expressions of anger.

Assertive responders are more likely to have trained themselves to think, act, and feel more constructively. They express their thoughts, preferences, and emotions directly to the other person in healthy ways that communicate a respect for the dignity and the rights of both themselves and others. Their response is more likely to move them toward achieving both their personal goals and their relational goals.

Many of us are not assertive responders. If you are not, the first step is to recognize your need. Assertive responders are expressing their feelings with love. Do you want that? If so, you need to learn to express your anger directly in a healthy manner. Chapter 14 will give you specific guidelines. Below is a description of how one passive reactor learned to change; her transformation should give hope to all passive and aggressive reactors.

Steve and Trish had been married for twelve years. They loved each other and their four children. However, like all normal couples, there were some aspects of each one's personality that triggered anger in the spouse. One of Trish's anger triggers was Steve's tendency to be late, especially for meals.

Trish grew up as a classic passive reactor. Whenever she felt anything close to anger she would either ignore it or think of some way she might be responsible for the problem. She was afraid of conflict, and this reaction pattern allowed her to avoid it. For most of their marriage Trish had ignored Steve's being late. Or at least she thought she had. She either told herself that it was unavoidable or that if she prepared better meals for him to come home to Steve would be on time.

But it didn't work. She continued to experience anger. It became harder and harder to ignore it. One day when Steve waltzed into the house more than forty minutes late, the years of repression, suppression, and denial exploded to the surface. The quiet and passive Trish became a volcanic Mt. St. Helens. Trish decided that she needed some help in dealing with her "anger problem."

It took Trish a while to acknowledge that anger is a gift from God and not inherently bad. She had to dismiss the powerful anger myth that all anger is sinful. In addition, she began to see that the problem really wasn't her anger. It was the unhealthy ways she reacted to it. She decided to ask God to help her move from being a passive reactor to an assertive responder.

"It took me a while to realize that my anger was a secondary emotion that signaled something was wrong," she told me. "When Steve came home late, that really triggered my anger, but I couldn't figure out why." As she thought about it, Trish realized that her secondary emotion of anger was really a response to her primary emotions of hurt and frustration.

She decided that she had been passive long enough. She needed to be proactive and communicate her concerns to Steve. She knew that if there was to be any change she had to work on a way to "speak the truth in love." After working on it for several weeks here's what she said to him:

"Steve, in the past two weeks there have been four times that you have been at least twenty minutes late for dinner without calling and letting me know. Every weeknight I work hard at preparing a nice dinner. When you are late I have to keep it warm and that often affects how it tastes. Your being late also throws everyone else off schedule. When you are late I feel hurt that we're not important enough for you to be on time.

"I also feel frustrated that the rest of the family has to pay for your lack of consideration. I would appreciate it if you would follow through on your commitment to be home by 5:45 every weeknight. I will have the dinner on the table and be ready to eat by 6:00. If you are going to be late, please call and let me know. If I don't hear from you we will go ahead with dinner, and you can eat when you get home."

Steve was surprised by the clarity and directness of Trish's confrontation. By choosing to respond with direct communication, in a warm yet firm manner, it was easier for Steve to hear what Trish had to say. She felt a lot better, and Steve's on-time performance improved significantly.

Like Trish, you will learn that any change will take time; becoming an assertive responder requires breaking deep-seated attitudes and habits. Remember, anger can be constructive, when it is rightly directed. In chapter 14, you will learn how to make your anger work for you.

Take Action

1. Few people express their anger in only one style. However, most people more consistently respond in one style more than the other two. On the next page I've listed some of the main distinctives of the passive reactor, the aggressive reactor, and the assertive responder. Read through each of the lists and ask yourself, "In the past three months how have I expressed my anger?" "What percentage has been passive, aggressive, or assertive?" Then put the percentages in the blanks below.

_____ Passive   _____ Aggressive   _____ Assertive

Distinctives of the Three Anger Styles

Passive Reactor	Assertive Responder	Aggressive Reactor
toxic	healthy	toxic
cold	warm	hot
soft	firm	hard
shame	claim	blame
avoid	approach	attack
repress/suppress	confess	express
resentment	indignation	rage
inactive	proactive	reactive
dependent	interdependent	independent
anger in	anger out	anger against
unhealthy	healthy	unhealthy
ineffective	effective	ineffective
may love but not speak truth	speaks truth in love	may speak truth but not in love
overresponsible	responsible	underresponsible
loses personal goals	achieves personal/ relationship goals	loses relationship goals
false inferiority	honest self-appraisal	false superiority
motivated by fear	motivated by love	motivated by fear
too few boundaries	appropriate boundaries	too many boundaries
understates/ deny issues	clarifies issues	overstates/blurs the issue
concern for others only	concern for self and others	concern only for self
I lose/you win	I win/you win	I win/you lose
values others	values self and others	values self

Notes

1. J. Grant Howard, *The Trauma of Transparency* (Portland, Oreg.: Multnomah, 1979), pp. 25-32.
2. James McTighe, *Roadside History of Colorado* (Boulder, Colo.: Johnson Publishing, 1989), pp. 143-45.
3. Harriet Goldhor Lerner, *The Dance Of Anger* (New York: Harper & Row, 1985), p. 19.
4. Gary Jackson Oliver, *Growing Strong Families* (Lincoln, Neb.: Back to the Bible, 1992), n.p.

5. Bert Ghezzi. *The Angry Christian* (Ann Arbor, Mich.: Servant, 1980), p. 99.

6. E.I. Megargee, P.E. Cook, and G.A. Mendelsohn, "The Development and Validation of an MMPI Scale of Assaultiveness in Overcontrolled Individuals," *Journal of Abnormal Psychology* 72 (1967) 519-28.

7. O. Carl Simonton, Stephanie Matthews-Simonton, and James L. Creighton, *Getting Well Again* (New York: Bantam, 1978), adapted.

8. Leo Madow, *Anger: How to Recognize and Cope with It* (New York: Charles Scribner's Sons, 1972), p. 85.

9. John Lee, "Anger and Grief," *Man! Men's Issues, Relationships, and Recovery*, a journal of the Austin (Texas) Men's Center, 9 (December 1990): 13.

10. Meyer Friedman and Diane Ulmer. *Treating Type A Behavior and Your Heart*, (New York : Alfred A. Knopf, 1984), p. 204-5, adapted.

11. David Augsburger. *Caring Enough to Confront* (Ventura, Calif.: Regal Books, 1981), p. 41.

12. E. K. Simpson and F. F. Bruce, *Commentary on the Epistles to the Ephesians and the Colossians* (Grand Rapids, Mich.: Eerdmans, 1970), p. 108.

13. Richard P. Walters, *Anger: Yours & Mine & What to Do About It* (Grand Rapids, Mich.: Zondervan, 1981), p. 17.

14. Ibid., p. 139.

14

MAKING ANGER WORK FOR YOU

I'm so discouraged." Jim said. "I don't know why I keep on trying. I make up my mind that I'm not going to lose my temper again, and then some little thing happens and I blow it. I get mad at myself, make the same resolution, but when the next time comes I do the same stupid thing all over again. I'm tired of feeling defeated. I'm not sure I can change my anger pattern."

Jim was a fine man. He loved the Lord, his wife, Donna, and their two children. He was a leader in his church and active in a discipleship ministry. However, for many years Jim had struggled with his limited ability to control his anger. He was an aggressive reactor. For most of his life his anger had worked against him rather than for him.

Jim had read many books and talked to a lot of people. He had much insight and knowledge about the emotion of anger. For years he had committed his anger to prayer on a regular basis. Yet he was still discouraged and defeated.

Most of us, like Jim, have great intentions. We want to change, but we find that change is difficult. Usually we are sincere, yet we discover that changing our anger reaction patterns can be especially difficult.

If our anger styles have produced desired results and given us the short-term relief we want, we will tend to react the same way again. If we are passive reactors, we may be afraid of our anger. If we are aggressive reactors, we may have become addicted to the power our anger has to numb us to our fear of facing the real issues.

The good news is that with God's help meaningful change is possible. We can learn to make our God-given emotion of anger work for us rather than against us. We can learn how to invest our anger-energy in constructive responses rather than spend it in destructive reactions.

The bad news is that the change won't take place overnight. It's unrealistic to think that a twenty-year pattern can be changed in two weeks. Deep-seated response patterns take time to change. However, you can become an assertive responder. Jim did. The starting point in the change process is to recognize your need to change and to communicate that need to God.

A Plan for Change

For change to occur, however, we need more than a strong desire and good intentions. We need a plan. We should follow the pattern of the prophet Daniel. When Daniel realized he would be taken as a prisoner of war to Babylon, he "purposed in his heart" not to defile himself by eating the meat of King Nebuchadnezzar (Daniel 1:8). And he didn't. Why? Because he decided in advance what he wanted to accomplish and what his response would be.

We can't wait until we are in the heat of anger to ponder our response. We can purpose in our hearts not to allow our anger to control us but rather to put our anger as well as our other emotions under God's control. Establishing new patterns of anger is like learning to waltz. You may step on a few toes, look silly, and feel awkward, but with a little practice you will begin to develop new responses. Over time those new responses will replace the old ones and become automatic. In our final chapter, we offer seven specific steps you can take to begin to experience the emotion of anger as the gift that God intended it to be.

STEP #1: Identify Your Specific Anger Pattern

"Don't tell me I'm angry!" Julie shouted. Her face got redder and her voice louder. "You're the one that's angry! I hate it when you can't even admit your own anger and then have the nerve to tell me *I'm* angry."

It's amazing how many people struggle with anger and either don't know when they are angry, can't admit it, or don't know what to do about it. A spouse or a child or a friend may be aware of your anger before you are. Why? Because anger can be such a strong emotion and the anger reaction can be so automatic, many people don't think they can change. You don't need to be afraid of or reject your anger.

The best time to begin to deal with anger is before you get angry. Before the anger recurs, you can study and learn from your past responses. You can identify aspects of your anger response that will help you to change. It doesn't matter if your responses have been successes or failures. God can use both kinds to help you grow.

Take an anger history profile of yourself. To complete your anger history, ask yourself the following questions:

1. What are the Anger Myths (chapter 3) that have influenced my misunderstanding of this important emotion? Where did they come from? Do I still function as if they are true?
2. What is my current anger style? Do I tend to be a passive reactor or an aggressive reactor? What specific behaviors characterize my response?
3. What kinds of situations are most likely to bring out my anger? Anger can manifest itself in different ways with the same person under different circumstances. For example, how do I react when someone cuts me off, when I'm running late and get a flat tire, when the kids are out of control, or when I've worked hard on a particular job and get criticized for the one thing I didn't do?
4. When am I most likely to experience anger? In the morning, afternoon, or evening? After a hard day at work? After a major success or victory?
5. How do I know when I am angry? How does my spouse know when I am angry? How do my kids know when I am angry? Look for the warning signs. Perhaps your volume, tone of voice, or speaking rate changes. You may start to use certain words or expressions such as "That really ticks me off," "I'm sick and tired of that," or "I've had it." Look at your physiological response and ask, "Does my heart beat faster? Do I start to per-

spire? Do I feel a knot in my stomach? Do my neck or shoulder muscles tighten?

6. What have I tried in the past that hasn't worked? Many people go through life reinventing the wheel. My favorite definition of crazy is to find out what doesn't work and keep on doing it. If the ways in which you are dealing with your anger aren't producing healthy results, then change them.

7. What will be the consequences of not working on my anger? This involves counting the cost of unhealthy anger. One person I worked with brought in the following list of consequences for not changing her anger pattern: Unhealthy anger limits my understanding, hinders my growth, gives Satan an opportunity, allows problems I could have solved grow into problems that are much more complex, keeps people away, encourages shallow relationships, and affects my physical health.

Your answer to these questions will give you a gold mine of information about your anger. If you are like most people you will be surprised at how helpful even this first step can be.

Another helpful way to identify and understand your anger pattern is to keep an Anger Log for one month. The log should include the date and time of your anger, the underlying emotion contributing to the anger, and the issue. For the contents and form of this log, see Take Action #1 (page 248)

After thirty days review your Anger Log. Do you see any patterns? Are there certain times of the day, the week or the month that you are more likely to experience anger? Are there certain primary emotions that more consistently lead to an anger response than others? Does your self-talk contain any distortions such as all-or-nothing thinking, overgeneralization, catastrophizing, or "should" statements?

When Jim completed step one, he realized that while growing up he had learned Anger Myth #7, which claims that the best way to deal with anger is to dump it, just get it out of your system. This contributed to his tendency to be an aggressive reactor. He also discovered that he was most likely to become aggressive when he was under a lot of pressure or at the end of the day when he came home from work.

Donna and the kids told him they could tell when he was starting to get angry because he would butt in and complete their sentences, he would talk faster and louder, and he would use more gestures. By identifying his pattern he was able to identify signs that alerted him to his anger and thus allowed him to quickly move on to Step #2. Over a period of several months he developed the skill of catching his anger more quickly and dealing with it before it got out of hand.

STEP #2: Admit Your Anger and Accept Responsibility for It

Whenever something goes wrong it's human nature to blame someone else. Adam and Eve did it and we do it. We can blame our spouse, our children, our boss, our friends, the weather, the mechanic, people we know, or people we have never met.

In many circles it has become popular for people to blame their parents. If you have been raised in a significantly dysfunctional family, it becomes easy to put *all* the responsibility for emotional problems and irresponsible behavior on Mom and Dad. However, as authors Minirth and Meier note, "It is easy to blame our parents for our present problems. The fact of the matter is that we have faced a lot of decisions and made many choices in life along the way. If we don't grow out of our problems and make the right choices, it is no one's fault but our own."[1]

Though other people can say or do things that influence when we experience anger, we are responsible for how we choose to express it. If we are angry it is our anger, not someone else's. Just as no one can make you "lose" your love or "lose" your concern, no one can make you "lose" your temper. What you do with your anger is your choice.

As soon as you become aware of your anger, confess it. Most people associate the word *confess* with admitting to doing something wrong. Although the word is often used that way there is another meaning. *Confess* can mean to "say the same as," or "to give accurate verbal expression of what is real." When I confess my anger I acknowledge it and I take responsibility for how I will deal with it. It doesn't mean admitting that I am guilty. It means admitting that I am angry and I am responsible for how I choose to express it.

When I confess my anger and accept responsibility for it, I am saying, "I am angry. There may or may not be good reasons for my anger. I can't control the fact that I am angry. But with God's help I can control how long I stay angry and how I express my anger. I choose not to hide or hurl my anger. I choose to deal with it in a way that will lead to understanding, growth and healing."

As Jim became more aware of when he was angry he found it easier to confess it. This helped to reinforce in his mind the difference between the experience of anger and the expression of anger. Up until this point he had functioned as if the experience and expression of anger were the same thing. As he acknowledged the experience he was aware of his freedom to choose his expression.

STEP #3: Determine Who or What Will Have Control

Step 3 is crucial. When we become aware that we are angry, we faced a key choice we must make within a matter of seconds. We can either allow the emotion of anger to intimidate and dominate us, or we can, with the help of the Holy Spirit, choose to control our expression of the anger and invest the anger-energy in healthy ways. Although we can't always control when we experience anger, we can with God's help choose how we express the anger.

The real problem isn't anger itself. The problem is with the degree to which we have disciplined our anger and stay in control of it. Any emotion that is undisciplined and that we allow to control us will become problematic rather than problem-solving. Fear that gets out of control often leads to paralyzing phobias; discouragement can lead to major depression; love can lead to a nauseating narcissism; and concern can lead to worry. Anger, not controlled, can lead to rage.

When any emotion is in control it interferes with our learning, narrows our perception, and causes us to have tunnel vision. It hinders our ability to do creative problem-solving, limits our ability to recall what we have learned, and wastes time and energy. Such a strong emotion also increases our vulnerability to other problems and can lead to impulsive behavior.

One of the best ways to make sure you stay in control is to take time to process your anger. "Do not be quickly provoked in your spirit, for anger resides in the lap of fools" (Ecclesiastes 7:9). James warns, "Be quick to hear, slow to speak, and slow to become angry, for man's anger does not bring about the righteous life that God desires" (1:19-20).

Determine in advance to be slow to express your anger. Delay action. It's one thing to strike when the iron is hot, it's another to strike when the head is hot. Hot words are never the result of cool judgment. In fact, if you speak when your anger is not under control, you will probably make the best speech you will ever regret. Delay is the greatest remedy for unhealthy anger.

If need be, take time out. You can always say, "I know this issue is important to you, but I need some time to sort my thoughts out." The old adage, "When angry, count to ten before speaking," is true. If you are very angry, count to 100—and then don't say anything for twenty-four hours.

Although we take time to understand our anger, it is important to deal with the anger as soon as possible. In other words, keep short accounts. Buried anger is always more difficult to deal with later. In Ephesians 4:26-27 we read, "Be angry, and yet do not sin; do not let the sun go down on your anger, and do not give the devil an opportunity." Christ warns, "Settle matters quickly with your adversary" (Matthew 5:25).

Anger is like water running through a hose. At low pressure anyone can handle it, but at high pressure it's much more difficult to control. The sooner we identify our anger the easier it will be to deal with it.

STEP #4: IDENTIFY THE CAUSE AND SOURCE OF THE ANGER

In chapters 6 and 7 we described ten major causes of anger. In our experience about 95 percent of the anger most people experience can be traced back to at least one of those ten causes. Lerner has written that "it is amazing how frequently we march off to battle without knowing what the war is all about. We may be putting our anger energy into trying to change or control a person who does not want to change, rather than putting that same energy into getting clear about our own position and choices."[2]

Anger often is the secondary emotion and therefore is hard to deal with; we mistakenly are treating only the symptom of a deeper problem. If we allow God to help us identify the root cause or causes of our anger we are much more likely to make meaningful progress. The biblical writer warns: "See to it that no one misses the grace of God and that no bitter root grows up to cause trouble and defile many" (Hebrews 12:15).

Remember that one of the several positive functions of anger is that it can serve as a warning or alarm system. The only problem is that sometimes it is a false alarm. When our alarm goes off we can learn to determine if it is a legitimate alarm or a false alarm. What's the difference?

A false alarm occurs when we have made an inaccurate interpretation of an event or situation. Frequently how we interpret a situation makes a big difference in what we feel since our interpretations trigger the feelings and the behaviors that follow. At times our interpretations are accurate. However, during other times our interpretations involve distortions. If our perception is inaccurate our anger is sounding a false alarm.

Both Dale and Linda have full-time jobs outside the home. They have three children and are active in their local church. They are a busy couple but have worked hard at making their marriage and family a priority. They have divided the household tasks in a way that is equitable for the entire family. When Dale's or Linda's load at work increases, the other family members pitch in to help. They have worked hard at dividing up the household chores so that each one carries his/her fair share.

Linda's division at work was facing a big deadline. Tuesday night was their usual family night, but on Monday afternoon her boss announced she would have to work late on Tuesday. That evening she prepared a special dish and asked Dale to put it in the oven after work Tuesday, so it would be ready when she arrived home.

Monday had been a rough day, and Tuesday was even worse. It seemed to Linda as if whatever could go wrong did go wrong. She even had to work later than she had thought. All the way home she looked forward to a great home-cooked meal and some relaxing time with her family. When Linda walked in the door she didn't smell any food cooking, the table wasn't set, and Dale and the kids were sitting in the family room watching TV.

"I can't believe it," she shouted. "I stayed up late last night to prepare a good meal and the only thing you had to do was put it in the oven. Give me a break! Is that too much to ask? What do you think I am around here? Your maid? I'm sick and tired of doing all of the work while you guys sit around and do nothing!"

Linda felt hurt and frustration, and those feelings quickly produced her anger. Unfortunately her anger was a false alarm. Because of several distortions she misinterpreted what she saw. Linda had experienced a long, hard day and had expected a meal to be waiting. What she expected to find when she walked in the door was not what she actually found. She assumed the worst, she jumped to conclusions, she overgeneralized the problem, she magnified the negative and minimized the positive.

"Honey, we decided to surprise you," Dale said quietly. "After a long day I thought you would enjoy going out for dinner with the famly. Then there would be no dishes to wash and no kitchen to clean up. I wanted to give you a surprise."

Linda looked at her excited children and her thoughtful husband and mumbled softly, "Well, you sure did." Linda's anger disappeared, and she apologized to Dale and the children.

Here are a few questions that can help you determine whether your anger is a false alarm or the real thing: "What do I expect of this person or situation? Is my anger due to real problems or to unrealistic expectations? Is my interpretation accurate or is my perspective distorted? Does the other person need to change, or do I need to change the way I am looking at and interpreting the situation? If an outside observer saw this, would he view my response as warranted, appropriate, and responsible?

"What am I telling myself about this situation? Is it rational or irrational? What's the evidence that this is true? How much control do I have over the situation? Can I control or change it? If not, can I influence it? If I can't control it or influence it I can do nothing about it."

Those are some of the questions thst Jim asked. As he defined his anger and identified its source Jim discovered that at least half the time his anger was a false alarm. His tendency to overgeneralize and jump to negative conclusions made it easy for him to assume the worst about a comment or situation. Then he would ventilate his anger toward Donna. When he followed Step 4, Jim began to check out and clarify interpretations and perceptions before responding.

STEP #5: CHOOSE AN APPROPRIATE RESPONSE

Once you verify your interpretations, you may decide that there is no need to respond. Either the anger is a false alarm or it is a situation that you can't control or influence and thus one you can do nothing about. If that's the case, by not reacting you've saved time and energy and possibly some word or deed that you might have regretted. However, you may decide that the situation demands a response. If so, you need to determine what kind of response is appropriate.

In order to make this decision you need to ask yourself a few questions. The first question is, "How important is this situation?" A quick way to answer this question is to rate the issue on a scale of 1 to 10; 1 means a minor matter, 10 means a crucial issue. If it's 1 through 5 it's a low-ticket issue; a rating of 6 through 10 makes it a high-ticket issue.

Typically passive and aggressive reactors respond to a situation inappropriately. Passive reactors often treat high-ticket issues as if they were low-ticket. Aggressive reactors tend to treat all issues as if they were high-ticket issues. Their reactions are disproportionate to the issues, and they are unable to discern what is truly important and what is not. They waste valuable energy over comparatively insignificant issues.

When an issue is legitimately important, however, be more careful in choosing your response. Ask yourself, "How can I express my anger in a way that is biblically consistent and that will enhance the probability of resolution? What do I hope will happen as a result of communicating my anger? How can I convey the information I want in such a way that the other person can accept it and that it will benefit him or her?" You may even take the other person's point of view. Ask yourself, "If I were the other person, how might I respond if someone said this to me in this way? What will make it easier for him (her) to hear my real message?"

There are many different ways to deal with our anger-energy. You can either spend it, or you can invest it. The passive reactor is likely to spend it by attacking himself. The aggressive reactor is likely to spend it by attacking someone else. In both cases there are no winners. Everyone loses. When you spend your anger-energy the results are almost always destructive.

When anger-energy is spent it usually hurts. Before you go any further you can choose to set aside the destructive responses. This involves saying to yourself, "With God's help I choose not to hide or hurl my anger by jumping to conclusions, attacking, blaming, lecturing, labeling, dumping, moralizing, ridiculing, or manipulating the other person."

Let's look at how these principles might apply to the two leading causes of anger—hurt and frustration. If you have determined that the primary cause is hurt, you are faced with a choice. The immediate reaction of many people to being hurt is to say or do something to hurt the other person for the pain caused you. This can be the beginning of a vicious cycle that can escalate way beyond the initial hurt. Or you can focus on forgiveness.

Anger and forgiveness need to be linked together. As you work through your anger it will be easier to forgive. When we choose to forgive it frees us from the resentment and the desire for revenge that can poison and gnaw away at us and eventually destroy us. Forgiveness isn't always easy, but it's always smart.

Forgiving doesn't mean forgetting. In fact it has nothing to do with forgetting. Forgiveness means "surrendering my right to hurt you back if you hurt me."[3] Or as Philip Yancey writes, "Forgiveness is another way of saying, 'I'm human. I make mistakes. I want to be granted that privilege, and so I grant you that privilege.'"[4]

You might say to yourself, "This jerk doesn't deserve my forgiveness. If she had said this about you, you'd feel the same way too." That may be true, but that's not the issue. The real issue is, are you going to choose to allow your emotions to control you and react in a way that will hurt? Or are you willing to, with God's help, control your emotions and choose a response that is more likely to lead to healing? Do you want to allow your bitterness and resentment to control your life? Do you want to nurse a grudge that can eventually poison your other relationships? No emotion is worth damaging your mental, spiritual, and overall emotional health.

Minirth and Paul Meier have noted,

> No matter how you verbalize your anger, you must forgive. Forgiving starts with an act of the will. Forgiving is a choice. It may take some time to work through the emotional feelings that are involved. We cannot immediately dismiss the feelings. Again, it takes time to reprogram our computer. It takes time to reprogram the feelings. However, we can forgive others immediately by an act of the will.[5]

If the cause of your anger is frustration there are several options. Once again start by rating the significance of the issue. On a scale from 1 to 10, is it a high- or low-ticket issue? Does it involve a situation that you can influence such as your associate getting his work to you on time? Or is it a situation you can't influence such as being caught in a traffic jam at a time when normally the traffic would be flowing?

Review your Anger Log to see if there are times when you experience more frustration that others. Jim discovered that he was more vulnerable to frustration when he was tired and under pressure. Some people find that after lunch their tolerance to frustration is lower. I've worked with many families who have realized that Sunday morning is a difficult time, especially if they have young children.

Ask yourself, "What is it about this situation that I can change?" If Sunday mornings are especially frustrating, perhaps you can start to get ready earlier, allow more time, have cold cereal rather than fixing bacon and eggs, or lay the clothes out the night before rather than trying to decide that morning what the kids will wear. There are usually a variety of things we can do to reduce the probability of a situation setting us up for an unhealthy expression of anger.

STEP #6: JUST DO IT!

Step six is where you apply your insights to a specific situation. Sounds easy doesn't it? Well, for many people it isn't. It's much easier to talk about change than it is to actually do it. You may be surprised to find out how powerful your habits can be. But go ahead. Do it.

Lewis Smedes has written: "Healthy anger drives us to do something to change what makes us angry; anger can energize us to make things better. Hate does not want to change things for the better; it wants to make things worse."[6]

If your response involves confronting someone, choose a time that will be good for both of you, rehearse what you are going to say in advance, and do it. The longer you put off mending a quarrel or allowing a misunderstanding to fester the more difficult it will be to deal with. Remember the nature of confrontation is to heal:

Confrontation is simply and essentially a sharing of facts and feeling. It is not a vindictive attack or an argument. It is not intended to alienate or change anyone. You do not confront someone for the purpose of releasing your anger against [him]. In fact, it is best to release your anger before a confrontation. You do not confront someone to punish him, get even with him, frighten him or make him suffer. Rather, confrontation is a way of bringing closure to a painful relationship from the past that would continue to fester if it was not openly discussed and dealt with.[7]

If the response involves a different approach to a situation you can't control, try the new response for at least several weeks. Many people try something once or twice and give up if it doesn't work immediately. Don't quit. In looking back at his attempts at change, Jim realized this was a mistake he had made.

STEP #7: REVIEW IT

The review process doesn't take long. Start by thanking God for His love and His faithfulness in this situation. Then ask yourself, "What worked and what didn't work? What did I learn? How have I grown? What can I do differently that will help me to be more effective next time?"

Jim felt anger well up inside. However, this time he knew he had a choice. He knew that he had a tendency towards being an aggressive reactor. His pattern was to leap before looking and speak before thinking. He reminded himself of the past consequences of the old patterns. He knew that most of the time his anger was caused by frustration. He reminded himself that while he couldn't always control his experience of anger he had a choice as to how he could express his anger. Over a period of six months Jim experienced significant and lasting change. With God's help and a refusal to give up, Jim changed from being a aggressive reactor to an assertive responder.

THE PATH TO CHANGE

For many Christians both the experience and expression of anger has become a habit. Habits can be hard to change and may take some time. The good news is that with God's help we can change, we can grow, we can become more than conquerors. Through the power of the Holy Spirit and the promises in God's Word, we can take old dysfunctional and unhealthy ways of reacting and develop new, healthy and biblically consistent emotional responses.

How do you know if you are changing? Remember that change takes time and often involves setbacks. Don't be discouraged by the setbacks; they are inevitable and form a normal part of the growth process. Setbacks can provide invaluable feedback and fresh motivation for continued growth and learning.

The Chinese have a unique way of forming the word "crisis" It consists of two symbols, one for danger and the other for opportunity. What we initially perceive as a crisis is in reality a crossroads between danger and opportunity. The danger is that we will stay stuck in the rut, be afraid of growth, and choose to react in the same dysfunctional way we always have. If we choose to see it as an opportunity to grow, we can maximize our growth and achieve greater maturity, stability, and long-term happiness.

When our emotional patterns are influenced by the promises and principles of God's Word, we will still have problems but those problems will not dominate or devastate us. Rather they will be able to be used of God to help us develop into the man or woman of His design.

TAKE ACTION

1. For the next thirty days maintain an Anger Log. Whenever you become aware of anger grab your Anger Log and record the following information:

   (1) The date and time of day.
   (2) Rate the intensity of your anger from 1-10, with 1 meaning the anger is barely noticeable, and a 10 means that you have gone beyond anger into rage. (In fact a 10 means that you are out of control.)
   (3) Where possible, identify the primary emotion or emotions that led to the secondary emotion of anger.
   (4) What is the issue that led to your anger? You will not always be able to identify the issue.
   (5) What is your self-talk about this situation? Does your self-talk reflect passive or aggressive reactions or an assertive response?

Here is a sample form for an entry into the Anger Log:

My Anger Log

Date: _____ Time: ____
Intensity: 1   2   3   4   5   6   7   8   9   10
Primary Emotion: (a) Hurt (b) Frustration (c) Fear (d) Other
Issue: _____
Self-Talk: _____
_____
_____
_____

Notes

1. Frank Minirth, Paul Meier, Richard Meier, and Don Hawkins, *The Healthy Christian Life* (Grand Rapids, Mich.: Baker, 1988), pp. 201-2.
2. Harriet Goldhor Lerner, *The Dance of Anger* (New York: Harper & Row, 1985), p. 13.
3. Archibald D. Hart, *Feeling Free* (Old Tappen, N.J.: Revell/Power, 1979), p. 85.
4. Philip Yancey, "An Unnatural Act," *Christianity Today,* April 8, 1991, p. 39.
5. Frank B. Minirth and Paul D. Meier, *Happiness Is a Choice* (Grand Rapids, Mich.: Baker, 1978), p. 156.
6. Lewis B. Smedes, *Forgive and Forget* (New York, N.Y.: Harper & Row, 1984), p. 21.
7. H. Norman Wright, *Always Daddy's Girl* (Ventura: Calif.: Regal, 1989), p. 218.

Moody Press, a ministry of the Moody Bible Institute,
is designed for education, evangelization, and edification.
If we may assist you in knowing more about Christ
and the Christian life, please write us without obligation:
Moody Press, c/o MLM, Chicago, Illinois 60610.